THE B LIST

ALSO FROM THE NATIONAL SOCIETY OF FILM CRITICS

*The A List: The National Society
of Film Critics' 100 Essential Films*
(edited by Jay Carr)

*The X List: The National Society of Film Critics'
Guide to the Movies That Turn Us On*
(edited by Jami Bernard)

THE B LIST

The National Society of Film Critics on the

LOW-BUDGET BEAUTIES, GENRE-BENDING MAVERICKS, AND CULT CLASSICS WE LOVE

EDITED BY DAVID STERRITT
AND JOHN ANDERSON

DA CAPO PRESS
A Member of the Perseus Books Group

Set in 10.5 point Berkeley Book by the Perseus Books Group

Published by Da Capo Press
A Member of the Perseus Books Group
www.dacapopress.com

Da Capo Press books are available at special discounts for bulk purchases in the U.S. by corporations, institutions, and other organizations. For more information, please contact the Special Markets Department at the Perseus Books Group, 2300 Chestnut Street, Suite 200, Philadelphia, PA 19103, or call (800) 810-4145, ext. 5000, or e-mail special.markets@perseusbooks.com.

Library of Congress Cataloging-in-Publication Data

The B list : the National Society of Film Critics on the low-budget beauties, genre-bending mavericks, and cult classics we love / edited by David Sterritt and John Anderson.
    p.   cm.
   Includes bibliographical references and index.
   ISBN 978-0-306-81566-9 (alk. paper)
   1. Motion pictures—Reviews. I. Sterritt, David. II. Anderson, John, 1955 March 10– III. National Society of Film Critics.
 PN1995.N354 2008
 791.43'75—dc22

                                             2008011055

10 9 8 7 6 5 4 3 2 1

Contents

Introduction

by David Sterritt and John Anderson

THE QUESTIONS: WHAT KIND OF COLLECTION COULD POSSIBLY find common ground among *The Son of Kong, Platoon,* and *Pink Flamingos?* What kind of fevered minds could conceive of such a list? What are the unheard-of qualities that tie them all together?

The answers: This book. The National Society of Film Critics. And the far-reaching excitement of the B movie itself. Once it was the Hollywood stepchild, the underbelly of the double feature, the scrambling lab rat of cinematic innovation. Today, we assert in this volume, it is a more inclusive category, embracing films that fall outside the mainstream by dint of their budgets, their visions, their grit, and frequently—sometimes essentially—their lack of what the culture cops call "good taste."

This is precisely where *The B List* takes a stand. Taste, at least in the sense of decency, decorum, and propriety, is subjective, transitory, and evolving. With that in mind, this book throws caution to the proverbial wind, zooming in on movies that demand attention despite their lowly births, squalid upbringings, and dubious character traits. What admirable qualities the pictures have—and they have such qualities galore—are cheerfully irrelevant to the properties that define Oscar movies, although some of our selections are, in fact, Oscar movies. The importance of these pictures lies in characteristics that are so offbeat, unpredictable, and idiosyncratic that only two generalizations can be made: some are important for what they are, and others are important for what they aren't.

No one, for example, would mistake *Reservoir Dogs* for a cookie-cutter Hollywood caper film; the violence is too extreme, the characters too eccentric, the motivations too arcane to provide a comfort zone for audiences brought up on more conventional thrillers. Yet the blood-soaked outbursts and contorted plot twists cooked up by Quentin Tarantino have influenced so many movies that they now seem like formulas themselves.

In the pages that follow, we and our critical colleagues address such genuine acts of genius as Francis Ford Coppola's prescient thriller *The Conversation* (the director's "tweener" movie, meaning it came between *Godfathers*) and Michael Powell's razor-sharp *Peeping Tom*, which virtually ended his brilliant career. We probe weird-fiction mentalities as different as the red-scare paranoia of *Invasion of the Body Snatchers*, the end-of-the-world ingenuity of *The Core*, the living-dead moodiness of *I Walked with a Zombie*, and the dream-world delirium of *Eraserhead*, which Jennifer Lynch, director David's daughter, has charmingly called "my baby album." We resurrect forgotten gems like *May* and *Mona*, find unsuspected depths in *Gun Crazy* and *King Creole*, and rediscover the delights of *Vampire's Kiss* and *The Big Bus*. Did you know *The Girl Can't Help It* resounds with modernist self-reference; *Red Planet Mars* is anti-Commie agitprop; and *The Rage: Carrie 2* is a crypto-feminist allegory steeped in beauty, terror, and intelligence? If so, you'll find much to treasure in these pages. If not, prepare for a string of cinematic jolts as galvanic as the Great Whatsit flare-up in *Kiss Me Deadly*.

At the risk of seeming grandiose, we think *The B List* subscribes to the same philosophy as radical scholars like Howard Zinn, who maintain that the evolution of a people, a culture, or a nation is rarely in sync with the Great Man theory's assumption that history is driven by singular acts of famous individuals. Transplanting this to the movie world, cinema is more than the pictures that have grossed the grossest, busted the most blocks, enriched their studios most fulsomely, and been statuetted most enthusiastically by the Academy of Motion Picture Arts and Sciences, whose membership has always been more interested in what's good for the business of filmmaking than what's good for filmmaking itself.

If you think movies aren't what they used to be, you can't blame the big movies, the self-congratulating Oscars, or the money-minded industry they represent. But you could blame us critics if we blindly echoed all the hype, so the best of us refuse to. Of course, we recognize the genius of the Hollywood system and the brilliant artists it has produced, but we also like peering into dark little corners where the marquee light doesn't shine. John Ford and Howard Hawks were great filmmakers, but so were Anthony Mann, Sam Fuller, and Budd Boetticher, who put their own distinctive imprints on the Western, too. Alfred Hitchcock was a master, but so is David Cronenberg, who has carved (and we mean it) his own niche in the body-conscious psycho-horror genre. Edgar G. Ulmer holds as important a place in American movies as directors much better known—see his inimitable *Detour* for Exhibit A—and watching Lee Marvin blast his way through *Point Blank* is as unnerving now as it was when John Boorman made the picture in 1967. Our fondness for these diamonds in the (very) rough, and a few dozen others, is the guiding force behind *The B List*.

Editing the book in the spirit of the movies it discusses, we've imposed no rules or regulations in matters of subject, style, or tone. To make the field manageable we've kept ourselves to English-language pictures, and most of the essays deal with American movies from the World War II era on. But writers could go in any directions they wanted as long as B productions were at stake. And don't look for a formal declaration, or even an informal one, of what a B picture is. Within the industry, the term originally meant a low-budget quickie destined for the bottom half of a double bill, and since the late 1950s, when double features bit the dust, it's come to mean a low-budget quickie, period. We've taken it in the broadest sense, referring to any and all movies made with modest means, maverick sensibilities, and a knack for bending familiar genres into fresh and unfamiliar shapes. Beyond this we've left it to the writers to follow their own magnificent obsessions in their own ornery ways, and the results of their labors have the anything-goes vitality of a dusk-to-dawn B marathon.

Critics are, by definition, outsiders. We observe, we judge, we maybe advise, but we'd be foolish to expect much affection in return. Perhaps that's why this particular volume is close to our hearts, celebrating the outré margins of mainstream American cinema. For every big Hollywood hit there are many, many also-rans that have not won popular acclaim, racked up huge profits, attracted the diligent scrutiny of PhD candidates, or secured the warm affections of Netflix and company. But that doesn't mean they never will. And in the meantime they deserve our attentions. Even our love.

Part ONE: Out of the Shadows

Film Noir

PSYCHOLOGICALLY GRAY, MORALLY AMBIGUOUS, AND EMOTIONALLY hair-triggered, noir came out of shadows—shadows of the Depression, creeping fascism, '30s pulp fiction, and a post-Darwinian universe—birthed in a caul of darkness and writhing its way into stepchildhood. More a cycle than a genre, "film noir" was named in 1946 by French critic Nino Frank, a Modernist who championed James Joyce and company. Its landmarks are bone-chilling tone poems of the '40s and '50s like *The Maltese Falcon, Double Indemnity,* and other hits with James M. Cain, Raymond Chandler, and Dashiell Hammett pedigrees. But today some bigger-budget studio noirs can seem like baby food, at least in relation to the hardest-boiled of the genre's nuggets; even Humphrey Bogart, outside *In a Lonely Place* (1950), is sometimes almost cuddly. What we discuss in this chapter is cinema made by men (our apologies to Ida Lupino) who toiled through much of their careers in the asphalt jungle of Hollywood's off-ramps, breathing an atmosphere of financial, technical, and artistic uncertainty, all of which is reflected on the screen, along with marvelous ingenuity and craft.

Fittingly, noir's best practitioners were yeomen. *Detour* was the strong-willed Edgar G. Ulmer's greatest artistic achievement, yet the 1945 masterpiece was produced on a rented soundstage in less than a week. *Pickup on South Street,* written and directed by Samuel Fuller in 1953, won an Oscar nomination for supporting actress Thelma Ritter, but it was hard recruiting someone for the big role Jean Peters eventually took. Nothing was easy in noir. If an air of the miraculous sometimes hangs over these films, it should be no surprise.

Few filmmakers have been more versatile than the best noir directors, for the simple reason that they *had* to be. Jacques Tourneur, who steps up more than once in this volume, was responsible for three of the most famous chillers

1

produced by B-movie king Val Lewton at RKO in the early '40s—*Cat People,* *I Walked with a Zombie,* and *The Leopard Man*—but he was equally ready for the challenge of *Out of the Past* in 1947, and no noir selection would be complete without it. The awesome stylist Joseph H. Lewis supervised the musical sequences in *The Jolson Story* in 1946, and by the '60s he was directing episodes of *The Rifleman* and *Bonanza;* but his 1950 stunner, *Gun Crazy,* aka *Deadly Is the Female,* is a towering noir achievement. Ditto for *Kiss Me Deadly* with its A-bomb coda, directed in 1955 by Robert Aldrich, the Zelig of mid-century motion pictures: he directed Burt Lancaster in *Apache* and *Vera Cruz* in 1954, led Bette Davis (as much as that was possible) through the '60s shockers *Whatever Happened to Baby Jane* and *Hush . . . Hush, Sweet Charlotte,* and oversaw an all-star cast in *The Dirty Dozen* in 1967, but he never outdid his work with Ralph Meeker as Mike Hammer in the greatest of Mickey Spillane movies. André de Toth made Westerns, African safari adventures, a whole lot of television, *and* the top-flight noir *Crime Wave,* one of four pictures he helmed in 1954. These were not prima donnas.

For some directors, noir offered a cheap way to be profound. It was a paycheck, of course, but it wasn't easy money. And what's more auteurist than auteurism under the gun? The films we call noir are often flat-out marvels, eight of which are discussed here.

Detour

Edgar G. Ulmer, 1945

by J. Hoberman

"YES, VIRGINIA, THERE IS AN EDGAR G. ULMER," ANDREW Sarris chuckled in *The American Cinema,* as though the idea of this unique director— a bargain-basement maestro who epitomized the category Sarris termed "expressive esoterica"—was even more remarkable than the director himself. But Edgar George Ulmer (1900–1972), a filmmaker who set up aesthetic shop in the recesses of Poverty Row, requires no indulgence. The man was a hero.

Reading the extensive interview that Peter Bogdanovich conducted with the ailing Ulmer in 1970, it's natural to wonder whether the filmmaker's bizarre trajectory from *The Cabinet of Dr. Caligari* (1920) through the Universal horror factory and the Ukrainian independent cinema to the Hollywood B-movie mill and eternal idiocies of *Beyond the Time Barrier* (1960) was Bogdanovich's invention. Here was a filmmaker whose major commercial success, *Damaged Lives* (1933), was a banned educational film on venereal disease that wound up grossing $1.4 million, and whose greatest artistic achievement, *Detour* (1945), was produced on a rented soundstage in under a week. Could such a vita be real?

Raised in imperial Vienna, where he studied architecture, Ulmer broke into movies as a teenager in post–World War I Berlin and, shuttling for the next decade between Germany and the United States, built sets for F. W. Murnau while directing Westerns for Carl Laemmle. A new sort of avant-gardist, Ulmer followed up a classic independent documentary in Berlin with the supremely perverse *The Black Cat,* Universal's top-grossing release for 1934. *The Black Cat* was *From Caligari to Hitler* in one lurid package, marooning a naïve pair of American honeymooners in Europe's heart of darkness as unwitting pawns in the death

3

struggle between a hysterical Hungarian psychiatrist (Bela Lugosi) and a proto-Nazi, Satan-worshipping Austrian architect (Boris Karloff) who has built his steel-and-glass deco castle on the site of World War I's bloodiest battlefield.

Wildly expressionist, bathed in Liszt and Chopin, trafficking in incest, necrophilia, human sacrifice, and sadism, The Black Cat somehow transcended the Production Code (not to mention the narrative incoherence resulting from extensive reshooting). The movie also established the Ulmer style—long, somewhat stolidly choreographed takes punctuated by close-ups all shot on the last day of production—which was designed to get the most out of the fewest number of camera setups. This pragmatism was put to the test when, in a career move without Hollywood precedent, Ulmer relocated to New York to make "ethnic" movies on budgets that sometimes failed to break five figures.

Ulmer's inventiveness was legendary—constructing a plywood shtetl in rural New Jersey as the backdrop for both his Ukrainian and Yiddish talkies, and shooting Moon over Harlem (1939) entirely with short ends. When he returned to Hollywood during World War II to direct six-day wonders for the B-movie studio PRC (Producers Releasing Corporation), Ulmer demonstrated a formidable capacity for making something from nothing. He created PRC's relatively lavish Isle of Forgotten Sins (1943) using leftover South Seas miniatures from John Ford's The Hurricane (1937). Even more minimal, Club Havana (1945) was shot entirely in the nightclub that might be generically termed The Ulmerocco.

Never lacking for adaptive strategies, Ulmer used the saga of a concert-hall cleaning woman as the premise for Carnegie Hall (1947), otherwise a succession of musical performances shot on location. (That this movie was produced by Boris Morros, the only Russian spy ever to have a Hollywood career, adds another improbable footnote to Ulmer's career.) The Amazing Transparent Man and Beyond the Time Barrier, the impressively crazy movies that Ulmer made for American-International Pictures in 1960, were shot simultaneously in Dallas, using a "futuristic" art exhibit at the Texas State Fairgrounds for postapocalyptic locations. Ulmer might have been the model for Ed Wood, but unlike Wood (or the even more experimental Oscar Micheaux), his ultra-pragmatic craft is anything but desultory. Ulmerian mise-en-scène is synonymous with problem solving—and vice versa.

Having served his apprenticeship at UFA (Universum-Film AG), the world's largest movie studio and the citadel of German expressionism, Ulmer imbued his PRC productions with a surplus of craft. Far from artless, the filmmaker was, if anything, too arty. He cluttered his foregrounds with shrewdly placed bric-a-brac, contrived to dapple the most barren set with shadows, varied angles, and forced perspectives, and created "atmosphere" with a vengeance—no director ever made more adroit use of smoke pots and fog machines. Moreover, Ulmer had *kultur.* *Green Fields* (1937) adapts a Yiddish stage classic; *Strange Illusion* (1945) transposes Hamlet to contemporary Southern California; *Ruthless* (1948), written under a pseudonym by blacklisted Alvah Bessie, remakes *Citizen Kane* for the equivalent of Orson Welles's dinner allowance.

With the decline of the studio system, Ulmer switched to cheap sci-fi. Watching *The Man from Planet X* (1951), one need only squint a little (and screen out the corny dialogue) to see this juvenile quickie as a UFA fantasia filled with expressionist tropes—the spaceship that blinks like a jack-o'-lantern, the alien with the face of a Pacific Indian mask, the lonely castle on the blasted moor. As a filmmaker, Ulmer is actually quite rigorous in proposing his threadbare productions and ridiculous scenarios as a sign system. Not for nothing did the critic Myron Meisel, who used to bestow an annual Ulmer award, call his pioneering Ulmer paean "The Primacy of the Visual."

Indeed, given the music with which Ulmer characteristically drenched his movies, one wonders if he didn't conceive them as silent. The simpleminded but forceful reform-school drama *Girls in Chains* (1943)—which, thanks largely to its title (typically conceived before the script was written), was among PRC's biggest hits—ends with a wordless chase over the rooftops worthy of French director Louis Feuillade. *Beyond the Time Barrier,* which, among other things, envisions a civilization of mutant deaf-mutes, suggests an impoverished remake of the 1924 Soviet constructivist space opera *Aelita.*

The musical puppet show that provides the centerpiece for the often brilliant *Bluebeard* (1944) is almost a metaphor for Ulmer's method. There is finally no disjunction between style and content. In some mysterious way, the artist's stylistic conviction dignifies even the most atrocious script as authentic kindermärchen while raising absurdity to a form of primordial make-believe.

Shot on a thirty-thousand-dollar budget that included the rights to Martin Goldsmith's pulp novel, *Detour* was cheap even by B-movie standards. But the master of *arte povera* stylistics turned all the production's liabilities—back-projected locations, limited actors, six sets, abrupt ending—into formal tropes.

Detour is quintessential Ulmer and, with its flashback structure and overdetermined plot, quintessential noir—an example of un-American fatalism in an echt American world, populated by slangy, tough characters telling one another things like, "You're being a goon, that's how people wind up behind the eight-ball!"

In hitchhiking across America, the movie's luckless antihero (Tom Neal) transverses the two noir modes—moving, via rear-screen projection, from a shadowy

New York City to the harshly lit "realism" of the Southwest desert and his fateful rendezvous with a female blackmailer (the aptly named, indelible Ann Savage). This femme fatale is not so much evil as insane; the antihero isn't just innocent but also stupid and unbelievably depressed: Tipped ten dollars for his piano playing, he glumly refers to the bill as "a piece of paper crawling with germs." Earlier, he has told his movie-struck girlfriend that "people go out [to Hollywood] and start polishing cuspidors"; later, he'll tell us that "no matter what you do, no matter where you turn, fate sticks out its foot to trip you." Of course, this might be considered questionable in view of his own succession of blunders.

A stringently minimal exercise as paranoid as it is elemental, *Detour* is informed by a kind of lumpen James M. Cain existentialism and propelled by an overheated voiceover narration that, frequently at odds with Ulmer's stolidly mobile camera, does less to explain the story than to discredit the very notion of any rational understanding. "This nightmare of being a dead man would soon be over." *Detour* isn't just a masterpiece; it's a veritable moon rock, a jagged chunk of the American psyche. (Indeed, Neal—whose movie career fell apart in the early '50s after a well-publicized fistfight with Franchot Tone over tawdry starlet Barbara Payton—wound up serving six years in prison for shooting his third wife, Gale, in 1965.)

Although never reviewed by the *New York Times,* this visually exciting movie should be a required study for all prospective independent filmmakers. Ulmer has an inexhaustible sense of how to use fog, shadows, and outsize props to construct a dynamic frame. He never tires of giving being to nothingness. Who was this guy trying to impress? *Detour*'s surplus of effect is not unlike discovering a Rembrandt drawing wrapped around a wad of bubble gum.

Gun Crazy

Joseph H. Lewis, 1950

by Richard T. Jameson

IF YOU HAD TO SELECT A SINGLE FILM TO JUSTIFY THE present enthusiasm for film noir and define its allure, few movies could compete with *Gun Crazy*. The same goes for celebrating the potential of B movies to achieve grade-A flair, excitement, and artistic intelligence. The picture taps brazenly into a sexual, almost feral energy that makes it unique, even in a school of film known for perverse psychology and smoldering subtexts. And it achieves its ends on an observably limited budget, via two strategies that ought to clash but instead invigorate each other: the bold stylization of expressionistic, verging-on-minimalist settings, and the camera's embrace of the real world in adventurous, sustained takes that approach documentary realism . . . except that the keynote of documentaries is rarely frenzy.

The premise is elemental. Bart Tare, an orphaned boy in a small American town, has an obsession with guns—owning them, touching them, and especially shooting them with proficiency, which makes him "feel awful good inside, like I'm somebody." After several years in reform school and four more in the army, Bart the man (John Dall) comes home an earnestly pleasant young fellow, albeit with his obsession intact. When he crosses paths with Annie Laurie Starr (Peggy Cummins), a carnival trick shooter who happens to be, in the words of her spieler boss, "soooo appealing, soooo dangerous, soooo lovely to look at," no power on earth can keep them out of each other's arms. What Bart doesn't know till much later is that Laurie once killed a man (*Gun Crazy* was initially released under the title *Deadly Is the Female*), and before long she has persuaded him to join her in a cross-country crime spree that also plays like an extended honeymoon.

From the outset, the film is galvanized with an electricity we aren't always privy to. The main title plays over an empty street corner at night, with a neon sign or two and a silver wash of rain. As the credits end, Bart (played at this preadolescent stage by Rusty Tamblyn) rounds the corner, pauses, then advances across the street toward the camera. The camera obligingly backs off, and we realize that all this time we have been looking out the window of a gun store—we've been inside Bart's gun craziness, as it were. After gazing raptly for a moment, Bart smashes the glass, then turns his back, his arms spread across the hole in the window as if he could conceal what he's done. Turning again, he reaches in to seize a pistol, then spins around to flee. But he trips and falls on his face, his prize skittering away through the puddles—virtually swept along by the camera to stop at the feet of the town sheriff. Extreme low-angle shot looking up at this towering figure, then cut to a camera moving along near ground level to frame a close-up of the boy. But instead of a conventionally centered close-up, the composition crowds Bart's face into the lower left-hand corner of the frame, almost off the screen. After a moment, the focus ebbs away and the scene ends.

A great deal of *Gun Crazy*'s logic and dynamism is set up here. The normal world can take on a hallucinatory quality—albeit expressed in acceptably naturalistic terms—in sympathy with Bart's state of mind. The camera is attentive, responsive to Bart's assertive behavior; but it's also susceptible to quicksilver changes, and can turn almost predatory in catching him at a disadvantage. The strategy of pinning Bart ultra-close-up in a corner of the frame will recur at key moments, an acute visual index of his distress and impotence, but also a kind of milestone measuring a fatal progression, a pattern, outside Bart's ken. And the ebbing away of focus never operates merely as an alternative to a fadeout or soft cut; there's always an expressive overtone to it, a sense of shame, or loss of power, or orgasmic release.

Gun Crazy was directed by Joseph H. Lewis, who had come up from the editing bench to helm an el cheapo medley of Bowery Boys comedies, program Westerns, and Bela Lugosi vehicles, then scored with an authentic noir sleeper, the 1945 *My Name Is Julia Ross*. (Lewis would go on to direct one of the most corrosive entries in the classic noir cycle, *The Big Combo,* in 1955.) Even the least and/or most preposterous of his low-rent assignments contained an ambitious deep-focus composition or eccentric use of a character player to relieve the surrounding flatness and give a glimpse of a lively directorial intelligence. Yet nothing anticipates the wall-to-wall resourcefulness and stylistic commitment displayed in *Gun Crazy*.

Take that carny introduction of Annie Laurie Starr. She enters with guns blazing, literally, and because the camera is looking up as though from the point of view of someone in the carnival audience—Bart, say, who's been brought along by his boyhood chums for a homecoming celebration—the guns and then Laurie herself rise into the frame. Brief cut to Bart grinning, then back to Laurie, who twinklingly registers his gaze, returns it, and . . . points a gun at him and fires! Bart, of course, grins all the brighter.

Like Luis Buñuel's razor across the eye in *Un Chien Andalou,* that moment never fails to astonish. Besides rendering superfluous any sober essay on the relationship between gun power and sexuality, the scene is a classic example of how, if only a director puts his camera in the right place, at the right distance and angle, all manner of additional values and valences can blossom. The whole erectile, rising-into-view nature of Laurie's entrance is a natural function of someone walking from the back of a stage to the front; forward motion becomes vertical thrust only within the selective frame of a camera. Lewis also had the cunning not to make the camera's eye precisely synonymous with Bart's. Laurie is looking—and firing her blank shot—just past the camera, not directly into our eyes; like Bart's pals sitting beside him, we're close enough to appreciate Laurie's audacity and its impact on Bart, but this is strictly between the two of them. Still, we can enjoy the contact high.

Actually, you can get a contact high off the movie in general. Everything seems freshly seen, unexpected: throwaway details like the breathy exhilaration of Bart's older sister, Ruby, taking a phone call from her brother (Lewis had the actress, Anabel Shaw, run around the soundstage for a couple of minutes just before the take); or the late-night goofiness of the moment when a nameless cook in a greasy-spoon diner dismissively turns away from the distant figures of Bart and Laurie, takes a swig of bad coffee, and favors us with a sardonic grimace. There's always an extra dimension to things.

But Lewis's greatest coups are, again, integral to the movie's action and how he films it. When Bart goes up onto the carnival stage to try outshooting Laurie, the camera follows each of them upstage and down as they trade places. (She lights matches over his head; he lights matches over hers.) Given the aura of competition, attraction, and sexual energy, the camera movements not only build suspense but also eroticize the space the two are traversing. The strategy is soon echoed in the claustrophobic scene in Laurie's trailer when Bart replaces the carny owner (Berry Kroeger) as the man in Laurie's life. And in a kind of aesthetic sense memory, the eroticism attaches to another scene a few minutes later when Bart and Laurie, having committed their first holdup, back out of the scene: the camera advances, as if fearful of being left behind. Or maybe that's just us.

The tour de force for which *Gun Crazy* is most famous is a bank-robbery scene near the midpoint. The camera is planted in the backseat of a car the couple has just stolen. Laurie is driving; Bart—dressed in the showbiz cowboy garb he wore during his own brief turn as a carny—will be getting out to go in and commit the robbery. As they wind through several blocks' worth of the small town of Hampton on a busy Saturday morning, the actors seem as much on the spot as their characters: they know the whole scene must play out in a single take of several minutes' duration, including perhaps some improvised dialogue. And so it does, with only the adjustment of the camera swinging to aim through a window when Laurie has to climb out onto the sidewalk and chat up the cop who ambles into view just after Bart enters the bank. The shot continues through the sounding of the alarm, Bart running out, Laurie pistol-whipping the cop, and a rushing getaway with Bart at the wheel. And still the shot holds, with Laurie now crowded up against Bart and looking back, ostensibly watching for the police cars whose sirens we begin to hear, but really just burning with lust for the moment. The camera can't just sit there; it moves closer to the glow in her eyes . . . and then settles back again, satisfied, as the car surges away. Up the road.

Out of the Past

Jacques Tourneur, 1947

by Stephanie Zacharek

IN THE WORLD OF NOIR, FINDING LOVE WITH A NICE GIRL means nothing: it's obsession—which electrifies and overstimulates the soul, spoiling it for anything as pedestrian and comfortable as marital love—that rules the day. In Jacques Tourneur's *Out of the Past*—one of the greatest noirs, among the most unsparing and the most bleakly beautiful—the femme fatale is actually the femme *domestique*. Robert Mitchum's Jeff Markham has escaped a crooked past to build a new life as a mechanic in a small, placid town. There he's found a girl he loves, and he truly does love her, with a deeply touching, gentlemanly, dutiful decency. Virginia Huston's Ann seems to be a fine enough match for him, an intelligent young woman who doesn't recoil when Jeff's secrets begin to seep into daylight. Instead, she urges him to talk to her, to tell her everything about the man he was before he met her: she's tough enough to take it, bolstered by the womanly, and not wholly unrealistic, belief that providing shelter and support and understanding is the key to earning a man's love.

And so Jeff begins his story, about a treacherous but irresistible creature named Kathie (Jane Greer), whom he first saw in a café in Acapulco, a faux-angelic vision in a white dress and a saucer-shaped halo of a hat. He's tough and smart, and he knows better than to believe the lies she feeds him; the problem is that her treachery is actually the ultimate truth, so raw in its hungry calculation, and its overt sexual dominance, that it isn't really a lie at all.

The disparity between the nice girl and the dangerous one is a linchpin of film noir: the good girl seems good enough, until the bad one comes along. And so in *Out of the Past,* Ann seems so terrifically nice, such a great girl to settle down with, until we get an eyeful of Kathie—appraising, predatory, so casually confident that her magnetism rivals the pull of the North Pole. Kathie doesn't have to work hard to be bad; she comes by it naturally, which makes her a woman without artifice. Her sin-dappled soul is as naked as her ambition.

And so in this twisted mirror world, Ann, the seemingly safe choice, the woman who has no desire for jewels, power, and dough, and who, unlike Kathie, would never dream of putting a bullet into another human being, is the danger-ous one. Her infinite understanding and patience will come with a price: she'll want Jeff home with her in the evenings; she'll want babies, a family—she wants only to give life, not take it.

But can we picture Mitchum's Jeff in that setting, trundling home in his coveralls after a hard day's work, washing his hands in the sink, dandling a baby on his knee? We can't—because he's most alive to us in that faintly rumpled trenchcoat, his tipped fedora only partly shading those perpetually half-doubting, half-believing-everything eyes. In the hushed, velvety, black-and-white universe of film noir—a bitterly poetic landscape of desiring and not getting, compared with the false cheer of the real-life postwar world, in which GIs returned to put their noses to the grindstone in pursuit of happiness, prosperity, and the build-ing of families—domestic bliss is life-sapping. In *Out of the Past,* it's Kathie who gives Jeff context, and thus everlasting life.

And so Kathie's cruelty is a kind of generosity. Jeff first yields to her, accepting, and then tries to resist, only to realize he can't escape her. Greer and Mitchum are perfectly matched here, partly because Mitchum—a man we think of as an indeli-ble symbol of masculinity—is so submissive to her, even against his better judg-ment. In a pivotal scene in which Kathie shoots one of Jeff's old colleagues, he turns around in horror to face her, the gun still hot in her hand; her ruthlessness is a cruel surprise. Later—after he's supposedly left her behind, eager to begin his life with Ann—he sees her again, and although he recoils from her, it's as if she's breathing life into him once again, a goddess of both destruction and rebirth. Recognizing what she is, in all its terrible splendor, repulses him, but it also sets something alight in him.

Mitchum was around thirty at the time the picture was made, and his youth-ful beauty is resplendent. (Even in the last years of his life, his face kept its aura of boyish vulnerability, although later you had to look a little harder for it.) In *Out of the Past,* his vulnerability is practically luminous. That's partly because of the way he's lit: as with all the great noirs, the movie's surface (the cinematogra-pher is Nicholas Musuraca) is so tactile that if you were unlucky enough to suffer a horrible blinding accident tomorrow, you could easily summon the contours of Mitchum's face as if they were sculpture.

But what makes the performance so wrenching is the way Mitchum mingles that searching, open quality with skepticism. The last thing he wants is to be taken in—the sensible downward curve of his mouth clues us in to his resolve—and yet he knows it's going to happen anyway. And how could he resist Greer's Kathie? At first her lips look all wrong, a bit too big for her face, borrowed—or stolen—from some other woman. But scene by scene, we get used to them, until they're nothing but bewitching. Greer's eyes have that dewy, melting quality, but not the kind of melting that suggests she's going weak at the knees. Their softness is a riddle, a dare: Come on in, the water's fine. They're welcoming eyes, bidding the dreamer to nestle deep inside this dream of a dame.

Jeff tries to find his way out of her strong undersea grasp, into a life of security, respectability, and love, the life Jeff would have built with Ann. Is it tragic that he's unable to do it? The movie's ending *is* tragic, but what makes *Out of the Past* so unsettling is that even its somber resolution suggests that Jeff has averted a greater tragedy. Love can sustain you for a lifetime, or it can be mere life support. From the moment Jeff met Kathie, he was of no use to anyone else. She's the woman who makes him most alive. She's the killer inside him.

Pickup on South Street

Samuel Fuller, 1953

by Ty Burr

PICKUP ON SOUTH STREET OPENS WITH THE IMAGE OF A New York City subway train slashing diagonally across the screen, its windows a scream of overmodulated brightness against a field of black. Then we're inside the car, but it's not one of those studio sets where everyone has a seat and enough room to unfold a highway map. No, it's the morning rush in midsummer, and air conditioning is a futuristic fantasy. Each commuter is jammed up against a slick, sweating stranger, trying to maintain the dignity of personal space that doesn't exist.

Because it's a subway car in a Samuel Fuller movie, things are happening even when it looks like they aren't. The guy with the snappy fedora and the weirdly taut face, leaning across the pole into the floozy opposite him—he's picking the wallet right out of her purse. The two suits watching the lift from several people over in the crowd, not sure what's happening—they're government agents, tracing the trail of top-secret microfilm from scientist seller to treacherous Communist buyer.

The girl's a courier, doesn't know she's carrying the equivalent of radioactive waste in her wallet. The pickpocket doesn't know what he just boosted. Nobody knows anything, but it's a Fuller movie, so they go down fighting anyway. The noirest of the noir, the best of the Bs, Fuller's films are gutter operas in which the death struggle is the only evidence of life. *Pickup on South Street* begins and climaxes in the subway, but metaphorically it never leaves the packed, hurtling train in which, as Fuller sees it, we're born and we die.

The pickpocket, Skip McCoy—a "cannon" in *Pickup*'s surreal argot—is played by Richard Widmark, the go-to weasel of early '50s noir. The girl—the "muffin"—

14

is named Candy, played by Jean Peters as one step from a streetwalker, either in the past or the future. (In reality, Peters would marry billionaire Howard Hughes four years later, staying with him until 1971.) The cannon and the muffin will fall hard for each other in the course of the movie, but even the sex looks like war here. When Skip and Candy kiss, their faces mash together like pieces of meat.

As in a Hitchcock movie, the microfilm is a MacGuffin—the thing that gets the characters hot and bothered—and you can tell Fuller doesn't worry too much about the Commies, either. It's 1953, you need something nightmarish on the horizon, so fine, yell "Pinko" in a crowded movie house and watch the panic. The political analysis in *Pickup* doesn't go any deeper than Moe's comment, "What do I know about Commies? I just know I don't like 'em."

Wait, who's Moe? She's this old lady who sells neckties on the street and information on the side, and the federal agent on Candy's tail—"the big thumb," a city cop calls him—brings her in to find the pickpocket. She listens to the agent's description of the boost and nails Skip based on his technique alone, but she'll spill only if she gets fifty dollars to help pay for her burial plot out on Long Island. "If I was buried in Potter's Field, it'd kill me," says Moe, and that, my friends, is the world according to Sam Fuller in a soot-specked koan.

Moe is played by the great Thelma Ritter (*Rear Window,* among many others), who gives the character a weary, quiet death scene that can bring grown men to tears. Ritter was actually Oscar-nominated for the role (one of six career supporting actress nods; she never won), proof that someone saw *Pickup* and realized her performance couldn't be denied.

Otherwise, the governing culture of 1953 pretended this terse, agonized, cartoonish, beautifully shot black-and-white slice of urban existentialism never existed. An uncredited staff reviewer for *Variety* dismissed the film: "for the most part falls flat on its face and borders on presumably unintended comedy." Bosley Crowther in the *New York Times* was equally unimpressed: "Indeed, the climate is so brutish and the business so sadistic . . . that the whole thing becomes a trifle silly as it slashes and slambangs along. . . . Sam Fuller, who wrote it and directed, appears to have been more concerned with firing a barrage of sensations than with telling a story to be believed."

Oh my. What a precise explanation of what film noir meant and why Fuller matters, and it's not surprising it came from the critic who lost his job after panning *Bonnie and Clyde* fourteen years later. Of *course* the filmmaker who was once the youngest crime reporter in New York City was "concerned with firing barrages of sensations." That is what a visual medium like movies is for. This is what art is for. "This is called instinct!" Fuller howls in an interview included on the Criterion Collection DVD of *Pickup*. "I write with the camera . . . Once I'm on the set, I use the camera as a typewriter."

What the Crowthers of the world never understood is that *Pickup*, both despite and because of its slightly loony exaggeration, its inarticulate urgency, captured 1953 culture far more cogently than A-list properties like *From Here to Eternity* (whose Donna Reed, playing a dewy-eyed whore, won the supporting actress Oscar that Ritter should have taken home). The Eisenhower era sprayed sunlight everywhere, but noir is where the shadows went, and in those shadows hid all the things the mainstream denied. You can call it a manifestation of cultural id, if you want. Fuller called it a "cinema fist."

That's why Joseph MacDonald's camera work doesn't give the characters any wiggle room, pinning them to their fates like moths on corkboard. And, okay, Skip McCoy the social outcast lives in a metaphor so bald-faced it's a bit of a giggle: an East River shack tenuously connected to the mainland by a gangplank. You can't live any farther out in Manhattan and still actually be *in* Manhattan. What reels him back? What gets him so riled up that he has to bash Candy's no-good boyfriend (Richard Kiley) right over the subway stile? Not patriotism, certainly. Not even Candy, who's taken a bullet for Skip and gone down the way people rarely do in movies, with an ugly little cry and a thud.

No, it's Moe who does it—or rather, it's her death, which Skip saves from Potter's Field anonymity in the first altruistic act of his entire life. And once he has saved her, he has to save himself (and Candy, too; why not?). Fuller knows that once the other passengers on the subway see you for who you are, the scam's over and a bigger game's just beginning.

The difference is, there's personal space this time.

Kiss Me Deadly

Robert Aldrich, 1955

by Desson Thomson

WHEN THEY MADE **KISS ME DEADLY**, PRODUCER-DIRECTOR Robert Aldrich and his screenwriter, A. I. Bezzerides, knew that a little subtext about nuclear destruction would go a long way.

They were neck deep, after all, in the cold-war paranoia of the 1950s: the duck-under-the-desk drills in the classroom, the basement dugouts at home, the search for Communist spies in Congress. Their instincts proved right, albeit in a backhanded way. The government's Kefauver Commission would soon declare *Kiss Me Deadly* the year's most pernicious influence on American youth.

Clearly, this 1955 film noir, centering on the pursuit of a deadly black box containing deadly plutonium, had struck a cultural nerve. And half a century later, the movie still resonates as a terrifying and timely cautionary tale. Its white-coated villains—who pursue, torture, and kill anyone who threatens their secret nuclear project—don't seem out of date amid today's buildup of atomic arsenals in developing countries, the threat of terrorist dirty bombs, and out-of-control government surveillance and torture.

But even as we remember *Kiss Me Deadly* for its apocalyptic menace, another theme hits home perhaps even more perniciously. It is a creeping misogyny, emanating most obviously from Mike Hammer (Ralph Meeker), the hard-boiled detective at the center of the story, but also from the movie's tacit implications about the women's misery index of the time. While the film's male characters grapple with the prospect of being bombed into the Stone Age, it seems these women already live in that dark place. And that sense of social oppression becomes the movie's proverbial elephant in the living room.

We feel this societal contempt in the movie's opening scene as a terrified woman, barefoot and naked but for her overcoat, runs frantically along a California mountain pass. Stopping Hammer's speeding convertible by standing directly in front of it, she forces him off the road.

"Let me guess," says Mike, reluctantly inviting Christina (Cloris Leachman) into his car. "You were out with some guy who thought 'no' was a three-letter word."

To Mike, her obvious desperation means nothing—even when she tells him she's being pursued by killers. Her wanton appearance is the issue, and we have little doubt that Christina's screen minutes are numbered. Soon enough, we watch her inevitable comeuppance, as her legs wriggle and kick, and her unseen head screams out her final moments. Those shrieks, which seem to reverberate forever, eerily evoke the aura of terrorist beheading videos of late—there's the same sense of rapacious physicality and our disconcerting involvement in it for even watching.

While Christina suffers horribly in the physical sense, another woman—Mike's secretary and lover, Velda (Maxine Cooper)—undergoes the emotional equivalent. Desperately in love with Mike, she's happy to satisfy his physical impulses, dreaming about a life with him. She exercises strenuously to remain attractive and waits forlornly for his return. ("I'm always glad when you're in trouble because then you come to me," says this darker version of Miss Moneypenny.) She's so focused on him, she's even resentful of the attention he gives to finding that nuclear device, which she dismissively dubs "the Great Whatsit."

Kiss Me Deadly is much more than a weirdly trenchant reflection of yesteryear. By showing malevolent hostility and frustration between the genders, it offers the unsavory idea that the human race's demise would be well deserved. If Mike Hammer—that walking, talking black hole—is our future, there is potent reason to doubt whether anyone is worth saving. And while that misanthropic philosophy would never see the light of day in a major Hollywood production, it makes a salient and powerful punch line here. Like so many other great B movies of the past, *Kiss Me Deadly* uses an ironic funhouse-mirror perspective to expose dark revelations about society. The outlook may be distorted and exaggerated, but we are still gazing directly into humanity's looking glass.

Crime Wave

André de Toth, 1954

by Richard Schickel

WE HAVE TO WONDER IF THE TITLE IS MEANT IRONICALLY, because as crime waves go, *Crime Wave*'s is nothing very much: a couple of jailbirds (Ted de Corsia and Charles Bronson—still playing under his real name, Charles Buchinsky) make their way toward Los Angeles, financing their trip with petty gas-station and convenience-store holdups. They might have escaped police attention if they hadn't accidentally bumped off a cop—in the film's opening sequence—who interrupts one of the depredations.

Their larger plan is to hold up a bank in Glendale, and they want to enlist a former inmate pal in the heist. He is Steve Lacey (played by sometime song-and-dance man Gene Nelson), newly married to nice Ellen (Phyllis Kirk) and trying to go straight. Alas for Steve, he's an aircraft mechanic and the bad guys need access to one of his planes for their escape. Even more alas for him, Detective Lieutenant Sims (Sterling Hayden) has a suspicious eye on him. And he's trying to stop smoking, which, if possible, makes him even crankier than usual. He shreds many a toothpick as he attempts simultaneously to satisfy his oral fixation and thwart the miscreants.

What we have here is, of course, a classic B picture—nasty, brutish, and, at seventy-three minutes, short. It is the kind of small program feature Hollywood was beginning to phase out in 1954, the year of its release. It is also the kind of movie that requires a strong, no-nonsense director if it is going to make its mark. And that's where André de Toth comes in. He was born in Hungary and began his career there before coming to America, where his first English-language feature was *Passport to Suez* (1943), one of the "Lone Wolf" series that starred the fading

Warren William. Thereafter he made twenty-six other movies, many of them low-budget Westerns and crime pictures, while also writing, producing, and working as a second-unit director. He was married for a time to Veronica Lake, and if he is remembered at all today, it's as the director of *House of Wax* (1953), generally thought to be the best of the 3-D films, and occasionally, wonderingly footnoted by cinephiles because André had only one eye, which should have interfered with his depth perception, but rather obviously did not.

I came to know André late in his life and I liked him enormously. He was a boisterous, opinionated, deeply amusing man who made his last movie in 1968 and filled his later years with sculpture and writing. (His autobiography, *Fragments,* is a great, disorganized, fascinating read.) He was also, several times in his life, a great director. I think particularly of *None Shall Escape* (1944), a psychologically acute study of a man succumbing to Nazism during the interwar years, and *Pitfall* (1948), a superb film noir, which brought that genre's dark style (and even darker sexuality) to the suburban doorstep of postwar America. These movies, like *Crime Wave,* like all of the de Toth movies I've managed to see, are brisk, unsentimental, and very objective in manner. You can get away with that attitude in B pictures, where the emphasis is on action and no one at the studio much cares about establishing the audience's "rooting interest" in the main characters—or for that matter about anything other than bringing the picture in on time, on budget.

Thus in *None Shall Escape* Alexander Knox plays perhaps the coldest and most unfeeling Nazi in movie history; in *Pitfall* Dick Powell achieves the sardonic heights he had been aspiring to since he abandoned his song-and-dance beginnings; and in *Crime Wave* Hayden, possibly the movies' hardest hard guy, achieved his frozen-faced apotheosis. If you wanted not to be loved—only a rare and treasurable handful of actors have aspired to that condition—André de Toth was your man.

He was perhaps not so much your man if you were Gene Nelson or Phyllis Kirk (also his leading lady in *House of Wax*). I wouldn't say that he's contemptuous of their bourgeois aspirations, but neither here nor elsewhere did he ever show much interest in such matters. André was one of those Europeans who had been blown every which way by the vast dislocations of twentieth-century history. The Laceys' desire for middle-class comfort and respectability clearly strikes him as naïve, ever subject to possibly fatal contingency. Indeed, in *Crime Wave,* Buchinsky's character is a constant, rapacious menace to Kirk's Ellen. He's always lurking in the corner of the frame, eyeing her, making salacious, sotto voce comments about her.

The script by Crane Wilbur, a sometime actor, occasional director, and creator of an endless filmography of B-picture screenplays, is terse and taut and makes gestures toward the semidocumentary manner often favored in postwar crime dramas. There are many shots of the police dispatch room, with cops barking into microphones or, conversely, being barked at by Hayden. These do not long detain de Toth: he obviously likes the ironic contrast between the vast resources the police can bring to bear on this case and the relative powerlessness of the victimized couple, but he does not require a lot of footage to make that point.

What he loves best is location shooting, and his deglamorized vision of Los Angeles is wonderfully realized in *Crime Wave*. It is, one might say, not a place that Lindsay Lohan or Paris Hilton would recognize. There are no movie stars, clubs, or paparazzi visible in this city. It is all dark, anonymous avenues, down which squad cars constantly race. The lights of the opening sequence's filling station are what the picture has for a bright spot. The apartment the Laceys inhabit is perfectly characterless, existing at the low end of respectability—not quite a slum, but aspiring to nothing more than shabby gentility. The standard visual tropes of film noir—slanted light coming through Venetian blinds, rain-wet streets, blinking neon signs—are not particularly stressed. That's equally so in the daylight hours. The city is seen in a flat, unmodulated light—characterless buildings squatting, without menace or promise, over streets jammed with buzzing traffic.

Putting the matter simply, there is nothing eye-catching in de Toth's mise-en-scène. His aesthetic is an antiaesthetic, blunt and without frills, just like the film's overall psychology. There is no explanation for the detective's sourness or for the crooks' psychopathy, or, come to think of it, for Steve's desire to go straight. It is typical of the best B-picture filmmaking that subtexts are elided. Their people are simply fated, like the characters in a naturalistic novel, to follow their preordained paths.

In de Toth's world, backstories are for sissies and smooth sociopsychological explanations for behavior, good or bad, are a waste of time. This particular narrative works out all right for the entrapped youngsters; nevertheless, we are rendered uneasy by their escape, not the least bit confident that they—or anyone—will avoid fate's blind pawings in the future. In essence, the unyielding bleakness of this movie triumphs over its conventionally "happy" ending. That's true of many low-budget film noirs of its era. (I think of *Side Street* [1950], *Act of Violence* [1948], *Railroaded!* [1947], and *Raw Deal* [1948], among many others.) As symbols of our postwar unease (or just as terrific little movies, so much more intense and ambiguous than the official great movies of their era) they are in need of rediscovery. *Crime Wave,* finally rereleased on DVD, is an excellent place to begin.

Murder by Contract

Irving Lerner, 1958

by Jay Carr

WHEN MARTIN SCORSESE DEDICATED **NEW YORK, NEW YORK**
to the memory of Irving Lerner (1909–1976), it wasn't because Scorsese's somber,
fatalistic musical had anything in common with Lerner's handful of noirs, apart
from spiritual darkness. Of Lerner's small output, the film that Scorsese was most
influenced by, and cited frequently, was *Murder by Contract*. A quickie shot in eight
days on a microscopic budget, it's a potent reminder of how less can be more, centered on Vince Edwards's loner killer for hire. Cool on the outside, tightly coiled
on the inside, Edwards's Claude, priding himself on having put his emotions on
ice, exemplifies a sort of cusp noir, a harbinger of postwar American change.

There's a surliness in Edwards's bottled-up Claude. (It later served him well as
TV's *Ben Casey,* which ran from 1961 to 1966, with Lerner directing 13 of its 153
episodes.) But Claude is more about control, and self-control, than anything else,
at least at the outset. In a deadpan subverting of the American dream, he declares
that he just wants to buy a house on the Ohio River and will be able to pay for it
much faster as an assassin, at five hundred dollars a pop, than as a wage slave.
His intro to a prospective client parodies a corporate job interview. When he's told
to go home and wait for the phone to ring, he does so for two weeks, in his
monk's cell of a furnished room, passing the time exercising and immersing himself in minutely detailed routine.

When the call comes, he's ready. Claude's meticulousness extends to killing only
with legal weapons—a knife, his hands, a rope, a razor. In every respect save voca-
tionally, he's scrupulously law abiding. He never speeds, doesn't carry a gun. He's a
careful craftsman whose attention to detail is always rendered discreetly; we never

see the killings, only Claude advancing on his victims as they—and we—yield to blackouts, or the sounds of death offscreen. Never asking questions, Claude is the model servitor, patiently executing hit after hit, recording five-hundred-dollar payment after five-hundred-dollar payment on a little pad, edging, step by step, toward his retirement cottage, à la Sterling Hayden in *The Asphalt Jungle* (1950).

But John Huston's noir landmark and Lerner's taut little study couldn't be more different in their underlying assumptions and even their cinematic language. The documentary approach that found its way into mainstream American film during and after World War II was more pronounced by the late '50s. Besides, Lerner, the New York–born leftist intellectual, came from making anthropological films at NYU. While Huston was making the now-classic combat documentary *The Battle of San Pietro* in 1944, Lerner shot a documentary on the legendary maestro Arturo Toscanini. While *The Asphalt Jungle,* with its nocturnal world of shadows and rain-slicked streets, was steeped in the noir lexicon, *Murder by Contract* stood the visual language of noir on its ear by dragging it into the sunlight.

There's a seismic change in tone and focus when the film shifts from the East, where Claude's killings had gone off without a hitch, to Los Angeles. It's a big career opportunity for Claude, whose efficiency with smaller fry—including the man who originally hired him (Michael Granger's Mr. Moon)—has led him up the ladder to a five-thousand-dollar payday for killing a gangster's former girlfriend (Caprice Toriel, whose character blurs gender-role lines by being named Billie). She's about to deliver damaging testimony to a grand jury. Avoiding Union Station, the taciturn Claude is met at the train in Glendale by mob grunts Herschel Bernardi and Phillip Pine. They're comic relief, Shakespearean clowns, with their baffled grumbling at his inscrutable ways. But his insistence on spending the first few days driving around sightseeing, seemingly at random, isn't just a show of nonchalance and a way to reduce the pressure. He wants to make sure they're not being followed.

When he is sure, he goes into action, faced with assassinating a woman barricaded inside her house in the Hollywood Hills, surrounded by police guards inside and outside. It's during the setup of the job, and Claude's implementation of his plan, that the film's thematic shocks come clear. The great cinematographer Lucien Ballard, most famous for shooting Sam Peckinpah's wide-screen epics, started by loading trucks at Paramount and worked his way up to directing B movies for five years at Columbia when it was a B studio. He knew how to shoot with economy, and he knew the language of several genres, noir included. What's impressive is that he used so much natural light to make the film's point.

What anthropologically trained Lerner tapped into was American postwar change. Where historians saw an age of conformity, Lerner saw a release of pent-up energies, a metaphysical sprawl that was soon to have its analogue in suburban sprawl. In his brilliant study *Film Noir: The Spaces of Modernity*, Edward Dimendberg usefully makes a distinction between the centripetal force of the classic noir of the cities, with everything (including women, trapped in male sexualizing of women's roles) pulled toward the city's dark center, and the centifugal forces of the postwar world, with everything spiraling outward, including into the suburbs, away from older role models.

Thus Billie, his target, although superficially trapped in her own house, is there out of choice. It's her space, however compromised. Strong-willed enough to testify against powerful killers, she's also strong enough to refuse protective custody in a safe jail cell and insist that the guardians of public morality guard her in her own house, where she can play her piano and flash a temperament the police around her are forced to respect. She is, in short, anything but a sitting duck. Analogue for a new kind of woman who wasn't to fully emerge for another generation, she's nevertheless a prototype. Claude's problem, as his employers grow ever more anxious, is that he literally can't get to her, especially after another woman intervenes.

Glowering, craggy-browed Edwards (Lerner used him again in his follow-up noir, the 1959 *City of Fear*) begins to show signs that his controlled exterior is starting to crumble. "I don't like women," Claude snarls. "They're not dependable. I don't like killing people who're not dependable." Leaving aside the psychosexual dynamic of which Claude seems at best dimly aware, this particular woman is especially unruly. The camera tracks Claude's consternation. LA's relentless, atomizing glare becomes a visual analogue to the erosion of the control that the hitherto cool hit man had extended over the spaces where he dealt out death with assurance. As he clambers through the scrubby hills overlooking her house, with Ballard's camera pulling back and tracking him from a distance, we realize that the film is exchanging intimacy for a distanced study of the technician of death as a scrambling animal. We feel desperation in Claude for the first time. Maybe his sniper-scope plan won't work. Maybe he'll have to improvise (he's aware that not successfully making the kill is his own death warrant), literally and figuratively penetrating the house, penetrating his quarry's space. And if he does, who'll end up as the victim?

Clean, lean, and mean, tight, tense, and satisfyingly reverberant, *Murder by Contract* vaults over its Poverty Row origins. We can understand why the young Scorsese was much more taken by it than by the A movie on the double bill he saw. We see in Scorsese's *Taxi Driver* (1976) Travis Bickle's genuflections to Edwards's ascetic preparations. Scorsese says he recalled Perry Botkin's potent music for *Murder by Contract*—a single guitar, which Botkin played, redolent with hints of '50s Italo-pop and Anton Karas's zither music for *The Third Man* (1949). Years later, Howard Shore devised a similarly guitar-flavored score that underlined the web-of-fate element in Scorsese's Oscar-winning *The Departed* (2006). In its pared-down imperative, and its distant early warning signals of postwar societal upheaval, *Murder by Contract,* with its fade to white, is a big little film noir turned film blanc.

The Well

Leo C. Popkin and Russell Rouse, 1951

by David Sterritt

YOU CAN'T JUDGE A MOVIE BY ITS DVD BOX, BUT SOMETIMES the disconnect between packaging and content is downright hilarious. The belated DVD release of *The Well* is a great example. Look at the box and you'll see a garishly colored shot of a bare-chested man holding a half-swooning woman in his muscled arms, gazing rapturously into her face as she looks away with an undefined emotion—longing? temptation? fear?—in her sparkling blue eyes. If you like passionate romance, this is clearly the movie for you.

Not! If ever a Hollywood drama steered totally away from passion and romance, *The Well* is that picture. The things it's actually about are a lot more somber: the evils of racial bigotry, the dangers of police power, the dark side of small-town innocence, and the ability of ordinary people to band together for both constructive and destructive purposes. The hero never takes off his shirt. And those sparkling blue eyes—what were they thinking? The movie is in black and white.

All this aside, *The Well* is an engrossing picture that deserves to be better known. Although the acting and dialogue are shaky at times, the issues it raises are as relevant today as when the film was new.

The story starts quietly. A little African American girl is walking through a field, and in an eyeblink she drops abruptly out of sight. The camera moves in, and we see that she's fallen into a well half hidden by grass and brush. We have no way of knowing how deep the well is, whether the girl survived her plunge, or how anyone could ever find her.

Back home, her parents are less worried than angry, because this isn't the first time she's wandered away without telling anyone. They grow increasingly

26

concerned as the hours pass, finally contacting the police to search for her. Questioning people in the town, the sheriff and his deputies learn she was last seen in the company of a white stranger who held her hand and bought her flowers. The cops eventually find the stranger, who's the visiting nephew of a local businessman. He claims he bought the flowers on a kindly whim, held the girl's hand to help her cross the street, and knows nothing of her whereabouts after that. None of this convinces the lawmen, who keep up a relentless interrogation in hopes of wrenching a confession out of him.

And still the tale is just beginning. Rumors circulate: a black girl has been kidnapped, or molested, or even killed by a white man. Tempers rise, along with confusion, since the racially mixed town hasn't experienced serious tensions in the past and people aren't sure how to react. Soon black folks are wondering if a cover-up is taking place—if the "culprit" has been caught, why hasn't the missing girl been found?—and white folks are all too eager to "protect themselves" from hostile blacks. This becomes a self-fulfilling prophecy, leading to mob hysteria and vigilante violence.

I won't reveal how this comes out, but the plot still has a long way to go. The missing girl is finally found—alive or dead, we still can't tell—and the town rallies around in sympathy, or at least curiosity, as rescuers try to reach her in the well. This makes for harrowing suspense and surprisingly visceral cinema. (It's not very true to the 1949 case of little Kathy Fiscus, though, which inspired this portion of the film; the same incident, which had a very different outcome, also plays a part in Woody Allen's nostalgic 1987 comedy-drama *Radio Days*.)

The Well was codirected by Leo C. Popkin and Russell Rouse, an effective team. It was the first directorial effort for Rouse, who was primarily a screenwriter and penned *The Well* with Clarence Greene, his frequent partner. It was the last directorial effort for Popkin, who had produced a handful of films with African American subjects in the late 1930s and early 1940s. He's best known for producing *D.O.A.,* the respected Rudolph Maté noir of 1950; it's an interesting footnote that Rouse and Greene got story credit (with a third writer) for that movie's 1988 remake.

The Well is efficiently directed almost all the way through—in terms of action and suspense, if not casting and acting—but it really comes alive in the last half hour, as experts work to retrieve the trapped little girl. Viewing this entirely from above ground, we watch a hardworking crew punch a new hole deep into the earth, see rescuers disappear down a narrow pipeline, and hear the agonizingly slow progress reports they provide through a hastily assembled sound system.

While the decision not to show any of the belowground activity was surely dictated by budget and logistics, it pays terrific dividends by forcing the viewer's imagination to work overtime. At its best, this lengthy scene recalls Jacques Becker's excellent 1960 prison-break picture, *Le Trou,* which also finds enormous drama in people digging a hole. In complementary ways, both pictures are first-rate filmmaking.

The strongest performance in *The Well* comes from Henry Morgan, aka Harry Morgan, best known for *M*A*S*H* on television but a hugely prolific movie actor from the early '40s through the late '90s. He plays the little girl's alleged kidnapper/abuser/killer, and his outrage at the cops is almost palpable. Everyone else in the cast—well, almost everyone else—is adequate. Ditto for Dimitri Tiomkin's music.

In its racial-tension scenes, *The Well* is a more-than-respectable entry in the cycle of "problem pictures" made by Hollywood in the post–World War II years; in the rescue scenes, it's genuinely gripping. The movie received two Academy Award nominations, well deserved, for film editing and screenwriting. But its deepest appeal lies in the things it doesn't show. This is sophisticated cinema, in a scruffy sort of way, and its praises need to be sung. B pictures don't come much more involving, engaging, and smart.

Part TWO: Nightmares in Technicolor

Neo-Noir

THERE'S SOMETHING PERVERSE ABOUT DAYLIT NOIR—IT'S like Harvey Keitel wearing a tuxedo at nine in the morning (see *Pulp Fiction*). You can't quite put your finger on it, but it's wrong. It's inappropriate. It's twisted. It's *perfect.*

You remember these movies in black and white. Isn't *Reservoir Dogs,* Quentin Tarantino's 1992 explosion of violence and vengeance, a chamber piece for ashen men in black suits and white shirts, under a moral eclipse? Don't these movies tantalize our rods, rather than our cones? Then again, there's all that red . . .

Perhaps it's that these movies *should* be in black and white but got somehow misdirected to the Technicolor lab. Colors notwithstanding, they make shadows out of light, ambiguity out of certainty, anarchy out of what tamer films portray as an orderly universe. (Really, now, wasn't *Croupier* in black and white?)

Unlike their older noir counterparts, the makers of neo-noir are generally not struggling fringe dwellers on the service road to the trailer park near the back way out of Hollywood. John Boorman has had a long and illustrious career, with films including *Deliverance* and *Hope and Glory* in the '70s and '80s, and *The General* and *The Tailor of Panama* in the '90s and '00s. He was only on his third outing when he directed Lee Marvin in the enigmatic *Point Blank,* a 1967 crime drama that continues to confound and delight (and was remade, from the same Donald Westlake novel, into the Mel Gibson vehicle *Payback* [1999], which somehow isn't noir, neo or otherwise). William Friedkin is a virtual institution thanks to *The Exorcist* (1973) and the wonderfully warped sensibility that gave us the disturbing *Bug* in 2006; but *To Live and Die in L.A.* (1985) holds a special place in his oeuvre, and not only because its backward chase tried to outdo his own car extravaganza in *The French Connection* of 1971.

Even when he delves into the comedy of *You Kill Me* (2007), John Dahl maintains the moist moral dankness of early hits like *Red Rock West* (1992) and the singular *Last Seduction* (1994), which is addressed here. And Mike Hodges, who in 1971 made the seminal *Get Carter* with a viciously unhinged Michael Caine, took movie houses by storm in 2000 with *Croupier,* which made a star of Clive Owen and provided evidence, if any were needed, that occasionally a great movie needs time to build an audience and shouldn't be banished from the screen for not breaking box office records at the Friday afternoon show. A theater in Manhattan played *Croupier* for months. And sure enough, the film took hold.

Bottom line: what *Payback* and the inexplicable 2000 remake of *Get Carter* (with Sylvester Stallone!) demonstrate is that style, not content, is what makes an outstanding neo-noir a brand upon the brain. Herein we celebrate six of the best.

Reservoir Dogs

Quentin Tarantino, 1992

by Jami Bernard

MR. BROWN: *Mr. Brown, that's a little too close to Mr. Shit.*
MR. PINK: *Well, Mr. Pink sounds like Mr. Pussy. How about if I'm Mr. Purple?*
I mean, that sounds good to me. I'll be Mr. Purple.
JOE: *You're not Mr. Purple. Some guy on some other job is Mr. Purple. You're Mr. Pink.*

PINK, BLUE, ORANGE, BROWN, WHITE, BLONDE. THE MEMBERS of the heist team in *Reservoir Dogs*, strangers to one another when assembled for the initial planning session, argue over who gets which color. The code names are for their own protection—they can't rat each other out if they don't know anyone's real identity. That, fundamentally, is why the heist goes so horribly wrong—ending in gut wounds, betrayal, death, and a sliced ear—because you can't work a crew that isn't tight, and you can't keep a crew from *getting* tight just because you hand out colors for names.

Although the ear-slicing scene became the movie's major takeaway, with its bouncy Stealer's Wheels ditty and its amusement-park ratcheting up of anxiety, the "meat" of the movie is when the traitor among them confesses his identity to the partner who's trying to ease him into death. Ratting oneself out is the *ne plus ultra* of sacrifice in a den of thieves.

That scene is as close to genuine emotional vulnerability as it gets in a Quentin Tarantino movie, but in the case of *Reservoir Dogs,* it's enough: this is a movie about friendship and betrayal (and posturing), and so are most (all?) of Tarantino's movies.

"Who's a tough guy?" says Mr. White as he tries to comfort the gut-shot Mr. Orange. "I'm a tough guy," Mr. Orange sputters weakly. What could be more intimate?

Reservoir Dogs was Tarantino's first try at directing. He had desperately wanted to direct his scripts for *True Romance* (1993) and *Natural Born Killers* (1994), but he signed them away in exchange for the clout (and money) he'd need for future projects. That left *Reservoir Dogs* in the hopper—it was cheap and it was swift. Although it didn't win top prize when it debuted at Sundance in 1992, it is surely better remembered than Alexandre Rockwell's *In the Soup,* a perfect instance of the B movie—the one on the lower half of the double bill—getting more traction.

Reservoir Dogs opens with a 360-degree pan around eight men in a diner as they argue over the true meaning of Madonna's "Like a Virgin" and whether it is incumbent upon customers to tip when there's no refill on the coffee. The scene gives Tarantino, as Mr. Brown, a chance to have some dialogue before departing the movie. (For this, he appropriated the Madonna riff he had written for Steve Buscemi's Mr. Pink; you can't trust gang members or filmmakers when it comes to self-interest.)

That opening scene, though boisterous, serves as a quiet prelude and a way to show all the gang members together for the last time, a kind of "before" picture. The movie will plunge almost immediately into the bloody, noisy, confused, and blood-soaked aftermath of the botched heist.

After the galvanizing opening credits—the eight men stride slo-mo toward the camera in their black jackets, skinny ties, and sunglasses, the very picture of *Magnificent Seven* cool—the movie zooms right over the heist itself to its fallout: Mr. Orange (Tim Roth) screaming and bleeding in the backseat of a car, Mr. White (Harvey Keitel) consoling him while driving the car to the appointed rendezvous, an empty warehouse. Over the course of the movie, the surviving robbers show up at the warehouse and try to piece together what went wrong, who is left, and who to blame. Through flashbacks, we gradually learn how the men got together for the job, how they masked their identities from potential witnesses and from one another with color-coded names, and how one of them is an undercover cop who set them up. The movie finishes with a Mexican standoff of epic proportions.

The movie is bloody and wild, chatty and funny, a grab bag of steals from movies from Hollywood to Hong Kong. It was workshopped at the Sundance Institute and then shot over five weeks for approximately $1.2 million, qualifying it for that definition of "B movie" that insists it be threadbare and scattershot. It did poorly at the box office, a victim of its signature ear-slicing scene; every review contained a warning like the kind you get on a pack of cigarettes. But it did superbly on video and remains a cult favorite . . . if you can call Tarantino "cult."

What truly makes *Reservoir Dogs* a keeper is Tarantino's infectious enthusiasm for B movies—genre movies, bottom-of-the-double-bill movies, gangster-and-shoot-'em-up movies. The picture borrows liberally (some say too liberally) from pictures past, starting with the color-coded names from *The Taking of Pelham One Two Three* (1974). Tarantino has said the color theft was subconscious; in any case, having the men squabble over their colors is pure Tarantino—for two reasons that have much to do with the Tarantinoverse as a whole.

First, the cast really did argue over their colors before shooting the movie. In the script, the characters are color-blind except for the names; there were no distinguishing physical characteristics that would make one actor ill suited for another role. Tarantino offered Tim Roth a choice of Mr. Blonde or Mr. Pink as if asking him to choose a card for a magic trick, but Roth took Mr. Orange, a role that required him to spend most of the movie lying in a pool of blood. Tarantino wanted Michael Madsen for Mr. Blonde, the one who would bop around to "Stuck in the Middle with You" before slicing off another character's ear. But Madsen was holding out for Mr. Pink, and thought it was his until virtually the week of shooting; the Mr. Blonde character didn't appeal to him initially, because it had little dialogue and the ear-slicing scene was so sketchily described that it would depend on improv. (It was Madsen's idea to "talk" to the ear he took as a trophy, for example.)

Many of the real-life conversations in which Tarantino engages end up in his scripts: about breakfast cereal, quarter-pounders, foot massage, tipping waitresses, and the deeper meanings of lyrics. But the second ingredient of "pure Tarantino" is the before-and-after-ness of things. What happens to these movie characters before "Action" and after "Cut"? Movies with scenes involving jewelry thieves at work tend to show the characters at full macho throttle, but . . . before the heist, do they have petty arguments? Do they practice the tough-guy routine in front of the mirror? When do they go to the bathroom? If they've been shot but they're not dead yet, how long does it take to die, and does the wailing continue until it's annoying to others? (It does.)

Samuel L. Jackson has called Tarantino a "film sponge." But Tarantino not only absorbs movies and how they are shot, he also turns them over and shakes them to see whether the batteries fall out. That's why, when he references other movies, it's usually in the true spirit of homage: a reference plus a wink. But he is not always quite so deft, and there were hard feelings out there over his use of the back-and-forth structure of Stanley Kubrick's 1956 *The Killing,* and especially of the plot and scene-by-scene stack-up against the last twenty minutes of Ringo Lam's 1987 *City on Fire*.

Somewhat defensively, Tarantino once told me that "great artists steal, they don't do homages." And sometimes great artists do things that are neither one nor the other: the title *Reservoir Dogs* is a nod to when Tarantino worked as a clerk at Video Archives, where he couldn't always pronounce the titles of the artsy French films his customers wanted to rent. It's a long way from *Au revoir les enfants* to *Reservoir Dogs*, but Tarantino wears his failings with pride. The important thing about film geeks, he says, is that they have to "show a high regard for their own opinion. He with the most point of view wins. When I walk into a room, I always have the most point of view."

The Last Seduction

John Dahl, 1994

by John Anderson

THE LAST SEDUCTION ESTABLISHED JOHN DAHL AS A MASTER of daylit noir, raised the bar of badness for female protagonists, and made an ultimately futile bid for Oscar glory on behalf of ur-bitch Linda Fiorentino. (The film had played on television before its theatrical run, and was thus rendered ineligible by those oh-so-wizened mandarins of the Academy.) While there are many startling aspects to this gleefully sordid movie, among the more baffling things about it, thirteen years later, is the subsequent evaporation of its star—perhaps via Dorothy's water bucket, but certainly in a sulphurous eruption. Fiorentino is magnificently depraved and, watching her now, seems to have arrived on Dahl's doorstep having fallen off some dark, dark planet of the rattlesnake women to create a siren both sui generis and sociopathic. (Have we mentioned she has great legs?) She then, presumably, returned to her homeland, to frolic among the succubi.

Where is Fiorentino really? She made *Jade* in 1995, *Men in Black* in 1997, *Dogma* in 1999, and some others, but her semipermanent wave seems to have crested, and she was last heard of, professionally, making films in Germany. (Not including, although it would have been perfect, a remake of *Ilsa, She Wolf of the SS* of 1975.) We tend to think (and my experience interviewing her around the time of *Jade* leads me to say this) that somewhere she is running a concentration camp, performing unspeakable lab experiments on small, formerly furry animals, and/or ruling over an upriver Amazonian outpost, à la Colonel Kurtz. (The truth is apparently worse: she lives in Connecticut.)

It's a shame about our lack of Fiorentino, because without her today's bad girl is merely a brat. The unfortunately nonfictional Paris, Lindsay, Nikki, Britney, et al. are amateurs of dysfunction compared to Fiorentino's Bridget in *The Last Seduction,* a "total fucking bitch" (her words) and an unrepentant castrator. Barbara Stanwyck may be Fiorentino's patron saint; Kathleen Turner in *Body Heat* was perhaps an inspiration. But neither came close to the utterly heartless and self-serving calculation portrayed by Fiorentino. It's an epic performance, uncompromising, undiluted by sentiment or even regret. And the closing shot is so devoid of imminent perdition as to wreck the entire concept of karma.

It's the opening scene, however, that's the true key to the heroine's character. Amid a collage of legs, arms, ears, and telephones we hear Bridget before we see her, extolling, berating, and browbeating a crew of telemarketers hawking rare coin sets, telling them to make more sales, make more pitches, make more calls, in a cross-cubicle field holler of what's-the-matter-you-dickless-wonders passion. She's clearly the workingman's nightmare—a woman with power intent on retribution for gender crimes dating back to Eden. At home later, when she's slapped by her husband, Clay—an absolutely sublime Bill Pullman—whom she has called an idiot, the moment can be interpreted as setting the whole *Seduction* ball rolling. The real Bridget has been established, and Clay, who in fact *is* a pussy-addled idiot (along with every other man who crosses Bridget's path), is merely providing her an alibi for something she's already planned.

Clay. Let's talk about Clay, as in moldable, pliable, unformed. He's a doctor, not quite finished with his medical education but able to write prescriptions, and he's just completed a transaction involving a case full of pharmaceutical cocaine and seven hundred thousand dollars in cash. Which Bridget promptly steals. Half hanging out of his apartment window as he watches her disappear down their outerborough street, Clay doesn't seem very surprised that his wife has just left him one hundred thousand dollars in debt to a loan shark. "You better run," he bellows, but with a certain degree of chagrin.

The script by Steven Barancik is about stolen money, calculation, a quest for revenge, and a city slicker versus a country rube (Peter Berg, whom Bridget plays like a hay-congested accordion). But it's *really* about sex. Or rather, our perceptions of same. "They're soft," Bridget says, fondling Clay's . . . currency. "I thought they'd be stiff." Bridget looks at money the way men look at porn: it's mostly about promise, but it also has a power all its own. And if one man in the movie could figure that out about Bridget, the ending would be different. Barancik's brainstorm is that men perceive women the way they want women to be. And if more women could figure *that* out, life might be different. And a lot scarier.

So let's think of *The Last Seduction* as a horror movie. It certainly is for Mike, a nice guy living in Beston, where Bridget pulls up to a gas pump marked "self-serve only." He's well aware of his umbilical ties to the town and his lack of motivation to leave it. When Bridget barges in and immediately alienates a local bartender ("Who's a girl got to suck to get a drink around here?"), Mike is transfixed. "What do you see in her?" a bewildered friend asks him. "Maybe a new set of balls," Mike says, and he doesn't know how right he is. Not long after, they're coupled against a chain-link fence, Bridget hanging virtually upside down (think vampire bat) and silhouetted against a lamplight as other patrons blissfully head home. Bridget, now named Wendy Kroy—she has a curious talent for reading backward, and a return to New York is her goal—establishes herself in Beston, avoiding the phone taps and private detectives of her thoroughly pissed-off husband. She also sets up Mike, who has his own twisted history, the way Hitler set up Stalin.

The noir credentials of *The Last Seduction* are solid—the movie is all moral ambiguity and dank gray psychology—and it qualifies as a B partly because it was made for cable. It had a reasonably healthy theatrical life (an Oscar would have helped), but since the demise of the double bill, television has become the medium secondary to film in terms of esteem, if often the primary medium in terms of quality. (*The Sopranos,* for instance, taken in its totality, is the equal of much great cinema narrative.) *The Last Seduction* also raises the question of whether our culture is any more progressive, or at least open, than it was thirteen years ago. Probably not, and one reason it's difficult to imagine this picture being made today is that a lot of its allure comes from how boldly it breaks taboos about female character, expressed in small, tender gestures, such as Bridget putting out a cigarette in Mike's mother's apple pie, or nonchalantly tossing her wedding ring into the coin well in her car's console. Little things. Endearing things.

The bigger gestures—Fiorentino's acrobatic eye-rolls at any suggestion of sentiment, or the way she seems to sincerely consider the idea when Mike tells her she needs help—are all part of a performance that is so peculiar and singular it has no precedent and has left no legacy. That Fiorentino is so unbelievably sexy doesn't make the experience any less fascinating, or explicable. That she's sexy because she's bad is not a question. But is she bad because she's sexy? Fiorentino has created a criminal genius/hottie-libertine who's a moral bankrupt and can't quite stay in her heels, and we arrive at the question of what the viewer, male or female, makes of her, knowing nothing about her except her voracious appetites for money and sex, and her use of the latter to attain the former. She's an enigma, although since she's a woman, a history of oppression is assumed. But is that fair? Can't a character be female and still be purely evil, self-serving, manipulative, exploitative, sexually predatory, and bad, bad, bad? It seems only fair.

One False Move

Carl Franklin, 1992

by Sheila Benson

ONE FALSE MOVE WAS RELEASED—BARELY—IN 1992, WITH
only scattered distribution, just enough to enable a handful of supportive critics
to spread the word about the stunning, modestly made movie and about its director, Carl Franklin, in his feature-film debut. The following year, a critic at the
Edinburgh University Film Society wrote: "The characterization is superb, the performances wonderful, and the ending heart-stopping. *One False Move* should have
been huge. It should have been bigger than huge. It should have been enormous."

Why it wasn't is fascinating. The movie's wan little release certainly didn't help;
it's hard to build an audience with brief runs and virtually no advertising.
However, there may have been another stumbling point: what the film seems
to be, from its opening sequence, is a world away from what it is, but those first
minutes are so terrifying that they overwhelm you, and word of mouth may have
turned away some audiences. (On the DVD, Franklin said he watched his
then-agent walk out of an early screening; I myself watched a revered cinematographer stalk up yet another aisle—although his wife was leading the way.)

In the two opening scenes, Franklin pours out his rage at the carnage that punctuated many blockbusters of the day, where for an opening flourish scores of anonymous, characterless extras would be obliterated while we watched, untouched and
unmoved. Franklin challenges this: you want to know about the loss of a human
life? *One False Move*'s victims are partying and dancing, taping themselves on a new
video camera, when their coked-out "friend" Fantasia (Cynda Williams) joins them
and lets hell loose in South Central. Pluto (Michael Beach) and Ray (Billy Bob
Thornton), her boyfriend, remorseless killers both, are there, hunting drugs.

Franklin uses contrasts to stage his most indelible scene: as we see a woman, trussed up on the floor with duct tape over her mouth, we also watch her video image on the TV screen, dancing, laughing, vibrantly alive. While she struggles, during the awful minutes before Pluto uses his knife, we feel the agony of the waiting Clutter family or the students at Columbine—trying, useslessly, to hide— and of every victim anywhere.

Having made his point, Franklin moves smoothly into the real heart of his story. Learning that the three are bound for tiny Star City, Arkansas, a pair of veteran LA detectives (Earl Billings and Jim Metzler) fly there to wait for them, while the town's brash, becalmed sheriff, "Hurricane" Dixon (Bill Paxton), throws himself into becoming indispensable, whether he's wanted or not.

As the increasingly unstable killers veer through the Southwest, trying to sell their drug haul, the action cuts between their snarling panic and the tense quiet in Star City. Franklin gives his drama elements of almost mythic inevitability. Some of these are grounded in the screenplay by Thornton and Tom Epperson; it's uncommonly smart—in a bone-deep way that doesn't call attention to itself— in matters of guilt, human nature, and long-standing Southern bloodlines. It's also nicely studded with surprise.

Well out of their element, the LA cops settle warily into their wait, trailing Hurricane as he keeps the peace by sheer force of personality. (He hasn't had to draw his gun once in six years.) Over backyard barbecue and bourbon, his wife, Cheryl Ann (Natalie Canerday), quietly takes one of the detectives aside. She knows her husband and she's worried by how dangerously much he idolizes these pros who bark out commands with guns at the ready. "He doesn't know better," she warns. "He watches TV. I read nonfiction."

From his DVD commentary, it's clear that Franklin hand-picked his cast, down to nuances of age and skin color—details of no small importance in a story where race is, and isn't, an issue. Franklin began as an actor, and this seems to have given him a great, free, go-for-broke approach to casting. God knows no one else had seen Bill Paxton as a leading man before, but Franklin delayed production to get him, and Paxton's uncommon depth as the seemingly sunny Hurricane becomes the film's bedrock. (Don Cheadle as Mouse Alexander in *Devil in a Blue Dress* [1995] would be Franklin's next actor to take off running.)

I'm not sure if anyone could, or would, claim credit for Billy Bob's broad-scale talents—he's sui generis—but Franklin may have been the first (aside from Thornton himself) to see him as a plausible lover for Cynda Williams. Unappetizingly shirtless, with a skanky ponytail, Ray is one sorry specimen, a depth marker of how far down Fantasia has come.

As events collect toward the shattering ending, Franklin allows himself a quick director's indulgence: a high-angle *North by Northwest* homage with empty crossroads, crop duster, and all. Not just a throwaway gag, this actually heightens the sense of dead-end abandonment as one of the characters returns to Star City—which, we discover, is where it all began. Looking back, we realize that *One False Move* has been Fantasia's story all along; not a new one, certainly, old as the South itself, but no less tragic for that.

Even if Franklin has opened his first film with his deeply held feelings about cinema violence, he's not one to let violence be its lasting aftertaste. Not this director, who—after an onscreen death—momentarily stills the sound track's noises of birds and crickets, choosing silence to honor "the passing of a soul." Against all odds, Franklin embraces the power of redemption and closes *One False Move* on that belief, as a central character inches stubbornly, almost imperceptibly toward it.

Point Blank

John Boorman, 1967

by Charles Taylor

OF ALL THE DISJUNCTIONS IN JOHN BOORMAN'S SEMINAL 1967 noir *Point Blank,* none is more jarring than the one that occurs at the very beginning: the roaring MGM lion followed by a shot of a battered and dazed Lee Marvin with a psychedelic light show playing over his face. Here was Metro's big kitty, *the* symbol of Hollywood tradition, visually supplanted by the very countercultural weirdness that threatened to make Hollywood irrelevant. The MGM execs who were baffled by the movie must have been even more unsettled by what followed, a sudden, unexplained cut to a cell on deserted Alcatraz Island, where, under the credit, "Lee Marvin . . . Point Blank," the star himself is shot and left for dead. What the hell was going on here?

For one thing, the death of the studio system. By 1967 Hollywood was desperately trying to find a way to attract the new youth audience but was too scared to abandon its by-the-book methods. What resulted was often movies that wound up looking like a Jaycee in a Nehru jacket: the mod trappings couldn't disguise the square essence.

Several months before *Point Blank* was released, Arthur Penn's *Bonnie and Clyde* (1967) had reconnected American movies to the energy of their previous golden era, the 1930s, and heralded the new sensibility they would have in their next golden era, the 1970s. But Boorman didn't follow Penn's visionary lead. He did something more insidious: he let the rot show. In *Point Blank* cold, angular modernist design melds with the flat anonymity that characterized Hollywood production design during the studio system's death throes. It's Antonioni meets *Lover Come Back* (1961). Boorman also took a panoply of contract players—Lloyd

41

Bochner and Michael Strong and Keenan Wynn among them—who had made a living playing lawyers, doctors, small-time businessmen in B movies and TV shows, and cast them as mob bosses, hit men, slimy two-bit gofers. At times *Point Blank* feels like an uneasy amalgam of innovation and played-out convention. But the mix is finally startling, a kind of vampirism in reverse, with Boorman's stunning technique putting blood back into a desiccated genre corpse.

Beneath all the knockout visual preening that Boorman and cinematographer Philip Lathrop indulge in lies a standard revenge melodrama. Lee Marvin's Walker agrees to help old buddy Mal Reese (the wormy John Vernon) get out of debt by staging a heist at abandoned Alcatraz Island, where "The Organization" has a money drop. Reese, who's been sleeping with Walker's wife (Sharon Acker), improvises and shoots Walker, taking Walker's share of the money and leaving him to die. Walker survives and, with the help of Yost (Keenan Wynn), who wants to destroy The Organization for his own shadowy purposes, sets out to get his revenge and his money.

The first thing that drew director and star together was shared contempt for the script. Credited to Alexander Jacobs and David and Rafe Newhouse, it could have been taken from any pulp novel. (In fact it's based on *The Hunter,* one of the books Donald E. Westlake wrote under the pseudonym Richard Stark; it was also the source of the Mel Gibson vehicle *Payback* [1999].) Having won an Oscar for *Cat Ballou* (1965), Marvin had approval of script, casting, and final cut, and impressed with how Boorman intended to rework the screenplay, he ceded those to the director. Making his Hollywood debut, Boorman had control normally reserved for the most powerful directors, and he made stunning use of it.

In pictures like *Breathless, Shoot the Piano Player,* and *Band of Outsiders*, filmmakers like François Truffaut and Jean-Luc Godard had poeticized the American gangster film. Boorman's method was closer to the puzzle movies of their nouvelle vague colleague Alain Resnais, though without the ennui that makes Resnais's movies so deadly. *Point Blank* is probably as pretentious as a movie can be and still be good.

The question movie geeks have always debated about *Point Blank* is whether Walker is in fact dead from the beginning and the movie is his dying fantasy. After he's gut shot, we see him rising from the cell, a jacket tied around his wound, plunging into the icy waters to swim to the mainland. On the sound track, a chirpy tour guide tells us no one is believed to have survived an escape from Alcatraz—and there seems no way Walker could, either. Back in civilization, he's dressed in a steel-gray suit that, with Marvin's white hair, gives him the appearance of an avenging wraith. A cocktail waitress greets him: "Walker, you still alive?"

Like Steven Soderbergh's *The Limey,* a movie that is in many ways an homage to *Point Blank* (Soderbergh interviews Boorman on the DVD of *Point Blank*), the movie is edited to dislocate us. In the most famous sequence, Boorman cuts between Walker striding furiously through LAX, the relentless clip-clop of his hard shoes echoing on the sound track, and Walker's wife going zombielike through her day, unaware that her "dead" husband is coming for her. The effect of *Point Blank* is both oblique and brutal, as if we'd been sucker punched without first being told why. The tension only occasionally breaks, as in the scene where that most delicate of movie broads, Angie Dickinson—superb, as she frequently is, as Walker's sister-in-law—stands in front of Marvin slapping him silly while he doesn't even blink, regarding her as no more effectual than an ape would a persistent fly.

What saves *Point Blank* from being *Bad Day at Marienbad* are the B-movie energy of the pulpy premise, the thumb-your-nose freedom in Boorman's rule bending, and the sense that both director and star are working out personal obsessions. On the commentary track of the DVD edition, Boorman says the movie is about the psyche of Lee Marvin. Marvin, who had snuck into the marines at age seventeen and come back marked by the brutalities he'd seen, made a career as a movie thug. Though there are exceptions (throwing a pot of boiling coffee in Gloria Grahame's face in *The Big Heat,* for example), Marvin was normally the least showy of villains. He presented the violence of his characters as a fact, without judgment. There was nothing sentimental about him. That's a plus in the *Point Blank* moment when he slips his wedding band onto his dead wife's ring finger. The fact is, her death doesn't deter him.

How can you be moved, or at least have a stake in, such a character? In *Point Blank* it's because the single-mindedness of Walker's quest for revenge and money is more recognizably human than the reptilian machinations around him. The criminal empires of earlier noirs have become, in *Point Blank,* as faceless and efficient as any other big business. Sustaining the organization takes precedence over the lust for greed or power or personal ambition. Walker is the hero because he's the one who resists turning himself into, in William H. Whyte's phrase, "The Organization Man." The irony is that even as he's tearing it to shreds, he's doing its nefarious bidding.

Which is why, at this distance, *Point Blank* can be read as a prophecy of the fight Boorman has waged throughout his career, trying to keep his own identity while working for the organization that is Hollywood. That's the implicit subject of his great, near-Shakespearean family comedy, *Where the Heart Is* (1990). If Boorman has beaten the odds by bringing gems like that picture (and *Excalibur,*

Hope and Glory, Beyond Rangoon, The General) to the screen, he's lost to the house in other ways. Disney, which neither liked nor understood *Where the Heart Is,* dumped it theatrically and then punished Boorman by not sending him any of the handful of rave reviews that appeared. At the end of *Point Blank* Walker recedes into the shadows he emerged from in the first shot. We're lucky that Boorman has refused to go so quietly.

To Live and Die in L.A.

William Friedkin, 1985

by Matt Zoller Seitz

WILLIAM FRIEDKIN'S **TO LIVE AND DIE IN L.A.** BOASTS SEVERAL closeups of men getting shot point-blank in the face. Friedkin has been painting actors' faces crimson since his breakthrough hit, the notoriously ruthless *policier The French Connection,* which included a just-for-the-hell of it close-up of a couple of disfigured accident victims who had no apparent connection to the film's main plot. In most cases, these images are a visual definition of the word "gratuitous." But in *L.A.,* Friedkin's horrific close-ups are integral aspects of the picture's down-and-dirty aesthetic and a rebuke to an especially irritating cliché: the movie character who sustains what would surely be a mortal wound in real life, only to show up a couple of scenes later with a cast on his arm. In Friedkin's Los Angeles, when characters die, they're dead, and Friedkin puts the camera right up in their freshly pulped faces so you know it's adios muchacho.

Friedkin's viciously blunt direction of *L.A.*—which he cowrote with cops-and-robbers novelist Gerald Petievich, from Petievich's best seller—mirrors the obsessive quest of its protagonist, U.S. Treasury agent Richard Chance (William Petersen), a surly jerk hell-bent on punishing his partner's killer, the suave counterfeiter and would-be painter Rick Masters (Willem Dafoe). Chance flouts rules and procedures in the name of justice and ego; Friedkin startles the audience by flagrantly disregarding conventions that encrusted Hollywood movies in the 1980s. That decade saw the rebel antiheroes of the Johnson-through-Ford eras supplanted by macho narcissists played by the likes of Sylvester Stallone, Arnold Schwarzenegger, Michael Douglas, and later, Bruce Willis; alpha males who walked all over everybody yet still earned a slow clap at the end. In the scenes of

Chance drawing his more straitlaced new partner, John Vukovich (John Pankow), deeper into his payback fantasy, the film puts an ironic spin on the arguments that straightforward '80s heroes used to justify their quasi-fascist hijinks. "I'm gonna bag Masters, and I don't give a shit how I do it," Chance declares. He sounds like Mickey Rourke's Stanley White in the Oliver Stone–scripted, Michael Cimino–directed *Year of the Dragon,* which came out the same year as Friedkin's movie (White's signature line: "How can anybody care too much?"). But there's a crucial difference: not for a moment does Friedkin's film encourage us to believe that Chance represents anyone's interests but his own.

There's a disquieting sense that Chance's fury originates not just in his resentment of lawbreakers and his grief over his partner's death but also in an overpowering feeling of emasculation. He prides himself on getting close to death—even courting it—without being affected by it. The film's prologue finds Chance interrupting an assassination attempt on the president by a Middle Eastern suicide bomber who exclaims, "God is great!" before leaping off a hotel rooftop and blowing himself up; the next time we see Chance, he's bungee-jumping off a bridge on the day of his partner's retirement—a sequence whose opening shots are deliberately framed to suggest a suicide attempt. Masters's menace is personal; his treachery rattled Chase, and the fact that the system won't let him exact revenge with deliberate speed amps up his restlessness and egomania and ultimately leads to his demise. The movie is attuned to the decade's Me First culture, and it's borderline nihilistic in a way that's true to its gutter milieu and the self-interested, often loathsome humanoids that scamper through it. At its heart, *L.A.* is a cautionary tale about a man who is denied instant gratification and then seeks it in his own way, destroying careers, property, and lives in the process.

In a DVD supplement, Friedkin describes *L.A.* as a story of "counterfeit lives" in which every major character is pretending to be something he's not. On a superficial level, that's accurate. (Chance and Vukovich go undercover as criminals, and Masters is a frustrated, mediocre painter who lives an art-world hero's life, financed with money from his counterfeiting operation.) But the description implies a sense of delusion that doesn't really jibe with the characters' single-mindedness. They know what they are, they have primal drives, and they do what they need to do to satisfy them. Except for a few moments of macho banter, there's little warmth onscreen, and there's nothing resembling a traditional movie "love interest." Chance's relationship with Ruth Lanier (Darlanne Fluegel), a parolee and single mom, is notably bereft of hearts and flowers. Chance and Ruth seem to need each other physically, and they betray a guarded vulnerability when they're together, but the relationship is mutually exploitive. He wants tips that he can use to nail Masters; she wants to stay out of prison and needs money to supplant her gig as a ticket taker at a strip joint. "How much do I get for the information I gave you on Waxman?" Ruth asks Chance in an early scene. "No arrest, no money," he replies. "It's my fault he's dead?" she counters. "It took me six months to get next to him. I got expenses, you know." "Guess what?" Chance snarls, "Uncle Sam don't give a shit about your expenses. You want bread, fuck a baker."

Chance's platonic seduction of Vukovich is far subtler. Chance uses his he-man flamboyance (hectoring righteousness, snotty asides, bow-legged gunfighter's strut) as an intoxicant. He gets Vukovich high on bad-boy swagger and loosens his standards one concession at a time, like a high-school stud taking all night to unbutton his prom date's gown. By the film's midpoint, Chance and Vukovich are cutting legal and procedural corners; by the end—after posing as potential customers of Masters and then being denied the down payment required to make a deal with him and bust him—they rob an unrelated drug courier who turns out to be an FBI agent, accidentally get him killed (repeating a twist from the end of *The French Connection*), then flee from the money's heavily armed presumptive owners. The film's final stretch is a turbocharged black comedy—a Keystone Cops chase going the wrong way on an LA freeway while Wang Chung's synthesized score chug-chugs like a cokehead's dance-floor heartbeat. The chase doesn't just build on Popeye Doyle's deranged pursuit of the El train in *The French Connection;* it improves on it by serving up a spectacular metaphor for the characters' progress through—and effect upon—their world. Tear-assing across Southern California while drug goons strafe them with rifle fire and oncoming cars and trucks swerve to avoid hitting them head-on, the treasury agents literally threaten the very society their improvisations are intended to protect.

Friedkin is a deeply untrustworthy director; if you don't believe it, seek out his have-it-both-ways defenses of the audience-jazzing ugliness in *The French Connection,* the blasphemous mayhem in *The Exorcist,* the sinister homophobia of *Cruising,* and the pro– and anti–capital punishment pandering woven throughout *Rampage.* But in *L.A.,* his coldly observant eye—that of a robber casing a bank— suits the subject matter, and the production's glorified underground aesthetic cranks up its energy and intensifies its themes.

At the time, Friedkin was reeling from a string of box-office disappointments. He shot *L.A.* outside the studio system with a nonunion crew, on a relatively modest $14 million budget, with a cast comprised mainly of unknown or barely known actors (including John Turturro as a busted courier whom Masters believes is going to turn state's witness). Friedkin's biggest name was Dean Stockwell, a supporting player who has a few effective scenes as Masters's sleazy sellout of a lawyer. Except for the complex action sequences, most of the film's scenes play out from one, two, or at most three camera angles. Friedkin often printed the first take, and in a few instances he told the actors they were just rehearsing, secretly rolled film, then called "Cut" and moved on. The result feels like what it is: a work of furious urgency. The director depicts the movie's amoral crooks and corner-cutting feds as animals fighting for survival and dominance: sharks that must keep moving or die.

Croupier

Mike Hodges, 1998

by Kenneth Turan

INTENSE, HYPNOTIC, ASSURED, **CROUPIER** MESMERIZES FROM its opening image of a roulette ball on the move. A taut journey inside the world of professional gambling, this enigmatic, beautifully made film crosses the traditions of film noir with a distinctly modern anomie with results as ice cold and potent as the vodka its protagonist keeps in his freezer.

It's been more than thirty-five years since *Croupier* director Mike Hodges made *Get Carter* (1971), arguably the most influential of British gangster movies, described by one disapproving critic as "a bottle of neat gin swallowed before breakfast." And it's been three decades since Paul Mayersberg wrote the screenplay for Nicolas Roeg's haunting *The Man Who Fell to Earth* (1976), starring David Bowie. Together for the first time, Hodges and Mayersberg fashioned in *Croupier* an elegant gem, hard and bright, where the austerity of Robert Bresson meets the laconic toughness of Raymond Chandler.

Our guide is Jack, a tyro writer with dyed blond hair compellingly played by Clive Owen. His detached habit of referring to himself in the third person in *Croupier*'s extensive voiceover gives him a distant, uninvolved air, but don't confuse his coldness with complete amorality. For Jack's lack of surface emotion masks passions he's had to bury, because in his world, no moment of humanity or warmth goes unpunished.

Jack is no more than half in love with Marion (*Notting Hill*'s Gina McKee), the London policewoman turned store detective he lives with. "You're an enigma, you are," she says fondly, to which Jack accurately responds, in the voiceover that only the audience hears, "not an enigma, a contradiction," someone whose unspoken credo is "hang on tightly, let go lightly."

Jack is trying to be a writer, but the only editor he knows is not exactly encouraging: "Celebrity is what sells books," the man tells him. "We can always find someone to do the writing." So when Jack's estranged, amoral father calls and says he's lined up a job for his boy at the Golden Lion casino, Jack is more receptive to the offer than he might have been otherwise.

For Jack, as it turns out, has had enough casino experience in South Africa to make him wary of returning to the pit. But the lure of regular income persuades him to take his hair back to its original, more sepulchral, jet black and accept a job as croupier, the person who rakes in the chips and pays the winners on games of chance from roulette to blackjack.

Though we never learn exactly why, Jack categorically refuses to gamble and has feelings close to contempt for the punters, those who do. Still, when he enters the mirror-walled Golden Lion for the first time, his ironic voiceover reminds him, "Welcome back, Jack, to the house of addiction." Later he elaborates in his usual third-person: "A wave of elation came over him. He was hooked again, watching people lose."

Photographed by Michael Garfath and edited by Les Healey, *Croupier* beautifully captures the tactile quality of the gaming world: the spin of the roulette wheel, the click of the chips, the whoosh of cards turning over on felt. The film also allows you to feel how and why all this becomes addictive, to experience the rush inside that airless world rather than simply have it described.

Being a croupier demands the nerves and skill of a close-up magician, and though Jack likes to behave like a detached voyeur, much given to those ironic comments, in fact the pressure is so unbearable that he literally shakes for hours after his shift. Ever the writer, Jack quotes Ernest Hemingway from *A Farewell to Arms* about his own situation: "The world breaks everyone and afterward many are strong at the broken places. But those that will not break it kills."

Despite his attachment to Marion, Jack is drawn to two very different women he meets through the casino. One, Bella (Kate Hardie), is a mousy fellow dealer he glances at before concluding, "She looks like trouble." The other, Jani de Villiers (*E.R.*'s Alex Kingston), is a glamorous gambler who's also spent time in South Africa. Mayersberg's intricate, carefully structured plot involves them all as they try their best to survive in a "bent world" where no one can be trusted, yourself least of all.

Part THREE: From Grindhouse to Art House

Madness and Melodrama

IF YOU'RE LOOKING FOR THRILLS SANS SPILLS, LOOK NO further than the half of *Grindhouse* directed by Quentin Tarantino, wherein Zoë Bell hangs on to Kurt Russell's car with the tenacity of an IRS agent, enduring twists, turns, bumps, jumps, and all the tortures of the vehicularly damned. If you want chills sans spills, check out Michael Powell's *Peeping Tom,* a creepshow of intellectual potency and acute soul disturbance that's also a Hitchcock-worthy critique of voyeurism, addressing every moviegoer who watches this film about a man who watches and makes (murderous) films. If you take your thrills *avec* chills and spills, any of the pictures in this chapter will unnerve you and perhaps disorient you, speaking to your body as well as your mind.

The challenge this category presents is figuring out what separates the B picture from the A. Certainly, anything made by Francis Ford Coppola between 1971 and 1975, a period that included the greatest *Godfather* epics, is by default an A picture in some sense; and when you consider the top-flight craft, inspired acting, and uncompromised ethics of *The Conversation* you have to ask, "To B, or not to B?" Yet Gene Hackman's performance as Harry Caul defines the darkness and etches the limitations inherent in the flawed American character; the movie's themes—emotional avarice, human disposability, and the admission that technological innovation comes with as many pitfalls as benefits—all resoundingly echo the B ethos.

Ditto for *Peeping Tom.* Can anything made by a visionary like Powell be considered anything but crème de la industry crème? Normally, no, but this time he had something very different in mind—a picture that lives on the fringe and wanders on the margins, a purposefully prurient movie that almost had to be a B to be at all. *Pretty Poison* and *The Stepfather* likewise deal with warped realities, delusional thinking, and the mayhem that results.

In the movies discussed here, there's a displacement of perception between malefactor and victim, Peeping Tom and lust object, the surveilling and the surveilled. It's in this murky middle territory that we find the adrenalin rush of clashing, crashing realities. Of course, smashing up a few cars can be nutritious, too, a vicarious primal scream that also echoes across these films.

Grindhouse

Quentin Tarantino, Robert Rodriguez, 2007

by Stephanie Zacharek

CONTEMPORARY AUDIENCES HAVE BECOME SPOILED BY movies that make sense, have great acting, and feature nudity only when absolutely necessary: no wonder hardly anyone goes to the movies anymore. We sit at home, alone in our semidarkened living rooms, hoping *About Schmidt* (2002) or *Little Miss Sunshine* (2006) will answer our deepest questions about the human predicament.

But what about our littler questions? Questions like, Can nuclear splooge really turn us into flesh-eating zombies? Is it such a good idea to go into the basement of the last house on the left? And that naked girl sure looks great zooming around on a motorcycle—but did she at least wipe the seat first?

To answer questions like those—or at least to render them academic—you need an audience, a large roomful of like-minded individuals, to hoot and holler at dialogue that sounds as if it had been written on a square of institutional-grade toilet paper, to jump when zombie-victim blood splatters the screen, to flinch collectively when the sniggering rapist gets an ax to the groin, to peer at the screen through parted fingers as the crazy speed demon on the dark country highway trails a carful of giggling, scantily clad teenage girls.

In your living room, no one can hear you scream. And where's the fun in that? As movies have gotten more sophisticated—at least technically—so have we, and in their double-feature B-movie homage, *Grindhouse,* Quentin Tarantino and Robert Rodriguez suggest, with the subtlety of a buzz saw headed for a villain's private parts, that we've lost something along the way. *Grindhouse* is the filmmakers' love letter to the cheaply made, rough-edged action and horror pictures that in the '60s, '70s, and early '80s would play the crummiest, most run-down movie houses in the worst part of town, or perhaps, if you lived in a more suburban locale, the drive-in. Typical fare included blaxploitation and/or women's prison pictures like Jack Hill's *Coffy* (1973) and *The Big Doll House* (1971); psycho-killer creep-outs like Wes Craven's *The Last House on the Left* (1972) and Herschell Gordon Lewis's *Blood Feast* (1963); el cheapo car-chase extravaganzas like H. B. Halicki's *Gone in 60 Seconds* (1974); and any number of other imported or domestic pictures (kung-fu adventures, sexploitation cheapies) that might put warm fannies in seats. These theaters would show three or four features at a stretch, which made them attractive havens for bums and assorted ne'er-do-wells: when I saw *Grindhouse,* the wag sitting next to me offered to pee on the floor to make the experience more authentic.

It was a chivalrous gesture, but an unnecessary one. *Grindhouse*—which consists of two full-length movies, one by Rodriguez and one by Tarantino, as well as several faux trailers by guest directors—is a grand collage of drooling zombies, bounteous breasts, spurting blood, and careering cars, a rambunctious and unapologetically disreputable entertainment as well as a comprehensive catalog of B-movie references. (For no discernible reason, the Rodriguez and Tarantino features have been released separately on DVD by the Weinstein Company. For the authentic *Grindhouse* experience, I recommend watching them back-to-back.)

Grindhouse is also recklessly joyous and deeply affectionate, a celebration not just of an all but lost approach to moviemaking but also of the nearly lost experience of communal moviegoing. The audience I saw *Grindhouse* with didn't pee on the floor (at least not as far as I could tell). But we did hoot and holler and groan together, united, if only temporarily, by the happy recognition that most of what we were seeing onscreen was sick as hell: We're sane, thank God; it's the world around us that's gone mad! Our sanity confirmed, we all settled in to watch Rose McGowan, as an amputee stripper, take out a slew of baddies with the machine gun attached to her stump. Why ever not?

The charming, saucy McGowan is one of the chief attractions of Rodriguez's *Planet Terror,* which makes up the first half of *Grindhouse*: with those cartoon-pussycat eyelashes, that distracted pout, those killer gams (both of them), she's its heart and its hottie. In *Planet Terror* a biohazardous leak of something-or-other turns people into cannibalistic zombies. It's up to McGowan and her bad-boy hero boyfriend (Freddy Rodriguez) to stop them. Marley Shelton plays an anesthesiologist with a killer arsenal of hypodermic needles (they're strapped to her leg in a specially fitted garter); Josh Brolin is her wacko doctor husband. Naveen Andrews shows up as a scientist with a scarf tied around his head and a single hoop earring—in other words, an "ethnic" villain. (He also carries a jarful of pick-led testicles around with him, but never mind.) Two young Venezuelan actresses, Elise and Electra Avellán, billed as the Crazy Babysitter Twins, play—what else?—crazy babysitter twins. (They're also Rodriguez's nieces.) Tarantino appears, in a small part, as a rapist—talk about grabbing the plum role for yourself.

Planet Terror is the sillier, more raucous of the two movies, a model of cheerful, demented, cartoonishly violent excess. Rodriguez, true to the movies that inspired him, goes for the gusto. More is more, especially when it comes to blood, which never just spurtles from squibs in tasteful quantities; it shoots out, geyserlike. (Legendary makeup artist Tom Savini, who designed the zombie effects for *Dawn of the Dead,* appears in *Planet Terror* as a clumsy deputy who loses a finger.)

Explosions, car chases, women cavorting in skirts the size of hankies: *Planet Terror* packs it all in, but even though the movie may seem haphazard, it was clearly made with a Zen master's meticulousness. The picture's surface has been scratched up in some places, and the film jerks and jitters raggedly through the projector in others; scenes are tinged pink or red, as if the print has been fading for years; and when the characters talk to each other, their dialogue sometimes sounds as if it were being beamed from a radio transmitter in Sheboygan. Back in the day, just a handful of prints of any one grindhouse-caliber movie would cir-culate among hundreds of theaters across the country. A picture's scraped and scratched surface, its fading and discoloration, its funky sound, were the scars of being run through too many ancient, badly maintained projectors—they'd become part of its identity. The prematurely aged look of *Planet Terror* is partly a novelty, but it also suggests the way movies—lousy ones as well as good ones—endure: in our memories, they outlive the fragile celluloid on which they're captured.

Love it or hate it, you sure get your money's worth with *Grindhouse*: Rodriguez and Tarantino enlisted modern-day schlock filmmakers to direct the phony trailers clustered around the two main features. Eli Roth, director of *Cabin Fever* (2002) and the *Hostel* pictures (2005, 2007)—he also has a small role in Tarantino's por-tion of *Grindhouse*—gives us the sickest one, for a slashfest called "Thanksgiving" (its superb tag line: "This year there will be no leftovers!"). The "Thanksgiving" trailer caused the MPAA ratings board to waggle its reproachful finger: Roth had to trim a few frames—involving a protruding butcher's knife and a gymnastically inclined topless cheerleader (use your imagination)—to get the all-important R rating, but the thing is still sufficiently depraved. Edgar Wright, director of *Shaun of the Dead* (2004), offers a sweetly twisted, tantalizingly vague promo for a horror pileup called simply "Don't." My personal favorite, though, is the one featuring the wonderful character actor Danny Trejo as a rebel peacekeeper and ladies' man (as evidenced by the naked cuties he cavorts with) in a hot little number called "Machete"—which also happens to be the name of the gadget whiz Trejo plays in Rodriguez's *Spy Kids* movies (2001, 2002, 2003), the first two of which are terrific.

The *Grindhouse* feature directed by Tarantino, *Death Proof,* is somewhat pokier than *Planet Terror.* But it's also, in the end, more exhilarating, and in its perverse, twisted way, more elegiac. In the first section of *Death Proof,* a posse of tough girls—played by Sydney (daughter of Sidney) Poitier, Vanessa Ferlito, and Jordan Ladd; their rival is played by McGowan, this time in hippie-blonde tresses—show up at their favorite local watering hole and encounter a seemingly benign older dude who goes by the name of Stuntman Mike (Kurt Russell). The second act of *Death Proof* features another set of girls (Rosario Dawson, Tracie Thoms, Mary Elizabeth Winstead, and Zoë Bell) and one very cool car: a 1970 Dodge Challenger, the same car featured in Richard C. Sarafian's groovily existential 1971 car-chase drama, *Vanishing Point,* a movie revered by two of the girls; the other two have never heard of it.

In the first half of *Death Proof,* Stuntman Mike is a laid-back charmer, an aging hunk who knows just what to say to melt a girl's heart, or at least get her, momentarily, to stop rolling her eyes: "There are few things as fetching as a bruised soul on a beautiful angel," he tells one. Later, he'll reassure another that as a former stuntman he's made sure his souped-up, skull-emblazoned car is "better than safe—it's death proof."

Some bad stuff happens in *Death Proof*—it chiefly involves flying limbs and decapitation—because Tarantino isn't just riffing on the style of these old movies; he's also capturing their heartlessness, the ways in which, even when they followed a rough code of justice, they didn't always bother with niceties like allowing characters we've grown to care about to live. But the sustained climax *Death Proof* builds to is purely a thing of beauty. At one point Stuntman Mike reflects that most stunt work is now, unlike in the old days, enhanced by computer graphics. In *Death Proof,* Tarantino does everything the old-fashioned way, with fast cars and real human beings doing crazy things. Even if you've seen it all before, you've never seen anything quite like it.

Death Proof has an unusual, loping rhythm: whole chunks of it focus chiefly on dialogue (Tarantino's specialty), featuring the girls yakking idly about what they do with their boyfriends, or about why they carry guns instead of knives (if you need the answer: "You know what happens to the folks who carry knives? They get shot!"). But the centerpiece of *Death Proof* is a car chase in which Bell, the New Zealand–born stuntwoman who was Uma Thurman's double in both of the *Kill Bill* movies (2003, 2004), and who makes her acting debut here, spends most of her time outside the Challenger, instead of driving it—while it's barreling down two-lane Tennessee blacktop. Bell is an extraordinary presence, supremely likable even as she radiates a sunny intensity. Dawson, with her perky bangs and high, original-Barbie-style ponytail, is a ballerina goofball; Poitier, a classy Amazon in short-shorts. (Tarantino, who acted as the movie's cinematographer, gives us a wonderful shot of her stretched languorously on a couch, a visual echo of the enormous blow-up of Brigitte Bardot in *The Night Heaven Fell* [1958] on the wall above her.)

Russell, superb as always, gets a great introduction here: the camera lingers on him, his face artfully and obliquely lit, as he demolishes a plate of nachos. It goes on for so long that each successive instance of finger licking and lip smacking is funnier and funnier. Russell's Stuntman Mike is a lost soul speeding toward hell, a man out of time in every way: he tries to impress a cluster of young women by telling them about the TV shows he's done stunt work on, like *The Virginian* (1962–1971) and *Vega$* (1978–1981). They stare at him blankly until he finally asks if they've ever heard of any of the shows he's talking about. When they say they haven't, he's not surprised, and neither are we.

The first half of *Death Proof* has a definite '70s vibe, while the second half is undeniably contemporary in its look and feel. It doesn't matter that Poitier uses a cell phone to text-message her boyfriend: when she sidles her bodacious booty up to the jukebox, it's Joe Tex's 1966 "The Love You Save (May Be Your Own)" that comes streaming out, a song that makes us forget what year it is and transports us, in a feat of supersonic magic, into a place called the past.

Death Proof straddles the past and the present: it's not sure where it should be living, or where it wants to live. Like all of Tarantino's movies—the bad ones as well as the good—it's marked, and energized, by restlessness. Tarantino is sometimes a marvelous director and sometimes a maddening one: volume 1 of the *Kill Bill* epic is a clutter of references with no emotional glue, but the second half, volume 2, is bitter, dark, and gorgeously poetic. I'm not a fan of *Pulp Fiction* (1994)—stylized violence served up with a smirk generally leaves me cold. But *Jackie Brown* (1997)—which Tarantino once called, aptly, his "Howard Hawks movie," and which took part of its inspiration from his love for Pam Grier—is, simply put, one of the finest pictures of the last decade.

And now Tarantino, formerly a renegade and a groundbreaker, has become something of an old-fashioned filmmaker. His movies have always been filled with references that only true movie eggheads would get. But as the original audience for his movies ages, younger moviegoers aren't as likely to get his jokes, his asides, his visual fillips. That isn't to say they won't enjoy his movies: Tarantino is a smart filmmaker, and a lively one—I think he'll always find his audience. But even at his relatively young age, he's already on his way to becoming Stuntman Quentin, the guy who recalls the pleasures of *Rio Bravo* (1959) and *Foxy Brown* (1974) as the youngsters gather 'round to listen. That's not the worst fate that can befall a director; we need filmmakers who can move us forward even as they maintain a sense of the past. To that end, *Grindhouse* captures a bit of rowdy movie history in a bell jar. Tarantino and Rodriguez can tell it like it was, because for better or worse, they know how it is.

Peeping Tom

Michael Powell, 1960

by Roger Ebert

THE MOVIES MAKE US INTO VOYEURS. WE SIT IN THE DARK, watching other people's lives. It is the bargain the cinema strikes with us, although most films are too well behaved to mention it. Michael Powell's *Peeping Tom,* a 1960 movie about a man who films his victims as they die, broke the rules and crossed the line. It was so loathed on its first release that it was pulled from theaters and effectively ended the career of one of Britain's greatest directors. Why did critics and the public hate it so? I think it's because the film doesn't allow the audience to lurk anonymously in the dark, but implicates us in the voyeurism of the title character.

Martin Scorsese once said that this movie and Federico Fellini's *8 1/2* contain all that can be said about directing. The Fellini film is about the world of deals and scripts and showbiz, and the Powell film is about the deep psychological process at work when a filmmaker tells his actors to do as he commands while he stands in the shadows and watches.

Scorsese is Powell's most famous admirer. As a child, he studied the films of The Archers, the team of Powell and Emeric Pressburger. Scorsese haunted the *Late Show* screenings of their films, drinking in their bold images and confident, unexpected story development. Teamed with Pressburger or alone, Powell made some of the best and most successful films of the 1940s and 1950s, including *The Thief of Bagdad* (1940), with its magical special effects; *The Life and Death of Colonel Blimp* (1943), with Roger Livesey's great performance spanning three wars; *A Matter of Life and Death,* aka *Stairway to Heaven* (1946), with David Niven as a dead airman; *Black Narcissus* (1947), with Deborah Kerr as a nun in the

Himalayas; and *The Red Shoes* (1948), with Moira Shearer as a ballet dancer. After these and more came Powell's *Peeping Tom*.

It is a movie about looking. Its central character is a focus puller at a British movie studio; his job is to tend the camera, as an acolyte might assist at mass. His secret life involves filming women with a camera that has a knife concealed in one leg of its tripod; as they realize their fate, he films their faces, and watches the footage over and over in the darkness of his rooms. He is working on a "documentary," he tells people, and only in the film's final shot do we realize it is not only about his crimes, but also about his death. He does not spare himself the fate of his victims.

This man, named Mark Lewis, has been made into a pitiful monster by his upbringing. When Helen (Anna Massey), the friendly girl who lives downstairs, shows an interest in his work, he shows her films taken by his own father. Films of Mark as a little boy, awakened in the night by a flashlight in his eyes. Films of his father dropping lizards onto his bedclothes as he slept. Tapes of his frightened cries. Mark's father, a psychologist specializing in the subject of fear, used his son for his experiments. When a police psychologist learns the story, he muses, "He has his father's eyes."

There is more. We see little Mark filmed beside his mother's dead body. Six weeks later, another film, as his father remarries. (Wheels within wheels: the father is played by Michael Powell, Mark's childhood home is the London house where Powell was raised, and Mark as a child is played by Powell's son.) At the wedding, Mark's father gives him a camera as a present. For Mark, the areas of sex, pain, fear, and filmmaking are connected. He identifies with his camera so much that when Helen kisses him, he responds by kissing the lens of his camera. When a policeman handles Mark's camera, Mark's hands and eyes restlessly mirror the officer's moves, as if Mark's body yearns for the camera and is governed by it. When Helen tries to decide whether she should wear a piece of jewelry on the shoulder or at the neckline, Mark's hands touch his own body in the same places, as if he is a camera, recording her gestures.

Powell originally thought to cast Laurence Harvey in the lead, but he settled instead on Carl Boehm (Karlheinz Böhm), an Austrian actor with such a slight accent in English that it sounds more like diffidence. Boehm was blond, handsome, soft, and tentative; Powell was interested to learn that his new star was the son of the famous symphony conductor. He might know something of overbearing fathers.

Boehm's performance creates a vicious killer who is shy and wounded. The movie despises him yet sympathizes with him. He is a very lonely man. He lives upstairs in a rooming house. The first room is conventional, with a table, a bed, and a kitchen area. The second room is like a mad scientist's laboratory, with cameras and film equipment, a laboratory, a screening area, and obscure equipment hanging from the ceiling.

Helen is startled when he reveals that the house is his childhood home and that he is the landlord: "You? But you walk around as if you can't afford the rent." Helen lives with her mother (Maxine Audley), who is alcoholic and blind, and listens to Mark's footsteps. When Helen tells her mother they're going out together, her mother says, "I don't trust a man who walks so softly." Later Mark surprises the mother inside his inner room, and she cuts right to the heart of his secret: "I visit this room every night. The blind always visit the rooms they live under. What am I seeing, Mark?"

Powell's film was released just months before *Psycho,* another shocking work by a British-born director. Hitchcock's film arguably had even more depraved subject matter than Powell's, and yet it was a boost for his career, perhaps because audiences expected the macabre from Hitchcock, but Powell was more identified with elegant and stylized films.

There is a major sequence in *Peeping Tom* that Hitchcock might have envied. After hours at the film studio, Mark persuades an extra (Moira Shearer) to stay behind so he can film her dancing. She is almost giddy to have her own solo shots, and dances around a set and even into a big blue trunk. The next day, the body is discovered inside the trunk as Mark, unseen, films the discovery.

The film's visual strategies implicate the audience in Mark's voyeurism. The opening shot is through Mark's viewfinder. Later, we see the same footage in Mark's screening room, in a remarkable shot from behind Mark's head. As the camera pulls back, the image on the screen moves in for a close-up, so the face of the victim effectively remains the same size as Mark's head shrinks. In one shot, Powell shows us a member of the audience being diminished by the power of the cinematic vision. Other movies let us enjoy voyeurism; this one extracts a price.

Powell (1905–1990) was a director who loved rich colors, and *Peeping Tom* is shot in a saturated Technicolor with shots like one where a victim's body under a bright red blanket stands out against a gray street. He was a virtuoso of camera use, and in *Peeping Tom* the basic strategy is to always suggest that we are not just seeing, but looking, too. His film is a masterpiece precisely because it doesn't let us off the hook, like all of those silly teenage slasher movies do. We cannot laugh and keep our distance: we are forced to acknowledge that we watch, horrified but fascinated.

Peeping Tom essentially finished Powell's career, although he managed to make a few more films. By the late 1970s, however, Scorsese was sponsoring revivals and restorations and joined Powell on the audio commentary tracks of several laser discs. Indeed, Powell fell in love with and married Scorsese's film editor, Thelma Schoonmaker, and she assisted him in writing the most remarkable directorial autobiographies, *A Life in Movies* (1986) and *Million-Dollar Movie* (1992). Hitchcock defused his macabre content with humor, while in *Peeping Tom* Powell played it straight. The result was a four-star film.

The Conversation

Francis Ford Coppola, 1974

by Peter Keough

HOW DOES **THE CONVERSATION** QUALIFY AS A B MOVIE? Traditionally, the term B movie refers to those cheap, readily accessible, generally lurid exploitation films from pulpy genres designed to fill the second billing for the main feature. *The Conversation,* meanwhile, defies genre, frustrates narrative expectations, and challenges and sometimes alienates viewers. It is subtle, complex, stark, fuguelike, self-conscious, and utterly ambitious. It was, however, cheap, or at least it was initially. Otherwise, it would seem to be the opposite of a B movie.

Francis Ford Coppola would be the one to know, having spent the first three years or so of his career making B movies, getting his first directorial credits with films like the German-produced *The Bellboy and the Playgirls* (perhaps it sounds better in German: *Mit Eva fing die Sünde an*), made in 3-D in 1962 ("In COLOR plus the new depth perception . . . it puts the girls right in your lap!"), and the legendary *Dementia 13* for Roger Corman in 1963.

But in 1972, when *The Conversation* went into production, Francis Ford Coppola was the most powerful filmmaker in Hollywood. *The Godfather* was making more money than any picture since *Gone with the Wind* and had won three Oscars, including one for best picture. The film's success intoxicated Coppola with dreams of artistic grandeur, but the process of making it had struck him as frustrating and demeaning. Making a big-budget film for a mass audience, adapting another writer's best-selling potboiler, working under the neurotic oversight of an oppressive corporate studio like Paramount—this did not fulfill his dream of being an auteur. *The Godfather*—ranked number two, just below the perennial

Citizen Kane, on the American Film Institute's list of the one hundred greatest Hollywood movies of all time—was not exactly a B movie, but it was a kind of work for hire, perhaps an immensely more successful *Finian's Rainbow.* But it did allow Coppola to make a film worthy of his talent and artistic vision—a film like *The Conversation.*

That probably wasn't how Paramount regarded *The Conversation,* however. For them it was a necessary investment (budgeted at around $1 million) to placate their genius director and make sure he followed through with the sequel to the astoundingly lucrative *Godfather.* In a sense, *The Conversation* was a new kind of B picture, one that would catch on in subsequent decades: a cheaply made auteurist indulgence made to stroke a talented, independent-minded director's ego in the gap between genuine money-making features.

This new kind of B picture, then, was an intensely personal expression of the filmmaker's soul. As such, it would include homages, in this case to Michelangelo Antonioni's *Blow-Up,* which Coppola acknowledges as an inspiration. Despite that pervasive influence (one scene in particular is a dishearteningly direct rip-off), *The Conversation,* certainly when seen in retrospect and in the context of Coppola's subsequent career, is so personal as to be almost solipsistically self-reflexive.

It starts with a technical tour de force by the filmmaker that also depicts the technical tour de force being performed by the film's protagonist. Harry Caul (played with nuanced nerdiness by Gene Hackman), the best undercover surveillance expert on the West Coast, has taken on the seemingly impossible assignment of recording the conversation of a couple walking around San Francisco's Union Square during a crowded lunch hour. Caul's method of solving the problem unreels in the film's first eight minutes; more important, though, this sequence demonstrates Coppola's own expertise in recording Caul's project, a logistics challenge requiring six cameras, four camera crews, and piles of sound equipment (good-bye budget, and good-bye also cinematographer Haskell Wexler).

A long, excruciatingly slow crane shot, calling to mind similar bravura shots by Alfred Hitchcock, Orson Welles, Robert Altman, and, of course, Antonioni, descends into the square, focusing finally on hangdog Caul in his perpetual plastic raincoat being trailed and imitated by an obnoxious mime. Cuts disclose an agent aiming what looks like a sniper rifle, the crosshairs finding the targeted couple. It's a shotgun mike, and with that and Caul's other eavesdropping devices— a guy with a mike in a shopping bag and another long-distance recorder in a hotel window—the surveillance team picks up random sonic squiggles, snatches of a band playing "When the Red, Red Robin Comes Bob, Bob, Bobbin' Along," and non-sequitur bits of seemingly inane dialogue. These spill into a bewildering audio collage, a puzzle that Caul, and the audience, must piece together.

And, presumably, Coppola also. At this point a lot of the script was up in the air and, like Caul, Coppola was faced with a bunch of tantalizing leads and disconnected directions that eluded final form. When Caul returns to his cavernous, Zoetrope-like factory-floor office and runs his recordings through a bank of reel-to-reels trying to orchestrate them into a coherent transcript, it probably echoes similar efforts by Coppola, or more likely "sound designer" Walter Murch, doing the same in the editing room with the movie. As Caul obsessively repeats bits of the conversation over and over again, together with flashbacks to the actual scene, the pieces cohere into a narrative, one drawing Caul, against his better judgment, more and more into an emotional involvement with his subject. For Caul is happy being a gun for hire. He doesn't want to know what the conversation is about, or who the couple conducting it are, or what the motives are of the mysterious businessmen who are paying him well to get the work done. He wants his satisfaction to be limited to technical prowess—the finesse, ingenuity, and panache with which he fulfills the task given him, however daunting.

Caul, then, is a threadbare version of Coppola himself. A brilliant cinematic technician, able to pull off the seemingly impossible task of taking on a trashy best seller; overwhelming egos ranging from Marlon Brando to Robert Evans; and the innumerable practical, moral, and aesthetic decisions, challenges, obstacles, and booby traps of a major studio production; and turning them into a box-office gold mine and, incidentally, a revered work of art. The secret, apparently, is not to think too much about it, just apply oneself to the job at hand.

Sound advice, but it ultimately fails Caul, and Coppola as well. As Caul's preoccupation with detail and secrecy and his fetishistic sexual nature (the shot of him in bed still in his raincoat embracing Teri Garr wearing white socks has to be the saddest love scene in movies) indicate, Caul's an obsessive-compulsive with a guilty streak as big as Union Square. Certain moments in the conversation—the man's plaintive "he'd kill us if he had a chance," the woman reflecting "he was once somebody's baby boy" while gazing at a wino lying on a bench who bears more than a passing resemblance to Caul himself—unnerve him. They remind him of another assignment in which he astounded his peers by his solution to a daunting challenge and where he didn't question who he was doing it for or why and, well, what happened afterward wasn't Harry's fault.

But, true professional that he is, Harry takes his finished tapes to his client, and for truly professional reasons refuses to hand them over because the conditions of the contract were not being exactly filled. And then he refuses because his conscience and his interpretation of the narrative presented by the tapes refuse to allow him to. And then it's too late, and Caul is left in futile search of the heart of darkness in the solitude of his stark apartment, a microcosm of the green vastness in which Coppola would lose himself in his ultimate B movie, *Apocalypse Now*.

The Stepfather

Joseph Ruben, 1987

by Eleanor Ringel Cater

IT HASN'T BEEN A GOOD YEAR FOR SIXTEEN-YEAR-OLD Stephanie (Jill Schoelen). She doesn't get along with her new stepfather, Jerry Blake (Terry O'Quinn), and she's just been suspended from school for brawling in art class. "What's your stepfather gonna do when he finds out?" asks a friend, and Stephanie morosely replies, "He's gonna kill me."

Bingo.

Jerry is gonna kill her. Not just for getting expelled or sassing him back or kissing the boy down the street, but ultimately for not being exactly like the oldest daughter on *The Brady Bunch*. That's what *The Stepfather,* an impish little gem of a movie, is all about. It's a black comedy–thriller about a murderous psychotic obsessed with sitcom perfection. Jerry, as he calls himself for most of the movie, likes to marry comely widows with cuddly kids, set up a home life that's flash-frozen Norman Rockwell (backyard barbecues, Thanksgiving dinners, etc.), and live happily ever after.

That is, until normal, everyday flawed reality starts leaving its messy footprints on his pristine family fantasy. When his home life unravels in the slightest—a sharp word, a sullen glare—Jerry unravels completely. Suddenly, the guy who brushes away a tear when he's carving the family turkey is giggling as he starts to carve up the family pup. Then he's gone—on to a new town, a new ready-made family—leaving blood in his tracks.

When we first meet Jerry, he's calling himself Henry Morrison and he's in the upstairs bathroom, ostensibly getting ready for another day at work. Only there are these flecks of blood all over his face, and he doesn't just shower and shave;

he transforms himself from a comfortably rumpled bearded type in a plaid shirt and glasses into a smooth-shaven, clean-cut yup with contacts and short hair (from Steven Spielberg to the Arrow shirt man, sort of).

He then goes downstairs—straightening a picture, picking up a toy one of the kids has carelessly left out, plumping a chair cushion—and heads out the door, briefcase in hand, "Camptown Races" on his lips. On the way, he passes a living room that looks as if the Manson family just dropped by. It's littered with the mutilated bodies of his family, the littlest girl still clutching a bloody teddy bear. Doo-dah, indeed.

Cut (sorry) to one year later. Henry has resettled. He has a new name (Jerry Blake), a new wife, Susan (Shelley Hack, perfectly cast as a Breck Girl mom), and the aforementioned resentful, suspicious stepdaughter, whose sessions with her shrink (Charles Lanyer) suggest all-too-normal stepfamily tensions. If only we hadn't seen that bloody teddy. . . .

But that's the great appeal of this marvelously clever and well-made film. Director Joseph Ruben and writer Donald E. Westlake aren't as interested in Jerry/Henry/whoever's murderous rampages (though they certainly don't skimp on them, either) as they are in their protagonist's behavior between outbursts. *The Stepfather* is a chilling, subversively comic look at a pathologically abnormal man doing his darnedest to ape normality—normality as he's seen it on *Father Knows Best* and *The Donna Reed Show*. A wonderful throwaway scene has him sitting on his bed, watching *Mr. Ed* and happily whinnying "Wilbur!" in imitation of the series' equine star.

Because its focus is on a counterfeit—Jerry's bogus Big Daddy—the film may feel a bit slight to some, as if it's just skimmed the surface of a fascinating sicko who has sprung full-blown, like Venus from the sea, from the frothy airwaves of our media. But that's what makes O'Quinn's performance so special. Notice how he uses his generic nice-guyness, his soap-opera-slick appeal. This isn't any nervous Norman Bates; this is the doting Daddy who pulls himself together with Pepto Bismol to make it to Sis's ballet recital, the devoted husband who swears his wife's choice of orange juice has made their marriage complete.

Yet Ruben and his cast never overdo the parody, never lose the gnawing menace underneath the American Dream platitudes, the shadows in the sunshine. (Not surprisingly, the film recalls Hitchcock's brilliant *Shadow of a Doubt* of 1943, which also had a plucky teen heroine.) When the newly expelled Stephanie, frantic to escape an evil she can't quite articulate, suggests she be sent off to boarding school, Jerry replies with utter sincerity, "But it's not a family without children."

And for an unsettling second, his eyes glaze over and he's like Hal the computer, about to go on permanent blink in *2001: A Space Odyssey*.

The Stepfather is a riveting mix of fright and fun. It's a blood-smeared Father's Day card reminding us that fewer cavities and a family dog aren't all it takes to make a happy home, and that making room for Daddy should be a matter of degree.

Pretty Poison

Noel Black, 1968

by Peter Rainer

"YOU ARE GOING INTO A VERY REAL AND VERY TOUGH WORLD. It's got no place at all for fantasies."

This warning at the start of *Pretty Poison,* issued to Dennis Pitt (Anthony Perkins) by his gruffly paternal case officer, Morton Azenauer (John Randolph), on the day of Dennis's discharge, is a confirmation of the young man's defenselessness. Dennis was institutionalized at fifteen for setting fire to his aunt's home with, unbeknownst to him, his aunt still inside it. He is out on his own now for the first time, and his parting joke to Azenauer—he says he'd prefer an interplanetary assignment to the factory job awaiting him—is not even a joke exactly. For Dennis, being out in the "very real" world is indeed a kind of science-fiction-style relocation. He's a stranger in a strange land. The tense, over-rehearsed manner in which he speaks—even in casual conversation he appears to be reading from a teleprompter—is his way of reining in a barely concealed hysteria.

When we next see Dennis he is employed at a mill in western Massachusetts that dumps toxic chemicals into the Housatonic River. He girds himself to become an ecoterrorist. (You get the feeling he's less interested in saving the planet than in playacting the role of saboteur.) Having violated his parole, he is tracked down by Azenauer, who can't bring himself to dash Dennis's future. "I'm not going back," he yells to Azenauer. "This is my life, my one and only life."

Released in 1968 without advance press screenings, *Pretty Poison* sank at the box office but became an instant succès d'estime—and remains so to this day. The fact that the movie didn't roll out with the usual Hollywood hype may have worked to its advantage. Audiences feel more proprietary toward orphaned movies, especially B movies.

But *Pretty Poison*—it was the debut feature of director Noel Black and was written by Lorenzo Semple Jr., based on a novel by Stephen Geller—is something of a B-movie manqué. Despite its low-budget trappings and rudimentary murder plot, the film is, from a psychological standpoint, almost bewilderingly complex. Nothing is as it seems, starting with Perkins's performance, which only the unenlightened would deem a Norman Bates redo.

He was never better than he is in *Pretty Poison*. Whereas even his best previous (and subsequent) work was often jangled by tics and stammers almost to the point of self-caricature, here he moves beyond all that. Or rather, to be exact, he gives us a clear, wide view into the psychosexual underpinnings of his signature mannerisms. It's like looking at a two-dimensional portrait that on closer inspection suddenly snaps into 3-D. Perkins was sometimes accused of playing adults as if they were arrested adolescents, but here his characterization makes perfect sense. Dennis is locked inside the mind-set of a traumatized fifteen-year-old. Throughout the film Black gives us a series of meltingly lyrical long shots of Dennis stretching out his gangly legs and racing through town, and it's as if in those brief moments Dennis is unlocking himself. The sheer joy of physical release has made him ecstatic.

The pathos of *Pretty Poison* is that despite his flippancies and junior G-man demeanor, Dennis is almost mordantly aware of his torments. They give him a greater appreciation of normality, and so he lives a kind of double life. Not entirely without cause, he imagines the world conspires against him. Worse, he conspires against himself, and on some barely perceived level, he knows it. He aches to be happy. This is why he is smitten the moment he spots the goddessy blonde high-school senior Sue Ann Stepanek, played by Tuesday Weld. Dennis sees romance as his redemption, and he woos Sue Ann the only way he knows how—by pretending to be a covert CIA operative enlisting her in a secret mission to sabotage the mill.

Like Perkins, Weld carries her own baggage from previous films, but even in her sex-kitten phase she had a sly knowingness about her allure. That's what she has here, too, except now her beauty is a deadly weapon. Sue Ann is the pretty poison. At the start of their courtship, Dennis involves her in his tricky, goofy missions; he can't believe his luck at landing a hometown sweetheart. But Sue Ann's blank prettiness masks a gargoyle. The black comedy of the piece is that the all-American Sue Ann turns out to be a great deal more disturbed than Dennis, the institutionalized arsonist.

He comes to realize this at the moment when, during a nighttime raid on the mill, the night watchman is injured and Sue Ann, with lascivious glee, finishes the old man off. Dennis looks at the dead man and all that secret-agent artifice of his instantly burns off. What we see is a morbidly afraid boy. Sue Ann, however, is sexually high from the experience and consummates the moment with Dennis, whose best and worst fantasies are thus simultaneously fulfilled.

And yet, because he still clings to his reverie of Sue Ann as a "clean true girl"—his words to Azenauer—he can't bear to see her as she is or admit he is afraid of her. He's stricken. After the long night, he goes by himself to a park and sits on a swing in the early dawn and seems horribly alone.

Sue Ann, of course, is not afraid of Dennis, because she has no capacity for fear. Particularly on a second viewing of the film, it's clear that Sue Ann is on to Dennis very early. He's the patsy she has been looking for to eliminate her harpy mother (Beverly Garland). Sue Ann is like Barbara Stanwyck's black widow from *Double Indemnity* (1944) transplanted to the environs of Norman Rockwell. But she is not as overtly calculating as the standard noir vamp, and this is, finally, the most disturbing thing about her. She's a sun-kissed psychotic with a killer instinct so primordial it's practically unconscious with her. Her murders are like dream walks.

Dennis can't save himself, because he can't shake off the blissful future he envisaged with Sue Ann. An added horror is that he comes to believe—wrongly, perhaps—that he was a goner long before he met her. The nightmare scenario he has entered into certifies his long-held self-image of personal depravity. He grows up in the end, though. He understands what has happened to him too late, but it is this understanding that rescues him even though he winds up behind bars. *Pretty Poison* is a coming-of-age movie about a kid who talks crazy to keep sane. The Dennis who looks out at us in the last scene is fiercely, desperately sane, and this newfound condition is both his glory and his prison.

Part FOUR: The Allure of the Unknown

Science Fictions

HAS THERE EVER BEEN A MORE PERFECTLY ALIGNED CONVERGENCE THAN the simultaneous revitalization of the sci-fi B picture and the barely repressed paranoia of the Commie-fearing 1950s? Born of acute postwar anxiety in the nascent nuclear age, the sci-fi B was a rejoinder to the Eisenhower-era mind, ringed as it was by intellectual picket fences while *Leave It to Beaver* played on the thirteen-channel DuMont TV inside. Sci-fi Bs about aliens, invasions, and machinations of an insidious Other intent on destroying truth, justice, and the American way mirrored a cultural unconscious marinating in some borscht-based infusion while Dad flipped burgers for his 2.5 children under a blue sky ripe with missile attacks *any minute now.*

It's a film movement with a legacy. The pod people in *Invasion of the Body Snatchers* hold a status reserved for Reagan among presidents and Halliburton among no-bid contractors. *The Space Children* portrays the seemingly innocent offspring of cold-war America in ways that echo the kids-against-parents betrayals of Nazi Germany. Those happened in Soviet Russia, too—or so we were told, which brings us to *Red Planet Mars,* a B that so shamelessly manipulates the dread of godless Commies that it puts "red" right in the title.

But not all sci-fi adventures are psychodramas. Taking a converse tack, *The Brother from Another Planet* remains one of writer-director John Sayles's best pictures, a satiric romp through '80s Harlem as seen through the eyes of a crash-landed extraterrestrial who happens to be black. It's not about a predatory Other but a benevolent one, whose experience parallels the immigrant's journey to America. Playing audaciously with the term "alien," Sayles flips the concept of strangers in a strange land like Dad flipped those burgers, raising the possibility that the guest knows the territory a lot more insightfully than the host. Cosmically speaking, of course.

The stuff of *Primer* is the allure of the unknown, its intrinsic fear-making potential, and the mind's capacity for wrestling with itself over vague threats and incomplete data. Although it premiered in 2004, *Primer* is a crystal-pure distillation of the fear factors that so enriched the '50s sci-fi scene. So sit back, munch some Wonder Bread, and get worried.

Invasion of the Body Snatchers

Don Siegel, 1956

by Michael Sragow

DON SIEGEL'S **INVASION OF THE BODY SNATCHERS** STILL PLAYS as the snappy thing it was more than fifty years ago: an exciting drive-in thriller with a subversive metaphoric edge. Released with a punch-pulling prologue and epilogue tacked on, and much of the comedy expurgated, it nonetheless became one of the most enduring of all cult movies. In the late 1950s and 1960s it was one of those teenage tribal totems, like vintage *Mad* comics and magazines, that got passed from town to town through pop-cultural osmosis. Even before *TV Guide* announced the news, entire high schools would know when it would grace some late-night creature-feature showcase. Young moviemakers could point to it as an example of how to sneak something substantive into the most frivolous genres, and as Siegel's own following grew with hard-boiled cop thrillers like *Coogan's Bluff* and *Madigan,* it attained almost legendary status.

Students can still use Siegel's film as a textbook on turning infirmity into strength—only a filmmaker with a gift for forthright camera work and relentless pacing could have made such an effective film on such a frayed shoestring budget. (He spent only fifteen thousand dollars for special effects.) In addition, he had the craftsmanship and the smarts to respect Jack Finney's scary metaphor for dehumanization and conformity. In Finney's 1954 *Collier's* magazine serial, "space spores" float down to a small California town, sprouting pods that replicate— and replace—the human population. These pod people resemble real people in all respects, except for everything that makes us individual and human: intangibles like personality and emotion.

Siegel relies on this central creepiness to carry the movie. The idea of the pods' enveloping evil is as much a menace as the actual pod people. From the moment a terrified young boy nearly careers into the car that's taking Kevin McCarthy, the sophisticated country doctor–hero, to pastoral Santa Mira, the film never lets up. If you view them with a clear head, the pods look like garden vegetables, the emerging people look more like smoothed-out mummies than fetuses, and their "placentas" look like bubble bath; but Siegel makes sure you're too terrified to notice.

The period feeling of this *Body Snatchers* also adds to its fascination: McCarthy looks like an organization man in a proper hat and business suit, but he's got a roguish glitter to his eye, and Dana Wynter, as his true love, struts her fetching 1950s décolletage to a career high point. They earn their status as stars—and as humans—by acting stalwart and sexy, just as King Donovan and Carolyn Jones, as the supporting couple, earn theirs by acting believably terrified. (Donovan plays a writer who smokes a pipe and wears a cardigan, talks of turning the mystery of the pods into a crime novel, and has some noirish posters on the wall behind his pool table.)

Although the same jabbing style that makes the film work doesn't allow for much subtlety, it's amazing how much atmospheric mileage Siegel gets out of a simple stop at a gas station, the ominously helpful attendants planting a pod in a trunk as they dispense seemingly nifty and friendly '50s service. And Siegel's masterful staging of such scenes as the new humanoid race dispersing pods from the town square helps make the noonday glare as frightening as any shadowy Walpurgisnacht. Everything about the film has a double dollop of edginess and drollery, including Sam Peckinpah's appearance as a gas-meter reader. The tough, burly provincial cops—their flesh itself seems to drawl—carry a comic depth charge. You expect these rednecks to consider themselves all-American, yet they're downright alien. And the pod peoples' main spokesperson is a hick's idea of a smooth-talking intellectual who would gladly trade away everything that makes us human and American for the sake of some abstract idea.

This film is both anti-Eisenhower-era conformity and anti-Communist. Siegel's *Invasion of the Body Snatchers,* like Phil Kaufman's 1978 variation on it, is a movie about space-age Darwinism that's got the right stuff to survive.

The Brother from Another Planet

John Sayles, 1984

by Carrie Rickey

ALONG WITH JOHN CARPENTER'S **STARMAN** AND JAMES Cameron's *The Terminator,* John Sayles's *The Brother from Another Planet* is one in a trio of imaginative 1984 social commentaries masquerading as sci-fi. In each, a higher life form lands in America, sees social ills, and heals them where he can. He also enjoys what you might call a cosmic one-night stand, but procreation is not so much the Brother's aim as is interspecies connection.

Sayles's answer film to Steven Spielberg's *E.T.: The Extra-Terrestrial* (1982) stars the astonishing Joe Morton as a mute extraterrestrial whose space jalopy crashes on Ellis Island, port of entry for generations of American immigrants. The Brother, as he is later nicknamed, is in more ways than one an illegal alien. Shifting the extraterrestrial from the suburbs to the inner city, Sayles makes the Brother's adventures in Harlem and Times Square a parable of alienation, assimilation, and integration, set to a steel-drum score.

For his enchanting performance, as great as that of any silent clown, Morton creates what you might call "livepan" comedy. His mobile face mirrors every oddity and discovery of his new world. Despite a slight shuffle (he lost his right foot on landing and cloned a replacement, still stiff as a new shoe), he carries the movie—and its serious message—with lightness and cheer.

Although his three-toed feet look like those of a sloth, the Brother otherwise resembles a human of African heritage. Because he can't speak (although he apparently understands English and Spanish), everyone he encounters in the nation of immigrants projects his or her ideas of his origins onto him. To one of the regulars in a Harlem bar, he must be African. To a Puerto Rican–born person at a video arcade where the Brother finds employment, he must be the descendant of slaves brought to the island. His planet of origin is never specified. But bounty hunters, the Men in Black (Sayles and David Strathairn, resembling robotic versions of Johnny Cash and Roy Orbison), have been sent to bring him back.

We do know that the Brother is a superior life form, an empath whose radiant touch heals broken bones and machines and can feel the pain and joy previously experienced on a barstool, bed, or subway bench. What we don't know: Were his gifts exploited on his home planet? Were his masters responsible for rendering him mute? (The Men in Black hunting the Brother *can* speak—like people who learned English from watching episodes of *Dragnet.*)

Fearful of men with badges; curious about the strange folks and folkways of this new land; unable to communicate easily with the natives; and needing food, shelter, and employment, the Brother represents every illegal immigrant who has ever tunneled, swum, or boated to American shores. He brings unusual skills, though: not only does he have a healing touch, but he also can detach one eye and use it as a device to monitor the street when he needs to be in two places at once.

Because he seems genuinely surprised when people with black skin speak and are spoken of differently from those with white skin, there are hints that the Brother comes from a place where the color of one's skin matters as little as that of one's eyes. He adapts to racialized Manhattan by trying to help neighborhood junkies, who are mostly black, and free them from the white master who has them enslaved to heroin.

The Brother's empathy is psychological as well as physical: he approaches almost every figure without prejudice, with open ears, hands, and heart. As one who believes that if you greet the unfamiliar with friendship you will be befriended in return, he is a model citizen of the cosmos.

Brother's warmth toward its characters and their contexts is as much an extension of Sayles's inclusive personality as it is of Ernest Dickerson's rosy cinematography. Dickerson, making his feature debut here (he previously shot Spike Lee's featurette *Joe's Bed-Stuy Barbershop* and then sealed his reputation on subsequent Lee films), bathes the principals and their settings in a light that turns homeys into heroes and ghettos (as Harlem was in pre-renewal 1984) into model communities.

Primer

Shane Carruth, 2004

by Amy Taubin

PRIMER PLAYS LIKE A SUCCESSION OF BRAINSTORMS HELD together by a nearly subliminal sound track of ghostly tinkling music and vaguely ominous effects. It would be an astonishing film had it been made by a veteran director, but in fact it is the filmmaking debut of Shane Carruth, who not only is the director, writer, editor, producer, and composer but also plays one of the two leading roles. Carruth was in his early thirties when *Primer* premiered at the 2004 Sundance Film Festival, where it won the grand prize. It had been three years in the making and cost a mere seven thousand dollars before the blow-up from the Super–16-millimeter negative to 35-millimeter added another thirty thousand dollars. The film had a brief theatrical run later that year, followed by a DVD release in 2005. Among the DVD extras is a commentary track in which Carruth details his production process shot by shot. For fledging directors, it's probably more useful than a year in film school.

A veritable hall of mirrors, *Primer* is an ingenious experiment in garage-band-style filmmaking, about a pair of hardware engineers who build a time machine in a suburban garage. Since movies are, in essence, time machines, and since Carruth held a series of engineering jobs before devoting himself to the time machine that is *Primer,* the film we see on the screen is in every way a metaphor for its own making. There are even a bunch of in-jokes that make fun of Aaron, the character Carruth plays, for being a penny-pincher. Just as Carruth relied on fifty dollars' worth of fluorescents bought at Wal-Mart to supplement available light, Aaron is so reluctant to spend money on his big invention that he strips his own fridge and his buddy's car for the necessary parts.

Carruth's most extravagant production choice was to shoot the movie on Super–16 film rather than on video, just because he preferred the way film looked. But since film is expensive, he couldn't afford to do more than one take of any scene. He was forced, therefore, to storyboard every shot and rehearse his almost entirely nonprofessional cast for a month in advance. These limitations, however, didn't prevent him from including elaborate dolly moves as a key element of the mise-en-scène. In the end, he claims to have exposed only two or three minutes of film that didn't make it into the seventy-eight-minute final cut, which took him more than a year to edit. It's a stunt that only someone reinventing the process of making a movie from scratch would dare. That the resulting film is complex, mysterious, and, for all its roughness, stunningly beautiful is proof that Carruth is a major talent.

The narrative setup is simple. Four bored engineers put their after-work energies into a hardware start-up company, hoping to invent a moneymaking gizmo that will allow them to quit their corporate jobs. More driven than their buddies, Aaron (Carruth) and Abe (David Sullivan) make an unexpected discovery while attempting to build a miniature superconductor in a portable box. They generate what seems to be a self-regulating feedback loop, which sends any object placed inside the box backward in time. Without consulting Aaron, Abe builds a bigger version of the device, lies down inside, and takes a little trip himself.

Time-machine movies form a subset of the science-fiction genre. For the most part, these films are fantasies that posit a wizard guide who helps an initiate hop a ride to the past, as in *Back to the Future* (1985) and the *Harry Potter* films (2001–). Even Chris Marker's terse, mind-over-matter *La Jetée* (1962), the inspiration for *Twelve Monkeys* (1995), leaves science out of the picture. Throughout *Primer,* however, Aaron and Abe employ the lingo of theoretical physics and math, much as the medical staff of *ER* (1994–) or the detectives of the various *CSI* series speak the specialized language of their professions. At the Sundance premiere, Carruth explained that the science was "all real," albeit theoretical, and he expected a lay audience would be able to understand 70 percent of what Aaron and Abe are up to. He later amended that to 60 percent. I'm not ashamed to admit that although I grasp something of the basic concept, the details seem pretty fuzzy, which hasn't diminished the pleasure of the movie for me in the least. After a half-dozen viewings I'm still unclear about how and why Aaron and Abe generate doubles of themselves in the course of their time travels. Does it happen only when they muck around with events in the past, or is it a problem of not catching or getting off the return shuttle at exactly the right moment?

No matter. Time travel is merely the pretext for a study of the behavior and ethics of a particular subculture: Southwest "techburbanites." When Abe and Aaron realize that their magic box has untold moneymaking potential, their immediate impulse is to keep it a secret from the other guys they've been working with. Later they begin keeping secrets from each other, quarrelling in both the present and the past over how they should use their power, and eventually fighting even with their own doubles. As the stakes get higher, friendship, loyalty, and trust fall by the wayside. In the early scenes, Aaron and Abe seem so alike they could be one person (this despite the fact that Aaron is married and has a young daughter while Abe is single and lives with a bunch of male roommates). But once they've experienced the power of their invention, latent character traits surface that send them in different directions.

From first to last, *Primer* is a memory piece, narrated in voiceover by Aaron or, perhaps, by one of Aaron's doubles. The voiceover is couched in the past tense, but given the paradox of the time machine, Aaron could be anywhere on the space-time continuum and still be looking back on the events of the movie. In its tone and rhythms, the voiceover is reminiscent of that in *La Jetée*. Combined with the repetitive musical score, sound effects, and ambient sound, it acts as an anchor for the more elliptically edited visuals. When I interviewed Carruth, he explained, rather sheepishly, that he had never seen Marker's film and that indeed his knowledge of film history was mostly garnered from watching TMC.

There is no doubt, however, that the concept of film as a time machine shaped *Primer's* fragmented editing strategy. At the end of the opening sequence, in which the routine of the after-hours start-up company is established, there is a series of images of the men working in Aaron's garage. The images are connected by dissolves, suggesting that these same men pass many such evenings in the same garage doing much the same activities. In conventional film-editing language, dissolves are a simple way of condensing time. In retrospect, however, this particular series of dissolves becomes a foreshadowing of Aaron and Abe's experiment in time travel. Much later in the film, Carruth uses similar dissolves specifically to demonstrate that Abe, returning from a harrowing trip into the past, is out of sync with himself—indeed, that there is no longer a single Abe, but many versions of Abe, each of them occupying a slightly different zone of time and space before they literally collapse into one.

If there is any director whose films seem to have influenced Carruth in both his mise-en-scène and editing, it's Steven Soderbergh. Like him, Carruth favors high-contrast, blown-out images with colors so acidic they seem radioactive and a nervous, jagged editing style, full of unpredictable changes of angle that give each shot the surprise and intensity of a new idea. "Heady" is the word for *Primer.* It's one of the most promising debut films of the first decade after the first century of cinema. Three years later, I'm still awaiting news of a follow-up.

Red Planet Mars

Harry Horner, 1952

by J. Hoberman

GIVEN THE WIDESPREAD EXPECTATION OF NUCLEAR WAR between the United States and the Soviet Union, the American science-fiction films of the 1950s could hardly be anything other than political allegories. With the cold war further conceptualized in theological terms, as a struggle to the death between Godless Communism and Godful Capitalism, this was also a period for religious movies—not just huge biblical spectaculars but also small productions like *The Miracle of the Bells* (1948), *The Next Voice You Hear* (1950), and *The Miracle of Our Lady of Fatima* (1952).

As the movie that dared to ask the question, "Is the Man from Nazareth the Man from Mars?" *Red Planet Mars* was both—the most visionary of the anti-Communist films released during the genre's highwater mark as well as the nuttiest of religious films. Stimulated by a shooting war in Korea and the oft-reiterated warning that this might be the prelude to World War III, not to mention the Spring 1951 second round of the House Un-American Activities Committee's investigation into Hollywood, one-third of all the anti-Communist movies produced between 1948 and 1954 were released in the presidential election year 1952.

Although the *Red Planet Mars* ads promised "The World Torn Asunder by a Threat from Outer Space," the danger was neither an oncoming comet nor a fleet of flying saucers piloted by carnivorous carrots but, as in the Soviet picture *Aelita* (1924), a transmission from our neighboring planet. Using plans for a "hydrogen tube" recovered from the rubble of Nazi Germany, independent scientists Chris and Linda Cronyn (Peter Graves and Andrea King) are trying to establish radio contact with Mars. So, too, it would seem, is the tube's bitter, ranting inventor—a German scientist named Calder (Herbert Berghof) who is now in the service of the Communists.

Thanks to Calder's trick transmissions, bounced off Mars from his secret hideout—a hut high in the Andes Mountains, beneath the giant statue of Jesus Christ—and picked up by the Cronyns, the world learns that Mars is far more technologically advanced than Earth. Knowledge of this super-civilization triggers a worldwide economic panic (shown on a futuristic wall-sized television set). As if it were the 1930s all over again, the Kremlin is ecstatic while the U.S. president is so concerned that he invokes national security to shut down the Cronyns' transmitter. But then Radio Mars sends a new sort of signal, quoting from Jesus's Sermon on the Mount. Linda, who, although a scientist, suffers from acute anxiety and technophobia, wants to broadcast this holy message to the world. So does the president: "Now we're following the star of Bethlehem."

Although internal evidence suggests that *Red Planet Mars* is set several years in the future, perhaps 1956 or 1957, the movie took its cues from the rhetoric of the day. In February 1950, Senator Joseph McCarthy's epochal Wheeling, West Virginia, speech had predicted all-out war between Christianity and "atheistic Communism." J. Edgar Hoover regularly defined Communism as "secularism on the march" and called Christianity its "moral foe." The American Legion was sponsoring a "Back to God" movement. The evangelist Billy Graham—the most admired American of the era, four times on the cover of *Life* between 1949 and 1955—characterized Communism as an invention of Satan and advised his fellow citizens that to "be a true patriot, then become a Christian."

In effect, God seems to be speaking from Mars, using the Voice of America to address the people of Earth—or at least some of them. (The montage of worldwide radio reception features only white listeners.) The transmission has its greatest impact on Soviet Russia; China is never mentioned. Now it is the Communists' turn to panic. "Speak English, you fool," the Russian leader screams at one of his agents: "Anything is preferable to your atrocious accent." The enormity of the crisis is indicated by mysterious stock footage of Russian peasants ripping portraits of Stalin off their walls and digging up vestments buried in 1917. Then, in a scene eliminated in most TV prints, an Orthodox priest is placed on the once-Romanov Russian throne.

While it is possible that Russia may yet again become a theocracy, *Red Planet Mars* was more immediately prophetic. Shot during the winter of 1951–1952, the movie opened a few weeks before the Republican convention that would nominate General Dwight Eisenhower to run for president. The movie's president is similarly a former military commander, and the actor Willis Bouchey strongly resembles Eisenhower. Indeed, Eisenhower—identified by the Republican National Convention as "the spiritual leader of our times"—began his inaugural address with a three-paragraph prayer addressed to "Almighty God," and subsequently became the first American president to be baptized in the White House.

Red Planet Mars was produced and cowritten by Anthony Veiller (who worked on Robert Siodmak's 1946 Hemingway adaptation *The Killers,* as well as Orson Welles's 1946 *The Stranger* and Frank Capra's 1948 *State of the Union*). Twenty-some years earlier, Veiller's collaborator John L. Balderston had adapted both *Dracula* and *Frankenstein* for the stage, subsequently writing the screenplays for *The Mummy* (1932), *Bride of Frankenstein* (1935), *The Lives of a Bengal Lancer* (1935), *The Last of the Mohicans* (1936), and *Gaslight* (1944). Brought up as an orthodox Quaker, Balderston had been a passionate advocate for American involvement in World War II.

Red Planet Mars was directed by Harry Horner, a Czech-born onetime assistant to Max Reinhardt, who came to the United States during the 1930s. Having worked mainly as an art director, Horner was perhaps responsible for touches like the ritual masks that decorate Calder's hut and the Cronyns' surprisingly elaborate lab. These are important because, despite its title, *Red Planet Mars* never leaves Earth or, for the most part, even California.

Although *Red Planet Mars* borrows a few homey notions from MGM's *The Next Voice You Hear,* in which God commandeers the radio for six successive nights to endorse the American way of life, it has an earlier source in the play *Red Planet,* cowritten by Balderston and J. E. Hoare. Opening on Broadway in December 1932 (perhaps the worst winter—at least economically—in American history), *Red Planet* was set in London. An astronomer couple establishes radio contact with Mars and receives a message that sounds like the Sermon on the Mount. The character types are similar: he is "a cold agnostic," and she "is a warm Episcopalian." The ensuing tumult is somewhat different: the streets of London are filled with hymn singers, a Jewish financier attempts to option the Bible and convert New York's movie theaters into churches, and an opportunistic British politician makes himself world dictator. The endings, however, are the same: God works in mysterious ways.

In the play's last act, the radio transmissions are revealed to be a hoax perpetrated by a hunchbacked scientist broadcasting from the Alps. In the movie, an avalanche sweeps away Calder's shack, yet he turns up at the Cronyns' lab to gleefully inform them of his cosmic prank. "What were you after?" they cry. His answer: "Shall I say . . . amusement?" Realizing that Calder is less a Communazi than a Satanist, the Cronyns contrive to blow up their lab, sacrificing themselves to destroy the Antichrist. That this is done to secure the future of the baby boom is implicit in Chris's declaration that their two young sons belong to a "blessed generation."

Red Planet Mars opened in New York City at the Criterion Theatre on June 14, 1952—the same day that President Truman dedicated America's first atomic-powered submarine, the *Nautilus,* and declared it the "Harbinger of a New Age." I am haunted by the image of that kindly lawyer Emmanuel Bloch, schlepping the two Rosenberg boys up to Sing Sing or out to Brooklyn for some Committee to Secure Justice in the Rosenberg Case meeting and then, as a special Saturday treat, to this educational documentary on our celestial neighbor.

Manny nods, but Robby and Michael are entranced. Moments before the explosion that martyrs the Cronyns, there is a final transmission from Mars. . . . The smoke clears on the president. To the sound of tolling church bells and celestial choirs, he reveals that the ultimate message was, "Ye have done well, my good and faithful servants." Then he smiles upon the newly orphaned Cronyn kids, "Lucky boys—you're their sons."

The Space Children

Jack Arnold, 1958

by Chris Fujiwara

THE SCIENCE-FICTION FILMS DIRECTED BY JACK ARNOLD—
beginning with *It Came from Outer Space* (1953) and continuing through *The Creature from the Black Lagoon* (1954), *Revenge of the Creature* (1955), *Tarantula* (1955), *The Incredible Shrinking Man* (1957), *The Space Children,* and *Monster on the Campus* (1958)—are central to the American sf-film boom of the '50s. The end of Arnold's involvement with the genre coincides with the end of the genre's golden age. Though it comes near the end of the cycle, *The Space Children* feels more like a transitional than a terminal film. An uneasy cross between the antinuclear genre of the '50s and the evil-children genre of the '60s and '70s, *The Space Children,* like all the director's major works, is a film of paradox.

Arnold is a master of atmospheres and of locating the unfamiliar within the familiar. *The Space Children* shows how little this mastery depends on special effects, makeup, and monster suits. The understated power of this neglected film comes largely from elements that are simple and somewhat banal: landscape, settings, and the portrayal of family relationships. Above all, *The Space Children* is, like Arnold's other science fictions, a reflection of the fears, tensions, and ideals of the '50s.

The intergenerational war of *The Space Children* takes place in appropriately extreme settings whose tonality is characteristic of Arnold. The monotonous sound of waves pounding the beach continues on and off throughout the film, underscoring its visual flatness. With so many scenes set on or near the beach, the film is visually dominated by rock and sand. Its manmade environments—an isolated missile base and a nearby trailer camp—are appropriately harsh and inhospitable, all metal, glass, and artificial light.

The first scene defines the mood and concerns of the film. As the Brewster family drives toward the base, which will be their new home, the vast expanses of ocean and sand give Anne Brewster (Peggy Webber) the uneasy sense—shared by so many of Arnold's heroes—of having entered an alien environment. "I feel as if I were in another world," she confides to her husband, Dave (Adam Williams).

Arnold shows right away that all is not well between the Brewsters and their two children. In the car, twelve-year-old Bud (Michel Ray) and his little brother, Ken (Johnny Crawford), hear a strange high-pitched sound and see a shaft of light descending from the sky to the beach. They try to point out these things to their parents, but the adults are preoccupied with their stalled car and shush the children. Later, angry with Bud and Ken for returning late at night to the family's trailer, their father threatens them ("I ought to wallop the both of you") with language and gestures resembling those of another base resident, Joe Gamble (Russell Johnson), whom we have seen drunkenly abuse his stepson, Tim (Johnny Washbrook).

The base children find a mysterious being from outer space in a nearby cave. Their discovery strengthens the children's group identity and gives them a line of defense against their fathers' violence. An invisible force knocks down Joe when he raises a stick to beat Tim. (The man subsequently becomes catatonic and dies.) Later, under the alien's telepathic guidance, the children take advantage of (or perhaps cause) a series of paranormal interventions in order to carry out their main project: sabotaging the preparations to launch the *Thunderer*, a missile designed to send a satellite armed with a hydrogen warhead into orbit around the earth.

A scene in the Brewsters' trailer succinctly depicts the power shift that the alien helps bring about. After establishing his new abilities by curing the momentary paralysis of his father's arm, Bud asks his parents to sit down and listen to him. They sit on a bed in the foreground of the shot, their backs to the camera, while Bud and his brother face them. This composition refers back to the opening scene in the car, which layered the two pairs in the same way, parents in the foreground and children in the background, but now the parents turn toward the background to pay attention to their children, which they refused to do in the earlier scene.

Bud and Ken hear the alien's call as summoning them to act as members of a cosmic community; later, their father, seemingly without being sensitive to the same message, merely bends before a superior force: ever the obedient employee, he recognizes in the alien a superboss. Of the family, only Anne sees the alien as a threat. It becomes the focus for the discontent and anxiety she has expressed since the beginning of the film. With the alien's intrusion into the domestic space of the trailer, her floating discomfort (which she describes, in terms that are explicitly relevant to the film's H-bomb theme, as "the feeling of living so close to the end of the world") acquires a concrete object.

As a visual creation, the alien can be criticized: it's hardly one of the more spectacular or imaginative outer-space creatures in '50s science fiction. At times, its presence seems to embarrass the film, as when Dave hides it under his coat to bring it to his trailer. More mineral than animal, an amalgam of glowing, pulsating gelatin and a hard support, with brainlike convolutions, the alien grows over the course of the film: initially the size and shape of a tortoise shell, it eventually becomes a giant heap. This size growth links *The Space Children* to Arnold's previous, better-known works, in particular *Tarantula* and *The Incredible Shrinking Man* (the apparent enlargement of all other creatures and objects in the second film being, of course, a function of the hero's diminution). In the two earlier films, rapid growth is both a sign of natural disturbance, suggesting nature's revolt against the unchecked advance of technology, and an object of fear and loathing. Unmotivated and unexplained, the alien's growth in *The Space Children* seems to occur only to make the thing more monstrous and repulsive.

If we ask why Arnold wants this effect, we confront a central ambivalence. On the one hand, the adults in the film are relentlessly criticized, including even Dr. Wahrman (Raymond Bailey), the chief scientist on the *Thunderer* project, who presents himself as a kindly idealist. (In a climactic confrontation, he tells the alien that he is "trying to make this world a better place—a world where the very children you're controlling can live in peace instead of fear.") Yet his very name, whenever it's uttered, sounds like the film's unmasking of the truth of what he stands for, and our faith in his moral purity is undermined as we watch him playing good cop/bad cop with the truculent Colonel Manley (Richard Shannon). Wahrman, too, is subject to the film's total critique of adult authority.

On the other hand, the children seem increasingly sinister as they carry out their campaign against the *Thunderer*. Bud's unexplained entrance into a control room unsettles Dave, who is trying to tell Manley and Wahrman about the alien, and causes Dave to lose his voice and then to collapse. When Bud and Ken visit the dispensary where their father is being treated, the camera's pan turns their sudden appearance in the doorway into a threat. Later, an eerie shot shows two cute toddlers eating ice cream and watching intently as the guard at a checkpoint station struggles with a malfunctioning phone.

The secret society formed by the children is clearly analogous to the military-scientific conspiracy of adults working on the missile project. The first sequence in the cave, where the kids hold their "secret club meetings," is intercut with Colonel Manley's briefing to the personnel at the base. The intercutting sets up a parallel between the two activities and invites us to see them as equivalent. Both groups are organized around powerful leaders: practically the alien's first move is to lay down that the children must follow Bud's commands.

Both Jack Arnold and Douglas Sirk did much of their best work at Universal-International (though *The Space Children,* anomalously, was released by Paramount). A somewhat neglected aspect of Arnold's career is that like Sirk's soap operas, Arnold's science-fiction films criticize the conservatism and conformism of American society and attack that society's icons. In *The Space Children,* while issuing an unambiguous warning against the threats posed by U.S. militarism and nuclear weapons, Arnold also finds an uncomfortable and resonant duality in a central icon of American sentimentality: the child. If the strange intensity of the film owes much to Arnold's visual style, which aficionados have justly celebrated, it also owes a great deal to Arnold's feeling for the contradictions of his time— contradictions that fifty years later have still not been resolved, any more than the threat of mass destruction from nuclear weapons has been dispelled.

Part FIVE: Dark and Disturbing Dreams

Films of Horror and Terror

THERE ARE HORROR FILMS, AND THERE ARE HORROR FILMS. *Psycho* is a horror film; so is *An Inconvenient Truth*. There are torture-porn shockers like *Hostel* and *Saw*; and there's the *implicitly* awful tale, such as *The Innocents* and *The Orphanage* and *The Haunting* (the original, that is). Some movies are unnerving because of what they show, and some pack the same punch through what they don't; some are scary because they might happen, and others are scary because they *are* happening. Now. Somewhere. *Maybe right behind you!*

But let's collect ourselves. One of the sadder developments in cinema over the past decade or two has been the damage done to our collective capacity for suspending disbelief: movies are routinely expected to do every conceivable thing—sink an ocean liner, empty Manhattan of people, send asteroids careening into Earth—and anything less than total "realism" is unacceptable. Yet while we're convinced, we're not impressed. Movies can do anything. So we don't care what they do.

Which takes us back to the old saw that what really makes a movie is story, not effects, despite the lofty claims of postproduction mavens. B movies have always relied on story, because state-of-the-art technique isn't readily available when your budget is as zombified as your protagonist. This helps explain why horror-movie B's remain powerful: while the technical aspects of moviemaking change and move on, story is timeless—even in the realms of the unreal, the horrible, the unthinkable.

These movies are parables. In *Tales from the Crypt* (1972), the characters get a chance to review their lives, and deaths; *The Fly* (the original of 1958) revisits the classic *Frankenstein* theme (there are things mankind was never meant to know . . .) with an ironic twist provided by the title insect; *I Walked with a Zombie*

(1943) is a cautionary variation on *Jane Eyre* about black magic, bad habits, and the lurking melancholy of family life gone off the rails.

And then there's *The Son of Kong,* which suffered all the indignities B pictures are heir to. For starters, it was badly underbudgeted, because RKO was convinced the success of *King Kong* earlier in 1933 would sell a sequel regardless of quality. (Haven't we seen *that* movie many times since?) The production was also beset by offscreen tragedies and a wickedly tight schedule. Still, Ernest B. Schoedsack, who had codirected the original *Kong* with Merian C. Cooper, managed to put out a flawed but valiant picture. And flawed but valiant beats expert and sterile any day.

Tales from the Crypt

Freddie Francis, 1972

by Roger Ebert

THE HORROR COMICS OF THE EARLY 1950S ETCHED THEMSELVES upon my mind in a series of disconnected scenes: a hand pushing up from a grave, a grinning skull with rubies for eyes, a little boy who didn't like cats. I devoured this stuff, and after a while I began to realize that some of it was superior to the rest. The titles published by E.C. Publications were more dramatically drawn, scarier, and unsurpassed in the department of divine retribution.

Six months or a year after I discovered *Tales from the Crypt* and the other E.C. comics, they were taken off the stands during a national anti-comics frenzy. *Seduction of the Innocent* by Dr. Frederick Wertham charged that kiddies were becoming sadists because of horror tales, and overnight we comics-lovers were flooded with talking magpies.

And so, alas, my career as a sadistic madman was nipped in the bud. It was not until 1969 that Richard Schickel's book *The Disney Version* fearlessly exposed the sadomasochistic tendencies of Mickey Mouse and friends, and by then it was too late. The E.C. comics had become collector's items.

There the story might have rested, if it weren't for Milton Subotsky, British producer of horror movies and old-time E.C. fan. Subotsky bought the movie rights for all the E.C. horror titles from their publisher, William M. Gaines, and *Tales from the Crypt* is the first film made from the material.

It's put together something like the comic books, with the old Crypt Keeper acting as host and narrator; in the movie version, he's played with suitable ham by Ralph Richardson. Five people are taking a conducted tour of a crypt (actually, London's Old Highgate Cemetery) when they suddenly find themselves in a creepy stone throne room. The Crypt Keeper enters, they ask what the hell is going on, and the answer is—wouldn't you know—hell itself.

The film's five stories all work on the principle that an evildoer should be punished, ironically, by his own misdeed. I don't want to reveal the punishments, of course; but I will say that the inmates of a home for the blind, led by Patrick Magee, the writer in *A Clockwork Orange* (1971), plan a particularly painful revenge upon their cruel superintendent (Nigel Patrick).

In addition to such distinguished names as Richardson, Magee, and Patrick, the movie also features good old horror-film superstars like Peter Cushing, Joan Collins, and (unless I'm mistaken) Vincent Price in an unbilled walk-on. The direction is by Freddie Francis, who has something of a cult following among horror fans, and the visuals and decor have been planned in bright basic colors and gray, so they look something like comic panels.

One further note: if Santa Claus knocks at your door tonight, don't answer.

The Fly

Kurt Neumann, 1958

by Chris Fujiwara

KURT NEUMANN'S **THE FLY** SUCCEEDS BY PLAYING OFF THE respectable against the outrageous, introducing the grotesque and the absurd within a carefully defined context of the familiar. Unlike David Cronenberg in his 1986 remake, Neumann steers *The Fly* away from tragedy and toward black comedy (which seems to have been what George Langelaan, the author of the short story on which the film is based, had in mind).

It's appropriate that the film should feel distant and somewhat cold; that so many scenes should take place in sumptuous or banal domestic settings under bright and even lighting; that most of the compositions should be medium shots (their impersonality accentuated by Neumann's rather doctrinaire use of CinemaScope). Everything in the film seems designed to convince us that its hero and heroine, scientist André Delambre (Al Hedison) and his devoted wife Hélène (Patricia Owens), are unremarkable and uninteresting, and that the world they live in is normal and boring. As a result, what happens to them seems all the more outrageous, unwarranted, and absurd—an assault on the values they stand for.

André invents an apparatus that disintegrates objects, moves their atoms through space, and reintegrates them. Unfortunately, when he transports himself through the device, his atoms get mixed with those of a fly, with the result that he comes out with the fly's head and one of its forelegs, while the fly gets André's head and one of his arms. André destroys his machine, burns his notes, and persuades the horrified Hélène to crush his body in a hydraulic press.

To put over the outrageous central premise (and the dubiousness of the science used to justify it), Neumann and screenwriter James Clavell link André's miracle to ordinary objects and themes. In the early scene in which he demonstrates his invention to his wife by disintegrating an ashtray, André explains the theory of matter transmission with an analogy: "Now take television. What happens? A stream of electrons, sound and picture impulses, are transmitted through wires or the air. The TV camera is the disintegrator. Your set unscrambles or integrates the electrons back into pictures and sound. . . . This is the same principle, exactly." Though Hélène instinctively realizes that matter transmission is different ("because it's impossible"), she finally accepts André's explanation.

Linking André's breakthrough with television may be the most subversive of the many attacks on television in films of the 1950s. Such attacks are particularly frequent in films produced by Twentieth Century-Fox, the studio that launched CinemaScope in an attempt to compete with TV, and they culminate in Frank Tashlin's 1957 *Will Success Spoil Rock Hunter?* which opens with a series of parodies of commercials and features an interlude in which the color-and-Scope image briefly shrinks to a tiny black-and-white square (so TV fans will feel at home). In *The Fly,* also a Twentieth Century-Fox release, television is convicted by its association with André's invention. Rather than a benevolent, transparent provider of entertainment, TV is a "disintegrator" that pulverizes, teleports, and "unscrambles" the world. Through André's analogy, the film hints that TV is leading humanity toward a world in which humans randomly trade body parts with insects.

When Hélène gives voice to a universal fear of technology ("Everything's going so fast, I—I'm—I'm just not ready to take it all in"), André sells her on the merits of his disintegrator/integrator by claiming that the ability to send supplies instantaneously will mean an end to famine. The idea of feeding the world excites Hélène, who appears to identify strongly with the traditionally feminine role of nurturer. The film repeatedly associates her with food, as when she brings a bowl of milk (laced with rum) and a dinner tray downstairs to her transformed husband, and when she spills sugar on a coffee table in an attempt to attract his fly counterpart. This latter detail reminds us that flies, whatever else they may mean in our lives, are creatures whose interactions with us usually come about because of their search for food. Late in the film, a dissolve from a kitchen scene to a shot of flies swarming over a garbage can expresses this connection succinctly.

One of the more grotesque aspects of André's predicament after his transformation is his difficulty in eating, which the film dwells on twice (both times emphasizing Hélène's appalled reaction). If Langelaan's uncanny concept of a man becoming a fly is somehow more modern than Kafka's metamorphosis of man into cockroach (or "monstrous vermin," as Joachim Neugroschel translates it), it may be because the fly (specifically the fruit fly) is well known as a preferred test subject for the very modern science of genetic research. The cockroach is repulsive, but in Kafka's story it serves as the image of what is still a *human* wretchedness. The fly is more apt, perhaps, than any other animal to express the *inhumanity* to which André is condemned by accident and technology (not by fate, which would be too human a word to describe what happens to him).

This inhumanity is the source of the half-comic, half-horrible, all-bleak power of the film. If the mutant-insect subgenre of the 1950s is a response to atomic-age fears, *The Fly* is a melodrama of domestic crisis in which these fears penetrate into the heart of the home in the most abrupt and catastrophic way. The deceptively neutral visual style adopted by Neumann and cinematographer Karl Struss sets up an ideal background for Hélène's preoccupation with finding the fly that has borrowed her husband's head, an activity that bewilders the people around her. ("Flies, madame?" repeats Kathleen Freeman's maid in stone-faced stupefaction.) The sound department joins in the game with gusto: the buzzing of flies accompanies numerous shots in the film—a device introduced in the striking title sequence, in which the noise alternates with composer Paul Sawtell's hopeful love theme. The use of CinemaScope (obligatory for a Twentieth Century-Fox production in the late 1950s), seemingly ill-suited to this story, sets up the most abstract of visual jokes when, in a number of close-ups, a fly is the sole occupant of the vast screen.

"It'd be funny if life weren't so sacred," André remarks to Hélène in recounting the transformation of their pet cat into a disembodied "stream of cat atoms." Neumann's film seems to suggest, however, that since life is no longer so sacred, such events may well be funny. The legendary scene of the man-headed fly caught in a spider's web (a pitiless restatement of the film's food theme) has been declared laughable by no less an authority than Vincent Price, who plays André's brother, François. The actor told an anecdote about the difficulty he and Herbert Marshall (playing a police inspector) had keeping straight faces while performing in front of the web in which André is supposedly imprisoned. At such a moment, horror and humor are indeed hard to separate, though Neumann pulls no punches in depicting the cruelty of the scene, in which the inspector comes to the aid of the terrified insect by crushing both it and its monstrous oppressor with a rock.

The Fly affirms that humanity can be corrupted, invaded, reduced, devoured, and squashed—that it can cease to exist and leave nothing behind. It may be true that as the hero of *The Incredible Shrinking Man* affirms at the end of Jack Arnold's 1957 film, "to God there is no zero," but for *The Fly* there *is* a zero: the total obliteration denoted by "impact: zero," the control setting of the metal press in which

Hélène annihilates André. ("That means level with the bed," François marvels; "it's never been set that way, never. Why, that would squeeze the metal to nothing.") Whereas *The Incredible Shrinking Man* questions but finally affirms the soul's ability to sustain itself under the most inhospitable physical conditions, in *The Fly* the characters come to acknowledge that under certain circumstances a man can degenerate into "a thing" (as Hélène and the inspector both call what André has become), losing the essence of humanity. The film faces this unpleasant realization with a hysteria and a disgust that stand out all the more sharply because of the stereotyped but believable blandness of the domestic background of the crisis. With its clever balancing of tones, *The Fly* achieves a memorable and unrepeatable style of sick cinema.

The Rage: Carrie 2

Katt Shea, 1999

By Stuart Klawans

MY FRIEND DENNIS PAOLI SAYS THERE ARE TWO KINDS OF
horror movies, and since his screenwriting credits include *Re-Animator* (1985), I
treat his categories with respect. Either you organize a movie around nine decap-
itations, he says, spacing them at ten-minute intervals, or else you work up to a
single big decapitation at the end.

Carrie is a notable example of the latter type: a movie with a long, long
buildup, culminating in general slaughter. The big question, then, is, "What happens on the way to the bloodbath?" In the case of *Carrie* (1976), the answer is,
"Not much." If you watch the picture today, twenty-three years after its release—
and you should, to get the most out of Katt Shea's *The Rage: Carrie 2*—you will
be struck by its lack of incident. The fatal prom takes up a full twenty-five minutes of the film; another fifteen or twenty are devoted to the bloodshed in the
prom's aftermath, and to the coda and closing credits. Nearly half the movie is
payoff, and that half is realized at the pace of an adagio, so that Brian De Palma
may demonstrate what his studies of Hitchcock have taught him.

It is not enough for De Palma to set a bucket of pig's blood over the spot where
Carrie will stand. He also must track the course of the attached rope, starting
from the lair of the pranksters and craning slowly to the rafters. Then, for good
measure, he retraces the route, following it through the eyes of good-girl Amy
Irving. I doubt the mechanics of a practical joke have ever been so exhaustively
demonstrated—especially when the response to the joke will defy the laws of
physics. And what is Sissy Spacek's Carrie doing while this minimal plot device
is being put into place? She's getting wet, literally and figuratively. From the

opening credit sequence (a montage of autoeroticism in the shower) to the prom itself, where Carrie deliquesces in the arms of her date, De Palma keeps his protagonist moist with anticipation, though for a climax other than the one she gets.

To give a more general answer to the question posed above: on the long road toward a horror movie's bloodbath, we learn why revenge will be taken. In *Carrie* the explicit reason for the rampage is that the protagonist has been mocked and ostracized. The implicit reason: she's been denied sexual pleasure. And then there's a third justification, which may be imputed not to the character but to De Palma himself. As master revenge-taker, he humiliates and destroys Carrie because she's the girl who won't put out. Take it from someone who is close to De Palma's age and can recall the sexual mythologies of the 1960s and '70s: all women were supposedly begging for it. Unfortunately, too many of them were repressed and wouldn't come through.

That this notion wouldn't occur to Katt Shea, the director of *The Rage: Carrie 2,* might be obvious merely from her credits. We first encounter her as an actress, whose career intersects in an interesting way with De Palma's. She appeared in the role of Woman at Babylon Club in his 1983 *Scarface*. Other notable roles of the era included an appearance as a mud wrestler in *My Tutor* (1983) and as Dee Dee (a name at last!) in *Hollywood Hot Tubs* (1984). Hired to be decorative and willing to do the job, Shea could not have felt that prudishness was the main problem in her life. Nor would she have seen herself as cowering before her sexuality, as De Palma imagined Carrie to do. A woman who can command money and attention through her body is someone whose power, however hampered, is real.

From actress to director and writer: with the occasional addition of the surname Ruben to her credits, Katt Shea began to make pictures of her own, beginning with the 1987 *Stripped to Kill* (the title in itself responds to De Palma) and continuing with movies that included the 1989 *Stripped to Kill II* (also known as *Live Girls*) and the gorgeously lurid *Poison Ivy* (1992). These pictures were remarkable for their disquieting themes (which had a lot to do with the possibilities and limits of a woman's sexual power), for their style (which was bold, fluent, and varied), and for being released at all. Over the past dozen years, only five or six American women besides Shea have managed to turn out a comparable number of commercial features. With that in mind—not to mention the low budgets, the genre trappings, the seven-year gap between *Poison Ivy* and 1999—I will pose my questions yet again. What happens on the way to the bloodbath? What wrong must be avenged? Or to put it another way, Does *The Rage* merely reenact *Carrie*, as we'd expect of a sequel? Or does Shea's movie exact a new punishment of its own?

The film starts: A brush, shown in close-up, dips into thick red paint and begins to trace a band across the walls of a shabby living room. We are back in the original *Carrie*'s atmosphere of overwrought religiosity, with candles burning everywhere and Mom (J. Smith-Cameron) huskily warning the devil away from her daughter. But already Shea has let the situation get out of control in a way that De Palma would not. His preacher mom was a half-sly, half-sadistic Jesus shouter, offered up for the audience's contempt. Shea's Mom is crazy. She paints her protective band heedlessly, smearing it over anything that gets in the way: furniture, windows, photos on the wall. What's more, when Mom is carted away, her little daughter feels devastated. For young Rachel, *The Rage* opens on a note of bewilderment and loss.

An overhead shot and a circling camera transform this child into the teenage Rachel, played by Emily Bergl. Note the baby-fat cheeks, the tidy nose, the Betty Boop lips over neat rows of little teeth. Were it not for the unmanageability of her dark curls and her funereal taste in nail-polish color, Rachel might seem half infantile. But as Shea and Bergl conceive her (aided by screenwriter Rafael Moreu), Rachel is not only young but also guarded, defiant, alert, sympathetic, and chatty by turns. When she feels the need, she will speak as if sunk two miles beneath her own surface. But unlike Carrie, who could barely meet anyone's eye, Rachel is also capable of bantering on the school bus with her best friend, Lisa (Mena Suvari). The topic is sex; and far from shying away from Lisa's tale of adventure, Rachel shares it eagerly, then responds by flashing a friends-forever sign: a view of the tattoo on her left arm, showing a heart encircled by ivy.

But for Rachel, forever does not last long. Lisa is already dressed like Ophelia, in trailing weeds. Within minutes (as you'll know if you've seen the trailer) she dives off the roof of Bates High School, having learned that her virginity meant nothing to the football hero to whom she'd given it. The trailer does not tell you where Shea will position the camera. (The choice, let's say, is made for maximum impact.) Nor will you understand, all at once and free of effort, the implications of the death. Yes, Lisa's suicide sets off Rachel's first big telekinetic blowout. But it's only upon reflection, and with the playing out of the film, that you appreciate the intensification of the theme. Whereas De Palma in *Carrie* kept going over the mechanics of his set, Shea doubles back on emotions. First there's the loss of the mother, then the loss of the girlfriend.

So the film sets out on the long road toward its preordained bloodbath. Here the way is full of incident, which makes *The Rage* a far richer, more absorbing film than *Carrie*. But more important, it's a film that does not cheat on its chosen theme of abandonment—even during the lighter moments, even when Rachel finds new companionship by falling in with Jesse (Jason London), the high school's only sensitive football hero. (In a reminiscence of the meet-cute between Claudette Colbert and Rudy Vallee in *The Palm Beach Story* of 1942, Rachel introduces herself to Jesse by shattering a strategic piece of glass.) The best thing about this deepening romance is that it actually deepens—which means that Jesse, estranged from the football brotherhood, becomes a virtual girl. (Trust me on this. It's a question of the haircut.) But contrary to the fantasies perpetuated by single-decapitation horror movies, some losses are irreparable. Amy Irving, returned from the original film as the sole survivor of the Bates High School prom, keeps pursuing Rachel, pressing offers of help on her and trying to expiate her own guilt about Carrie. You will see from the climactic bloodbath how well these things can be made up.

Why does Rachel kill everybody? The explicit reason is that she's been mocked and ostracized. The implicit reason is that her girlfriend died and her mother was driven crazy. And then there's the third reason, which emerges when the film's master revenge-taker, Katt Shea, appears on the screen. She has cast herself in *The Rage* as an assistant district attorney who briefly attempts to prosecute the high school's football heroes for using and discarding young women. To her disgust, she learns the job can't be done: the boys' club is too widespread, its power too entrenched.

Twenty-three years after De Palma joined the boys' club, scoring his definitive hit with *Carrie* in those golden, innovative '70s, who can pretend that the girls' ongoing loss is reparable? Look at the beauty and terror that Katt Shea can achieve, and ask whether there's motivation today for *The Rage*.

The Son of Kong

Ernest B. Schoedsack, 1933

by Gerald Peary

AS FRANKLIN ROOSEVELT MOVED INTO THE WHITE HOUSE IN spring of 1933, Americans saw RKO Pictures' *King Kong* in its original release. The film was such a startling artistic and financial success that RKO roped in the *Kong* crew—producer Merian C. Cooper, director Ernest Schoedsack, special effects expert Willis O'Brien, composer Max Steiner, screenwriter Ruth Rose—and rushed them back to work. Before another studio could capitalize on "big ape" movies, RKO would do so itself.

The studio realized that bringing back the actual Kong would be absurd: his tumble off the Empire State Building had finality. Instead, RKO invented an orphaned foundling (and motherless) child of the late simian monster. Six months after *King Kong*'s release, a seventy-minute B-movie sequel, *The Son of Kong,* arrived at neighborhood theaters.

The new film begins imposingly enough, with dramatic jungle music and a close-up of the mighty Kong himself at his ferocious best—all muscles, hair, and teeth. The camera dollies back: disappointingly, this Kong is a picture on a poster, an artifact hung on a wall. The locale is a drab, confined New York rooming house. Who resides here? It's Kong's maestro, Carl Denham (Robert Armstrong again), who has fallen on dire times. That's because Kong took blocks of Manhattan with him when he met his final destiny, and left behind his business manager to deal with the deaths and property damage. "Tell the public that Carl Denham, the smart guy who was going to make a million dollars off of King Kong, is flat broke," the deflated promoter tells a reporter. "Everyone in New York is suing me."

Denham is not only indigent but, much out of his *King Kong* character, peni-
tent about the havoc caused by the giant ape. "Don't you think I'm sorry for the
harm?" he asks, and not without feeling. "I wish I'd left him on the island. I'm
paying for what he did." The once-brash entrepreneur, now a Depression everyman, uses his last energy to flee New York on the back of a junk wagon. Eluding
a host of creditors, he's off to sea again.

King Kong was a pacesetter: bold of conception, stirring in content, a movie
that viewers responded to like none before it. *The Son of Kong* is conservative and
cautious (and low budget), a movie of quiet excitements and leisurely pace,
and derivative of the filmic past. Many of the scenes are recognizable variations
of sequences in the parent film. But modern audiences wouldn't know that
chunks of the plot are lifted from a lost silent movie from the Tiffany Corporation
called *The Enchanted Island* (1927), which had been inspired in turn by
Shakespeare's *The Tempest*.

The earlier film concerned a father (Henry B. Walthall) and his adolescent
daughter (Charlotte Stevens), stranded for fifteen years on a tropical island with
only their trained animals as companions. Three men land there: the hero, Bob
Hamilton; the villain, "Red" Blake; and Ulysses Abraham Washington, a "Negro"
cook. Hamilton falls in love with the girl and teaches her about the outside world.
Blake kills the father after a quarrel, and then he's done in by the cook during a
volcanic eruption. The lovers escape the molten lava and get rescued by the
inevitable passing cruiser.

Ruth Rose's script for *The Son of Kong* utilizes the above plot, with adjustments.
A young girl, Hilda (Helen Mack), and her alcoholic father have lived as expatri-
ates in the port of Dakang, supporting themselves with a sideshow act featuring
trained monkeys. Sailing into Dakang are the hero, Denham; the villain, Helstrom
(John Marston); the ship's captain (*Kong*'s Frank Reicher); and a Chinese cook,
Charley (*Kong*'s Victor Wong). Helstrom quarrels with Hilda's father and murders
him. Eventually, Helstrom is killed by a sea monster and buried beneath the
debris from a volcanic explosion. Denham and Hilda escape the molten lava as
the island sinks into the sea. They are rescued by a cruiser.

The Dakang of *The Son of Kong* is hardly an "enchanted island" setting; rather,
it's a dank hangout for lost sailors and drifters. Nor is Denham's meeting with
Hilda the stuff dreams are made of. He and the captain follow a sign pointing the
way to an evening of music with Belle Helene. Their trip ends on a flat bench in
a tent crowded with the lowest native element. They sit in stony silence watching a
dubious orchestra of monkeys, dressed as miniature bellhops, pound on instru-
ments in arhythmic counterpoint. The show's star attraction, Helene, is a mis-

placed American, Hilda, who strums a Hawaiian guitar in a clumsy attempt to appear exotic and sings badly in a high-pitched voice, "Oh, I've got the runaway blues today."

(This finely detailed, idiosyncratic scene was made possible by the global travels in the 1920s of the filmmakers, Cooper and Schoedsack, who were both early documentarians. In fact, Cooper, whose resemblance to actor Armstrong is uncanny, speaks of an analogous experience in his 1924 autobiographical journal, *The Sea Gypsy*. Cooper had landed in Jibuti, an Abbysinian port, where he was urged by locals to "See Arab dance, see Somali dance." Cooper wrote in his diary: "In a tiny tent, three Arab women swayed their bodies in the squat floor space between beds." He added the wry observation, "These dancers and the fly-ridden café are Jibuti's only amusements.")

Back to *The Son of Kong*. Denham is forgiving of Helene's shoddy stage act. More, he falls in love with her. *King Kong* fans must have found this a stretch, recalling the unapologetic misogynist of the earlier film: Denham had lectured sexy Ann Darrow that their relationship would be strictly business, and meant it. Now, Denham eagerly brings Hilda aboard to search for Kong's native land. A bashfully grinning courtier, he flirts with Hilda at sea under the moonlight.

The Son of Kong now shifts to concerns that *Kong* fans might wish for in a sequel. There's a return voyage to strange, surrealist Skull Island. The sailing party approaches the beach, greeted, as in *King Kong*, by Willis O'Brien's eerie black apparitions floating through the air like Furies. And by Max Steiner's chilling, flamboyant jungle music. Skull Island seems cleaned up a bit since the first visit, however, with the rougher prehistoric beasts missing, including the tyrannosaur and pterodactyl.

Denham and Hilda soon come across a distressing sight, the titular star of the movie up to his neck in quicksand, yelping like a puppy for assistance. At last, the long-awaited scion of Kong reveals himself. As with the kinder, gentler Denham, he is a diminished presence. This twelve-foot Kong will not trample on native villages or rampage through the streets of New York. He's a friendly prepubescent, and shows no Kong-like bestial desire for the heroine, Hilda.

Denham and Hilda pull Kong out of the mire (Denham: "I felt I owed his family something"). Kong Jr. lumbers after his saviors and, in gratitude, protects them against the native animals. In parodic imitation of the Darwinian battle to the death between King Kong and the ferocious tyrannosaur, little Kong takes on a nasty-tempered bear. (Yes, a bruin on Skull Island!) They box, wrestle, and tumble about the terrain, with more bluster than physical damage. Denham remarks, "Gee, can he scrape. Just like his old man."

Afterward, Skull Island seems at peace. Wandering through the forest maze, *The Son of Kong*'s heroes are separated from the other party of explorers. The new lovers bed down near each other for the night, with Kong Jr. keeping watch over them, like the lion in Rousseau's painting *The Sleeping Gypsy*. Here, the movie acquires a tranquil beauty reminiscent of Shakespearean romance. And, as often with the Bard, the movie splits into a counterpoint double plot.

PLOT A:

The enchanted greenery sanctifies a trinity of man, woman, and beast. Denham, Hilda, and Kong Jr. have a restful night of sleep and sanctuary, and the following day Denham discovers the hidden treasures of the island.

PLOT B:

The captain, the cook, and the villain, Helstrom—a mismatched threesome—have holed up in a bare-stone cavern. Outside, a raging prehistoric behemoth pounds against the rocks trying to get at them. These three get no sleep at all, and no treasures await them.

At this point *The Son of Kong* has found itself, evolving from a somewhat tenuous work into a narrative that is well structured and purposeful. Everything gained is quickly lost. Literally from nowhere, a mighty (unmotivated) storm breaks on the horizon. Skull Island, its volcanoes erupting, crumbles into the ocean, taking with it the last vestiges of prehistoric culture. And the dead body of the evil Helstrom.

The virtuous protagonists—Hilda, the captain, the Chinese cook—row away in the nick of time. (What happens to the black native populace on the other side of the island? Their plight is ignored.) Carl Denham is saved from Davy Jones's locker via the most valiant (and also sentimental) heroic sacrifice. Little Kong, noble savage, holds Denham above the waves in his gentle fist until a rescue is possible. Then, with Steiner's mournful string elegy soaring away (the same music that lay King Kong to rest), the young semi-giant ape is swallowed by the ocean.

"Poor little Kong. Do you think he knows he was saving my life?" Denham asks with dimwitted seriousness. At the fadeout, the romantic couple, aboard a rescue boat, turn to portioning out the treasure money. Kong Jr. is already forgotten by them. As for movie audiences, seventy-five years later hardly any King Kong fan remembers a son of Kong at all.

I Walked with a Zombie

Jacques Tourneur, 1943

By Carrie Rickey

We are not photographers, but artists.
—MAURICE TOURNEUR, 1917

JACQUES TOURNEUR, SON OF THE PIONEERING FILM DIRECTOR Maurice Tourneur, brought an artist's eye to atmospheric noirs, unapologetic B movies where silvery moonlight cannot fully penetrate the menacing shadows.

I Walked with a Zombie, the most elegant of his modest masterpieces, which include *Cat People* and *Out of the Past,* is an unpretentious trance-inducer that would haunt the work of Jean Rhys and Manuel Puig—and the dreams of everyone else. Rhys's 1966 novel *Wide Sargasso Sea* implicitly pays homage to *Zombie* by way of Charlotte Brontë's *Jane Eyre;* Puig's 1976 novel *Kiss of the Spider Woman* explicitly references it in the dialogue between its imprisoned characters.

Tourneur's poetic mélange of Brontë, Daphne du Maurier, and postcolonialism plucks a naïve young woman, Betsy Connell (Frances Dee), out of Canada, transplants her to a picturesque piece of West Indies real estate (a sugar-cane plantation on the island of San Sebastian), and dares her to bloom under the glower of its broody lord, Paul Holland (Tom Conway), whose somnambulant, vacant-eyed, and perhaps zombified wife she has come to nurse. Betsy soon becomes witness to the family and colonial drama that plays out in their family home, Fort Holland, where a persistent ill wind blows, unsettling shutters, natives, and nerves.

The pervasive gloom that suffuses *Zombie* is like that wind, invisible but ominous, illustrative of Tourneur's operating principle, purveyed by the film's producer, Val Lewton: what you can't see can hurt you. "If you make the screen dark enough," postulated Lewton, "the mind's eye will read anything into it you want."

And what did Tourneur want us to read into his sixty-nine-minute tone poem scored to the rhythms of calypso and Chopin? The calypso troubadours play the music brought to the New World by African slaves; the plantation owners, whose forebears operated one leg of the triangle trade route that exchanged sugar for slaves for rum, play the music brought to the New World by its settlers. A strange statue of "Ti-Misery," figurehead from a slave ship, sits in the garden of Fort Holland, its torso pierced by arrows like that of the human San Sebastian for whom the island is named.

The legacy of slavery surely is one theme Tourneur invites us to see—and to listen to. The insistent *beat beat beat* of the tom-tom and *plunk plunk plunk* of the piano keys underscore the asymmetrical duet between the colonized, brought to this Haiti-like country against their will, and the colonizers. While one group works the fields of San Sebastian and the other owns them, neither is fully at home on this wind-raked island that's a metaphorical middle passage between the homelands of the ancestors and the final resting place.

One who is physically stuck in the middle passage between life and death is Jessica Holland (Christine Gordon), Paul's zombie wife. Betsy learns through the lyrics of a calypso song that the otherworldly blonde was beloved by Paul's reckless half-brother, Wes (James Ellison). As Betsy strives to solve the mystery behind Jessica's malady, she struggles to resolve her own attraction to the half-brothers. Might the gloomy Rochester/Maxim de Winter type, Paul, be more honorable than the upbeat Wes, who has a taste for rum and women? Might the origins of Jessica's suspended animation be a voodoo ritual, perhaps a curse, as alluded to in Tourneur's most allusive of movies? (Audiences familiar with Alfred Hitchcock's 1940 *Rebecca* might have gotten an inside joke: Maxim's adversary in that similarly themed film was played by George Sanders, and the Maxim figure here is played by Sanders's brother, Tom Conway.) Summoned as if by a higher force, nurse accompanies patient to the nearby *houmfort,* or voodoo temple, where Betsy discovers that one shaman there is a sham. Yet in the leaf-shadowed recesses out of Betsy's range of vision, another shaman performs a ritual that exorcises the curse immobilizing Jessica. And that has the effect of mobilizing the other characters.

One of the rare Hollywood films that declined to trade in exoticism (contrast it to the 1940 Bob Hope comedy *The Ghost Breakers*), *I Walked with a Zombie* is relatively respectful of voodoo and its practitioners and critical of those who would exploit the rituals for personal gain. It is likewise critical of the picturesque. As Betsy inhales the tropical air and looks at the sea sparkling like diamonds, Paul interrupts her reverie. "That luminous water—it takes its gleam from millions of dead bodies, the glitter of putrescence," he warns, alluding to the decaying creatures that, like many figures in this movie, have yet to find a final resting place.

May

Lucky McKee, 2002

by Roger Ebert

MAY IS A HORROR FILM AND SOMETHING MORE AND DEEPER, something disturbing and oddly moving. It begins as the story of a strange young woman, it goes for laughs and gets them, it functions as a black comedy, but then it glides past the comedy and slides slowly down into a portrait of madness and sadness. The title performance by Angela Bettis is crucial to the film's success. She plays a twisted character who might easily go over the top into parody, and makes her believable, sympathetic, and terrifying.

The movie is inevitably compared with *Carrie* (1976), not least because Bettis starred in the 2002 television version of that story. Like *Carrie*, it's about a woman who has been wounded by society and finds a deadly revenge. But *May* is not a supernatural film. It follows the traditional outlines of a horror or slasher film up to a point—and then it fearlessly follows its character into full madness. We expect some kind of U-turn or cop-out, but no; the writer and director, Lucky McKee, never turns back from his story's implacable logic. This is his solo directing debut, and it's kind of amazing. You get the feeling he's the real thing.

Bettis plays May Canady, who as a girl had a "lazy eye" that made her an outcast at school. After a brief prologue, we meet her in her twenties, as an assistant in a veterinary clinic. She is shy, quirky, askew, but in a curiously sexy way, so that when she meets the good-looking Adam Stubbs (Jeremy Sisto), he is intrigued. "I'm weird," she tells him. "I like weird," he says. "I like weird a lot."

Uh huh. His idea of weird is attending the revival of a Dario Argento horror film. He shows May his own student film, which begins with a young couple kissing and caressing and then moves on inexorably into mutual cannibalism. May likes it. She snuggles closer to him on the sofa. Afterward, she gives him her review: "I don't think that she could have gotten his whole finger in one bite, though. That part was kind of far-fetched."

Bettis makes May peculiar but fully human. There are scenes here of such close observation, of such control of body language, voice, and behavior, evoking such ferocity and obsession, that we're reminded of Lady Macbeth. It is as hard to be excellent in a horror film as in Shakespeare. Harder, maybe, because the audience isn't expecting it. Sisto's performance as Adam is carefully calibrated to show an intelligent guy who is intrigued, up to a point, and then smart enough to prudently back away. He's not one of those horror movie dumbos who makes stupid mistakes. Notice the look in his eye after he asks May to describe some of the weird stuff that goes on at the animal hospital, and she does, more graphically than he requires.

May's colleague at the clinic is Polly (Anna Faris), a lesbian, always open to new experiences. One day when May cuts herself with a scalpel, Polly is fascinated. Then May unexpectedly cuts her. Polly recoils, screams, considers, and says, "I kind of liked it. Do me again." Like Adam, she is erotically stirred by May's oddness—up to a point. There's an erotic sequence involving May and Polly, not explicit but very evocative, and it's not just a "sex scene" but a way to show that for Polly sex is entertainment and for May it is of fundamental importance.

McKee uses various fetishes in an understated way. May is not a smoker, but she treasures a pack of cigarettes that Adam gave her, and the precious cigarettes are measured out one by one as accomplices to her actions. She has a doll from childhood that gazes from its glass cabinet; in a lesser movie, it would come alive, but in this one it does all the necessary living within May's mind. When May volunteers to work with blind kids, we fear some kind of exploitation, but the scenes are handled to engender suspense, not disrespect.

The movie subtly darkens its tone until, when the horrifying ending arrives, we can see how we got there. There is a final shot that would get laughs in another kind of film, but May earns the right to it, and it works, and we understand it.

There are so many bad horror movies. A good one is incredibly hard to make. It has to feel a fundamental sympathy for its monster, as movies as different as Frankenstein, Carrie, and The Silence of the Lambs do. It has to see that they suffer, too. The crimes of too many horror monsters seem to be for their own entertainment, or ours. In the best horror movies, the crimes are inescapable, and the monsters are driven toward them by the merciless urgency of their natures.

Part SIX: Burning Up the Blacktop

Road Movies

ROAD MOVIES COURSE THROUGH THE HISTORY OF AMERICAN cinema the way Route 80 cuts across the country itself. *The Big Trail* was a road movie in 1930; so was *Red River* in 1948, albeit of the quasi-homoerotic buddy-film variety. Arguably, *2001: A Space Odyssey* was a road movie, as were *Captain Blood* and *Fantastic Voyage.*

The yearning for forward motion is in our pioneer DNA—the thirst for forging ahead, blazing trails, violating frontiers, going on the road like Kerouac, cutting ties to place and even time. Its cinematic manifestation, the road movie, almost always achieves strong dramatic momentum, partly because it taps into our need to not sit still. (We have to sit still to watch one, of course, but viewing a road movie inside a moving non-airborne vehicle would be perfect, and is probably coming soon to an iPhone near you.) That the genre also provides a wide-ranging array of events, locales, and (especially) characters hasn't hurt its popularity, either. Over the history of B pictures it has bestowed on filmmakers a scope and scale they might not otherwise have found, unless set loose themselves on the open road with cameras in their knapsacks.

The highway and byway offer freedom, and with freedom sometimes comes insanity. See *The Big Bus,* in which James Frawley launches the first nuclear-powered bus on its maiden voyage from New York to Denver, complete with chirpy stewardess and anti-fallout gear. Moodier and more cerebral is *Two-Lane Blacktop,* the existential epic by B-movie maestro Monte Hellman, who uses nonactors in key roles (James Taylor, Dennis Wilson) and turns the road into a Homeric river of thwarted destiny. Equally fatalistic is *Vanishing Point,* which did more for the Dodge Challenger than any ad campaign devised under Detroit's fume-laden skies.

Stranger Than Paradise also appears in these pages, but isn't virtually every Jim Jarmusch film a road movie? *Permanent Vacation* is a road movie on foot; *Mystery Train* rides the freight car of Elvis's spirit; *Night on Earth* comes and goes by taxicab; and *Dead Man* travels on various primitive vehicles, including the human consciousness. *Year of the Horse* doesn't actually involve horses, but hey, Neil Young did a lot of traveling.

Where are we going with this? Why does it matter? Getting there is half the fun, and all of the meaning, when we take the movies on the road.

Stranger Than Paradise

Jim Jarmusch, 1984

by Amy Taubin

"COOL" HAS NEVER SEEMED AS DESPERATELY SAD AS IN Jim Jarmusch's *Stranger Than Paradise,* the indie picture that is to the road-movie genre what Jean-Luc Godard's *Breathless* (1960) is to the gangster noir. It was the second feature by Jarmusch, an Ohio-born NYU Film School graduate who was a central figure in the downtown New York arts scene during its pre-gentrification glory days. Made on a minuscule budget and with grainy black-and-white film stock left over from a Wim Wenders film, *Stranger* is rooted in the less-is-more aesthetic that defined punk rock (Jarmusch was a member of the post-punk group the Del Byzantines) and New York's underground film and theater scene in the 1970s and early 1980s. The film's major influences were the photography and films of Swiss-born Robert Frank and the work of Squat, an experimental theater company made up of Hungarian émigrés. Jarmusch found visual correlatives to his own alienated perspective in Frank's despairing, subversive *The Americans* (published in 1958 in Paris, 1959 in the U.S.), a book of photographs documenting Frank's road trips across the United States during the middle 1950s, and in *Pull My Daisy* (1959), Frank's avant-garde film portrait of a bunch of beat-generation luminaries hanging out in a run-down Bowery loft. The Squat connection provided Jarmusch with the film's central comic conceit—that from New York's East Village bohemia, to the industrialized Midwest, to the beaches of Florida, the landscape of the United States is every bit as bleak as anything in an Eastern European art movie.

But *Stranger Than Paradise* is less about a place than a state of mind. Its governing consciousness is Willie (John Lurie), a permanently depressed two-bit gambler who spends most of his time sitting around in his tiny, sparsely furnished apartment, either by himself or with his sad-sack friend Eddie (Richard Edson). Out of the blue, Willie's teenage cousin Eva (Eszter Balint, a member of Squat) arrives from Hungary to visit for a few days before going to Cleveland to live with their aunt (Cecillia Stark). Eva's presence stirs some faint memory of familial warmth in Willie; for a few seconds after she leaves, he feels his loneliness more acutely.

A year later, Willie and Eddie make some fast money cheating at poker and, to be safe, they decide to get out of town for a while. They drive to Cleveland to visit Eva, more out of default than desire—she's the only person they know. In the film's emblematic scene, Eva takes them on a sightseeing trip to the shore of Lake Erie. But because it's night and snow is falling hard, there's nothing to look at except a vast indeterminate field of gray—no water, no horizon line, just grayness everywhere. Then Eva mentions that it would be nice to go someplace warm, so they head for Florida, the Sunshine State. But it's cloudy all the time, the beach as gray as Lake Erie, and their motel room even more drab than Willie's New York apartment.

It was the spare, graceful yet rigorous form of *Stranger Than Paradise* that made such an impression when it first appeared. With few exceptions, American independent filmmakers made their differences with Hollywood known by embracing subject matter and characters that were regarded by the studios as "unappealing" (meaning poison at the box office). Far from challenging Hollywood conventions of realism and definitions of genre, however, they adopted them without question or mixed them with elements of neorealism for the sake of economy. For an American independent narrative filmmaker to take an aggressive approach to form—to shape film time and space in a way that countered received wisdom about narrative flow and dramatic tension—was radical; it was the kind of thing a European art filmmaker like Godard or an avant-garde filmmaker like Andy Warhol would do. Marrying the formalism of "foreign" art films to archetypal American settings and characters (albeit delivered with a twist), Jarmusch created a hybrid—the American art film—that has served as a model for his entire career.

What Jarmusch does in *Stranger Than Paradise* is to cover each sequence of the film in a single master shot, which can last anywhere from a few seconds to several minutes. Sometimes the camera is stationary, sometimes it moves; sometimes the characters move around, sometimes they don't. At the end of each shot (sequence) the screen goes black, and then after a few seconds the next shot (sequence) begins. Because there is no editing within the sequences, they appear on the screen in exactly the manner they were shot—that is to say, in real time.

The blackouts between the shots, however, can represent the passage of a year or a few seconds or anything in between. And because there is no editing within the sequences, there are no shifts in point of view. There are no character-point-of-view shots at all. The only point of view is that of the camera, which functions as the proverbial fly on the wall. In his program notes for the film's 1984 debut at Cannes, where it won the Camera d'Or, Jarmusch wrote, "the effect of the cinematography and the form of the film suggests a photo album where individual photos are surrounded by black spaces, each one on a separate page."

While *Stranger* is innovative in form, it follows the rules of the road in its sexual politics. I suspect this accounts for its popularity and the sense that it was, from the moment it appeared, a classic; the same could be said of *Breathless*. The film opens on the outskirts of a large New York airport. Standing alone at the edge of what appears to be a gravel pit, with her baggage at her feet, is the recently deplaned Eva. Something about her pose—although not her jaunty ponytail, a rattier version of the one worn by the heroine of Otto Preminger's once-scandalous *The Moon Is Blue* (1953)—recalls the female hitchhiker in one of Cindy Sherman's *Untitled Film Stills* from the late 1970s. She is the girl on the road destined to disrupt the lives of the male buddies in the front seat of the car. She will be the catalyst of either their destruction or their salvation, almost always at the expense of her life, or at least her soul.

In the blackout that follows the opening shot, Eva, whose dominant character trait is self-reliance, has managed to get from the airport to the city, where we see her walking along a deserted street, past a row of shop fronts covered by metal shutters, on one of which is scrawled, "U.S. out of everywhere! Yanqui go home!"—a ubiquitous slogan of political defiance in the Reagan years, here directed as much against any real estate developers who might be poking around one of the city's then-preeminent melting pots (or citadels of poverty and alienation) as against the CIA's war on the Left in Latin America. Eva pulls a brick of a tape recorder out of her bag and turns up the volume on Screamin' Jay Hawkins's "I Put a Spell on You." As we will find out, it's the only tape she has and she plays it on every possible occasion, much to the annoyance of Willie, whom we meet, as she does, in the next scene. One of the film's running gags is that Willie loathes Screamin' Jay and apparently all music, even though the actor who plays Willie is Lurie, the prominent jazz/"No Wave" composer/saxophonist who wrote the incidental music for *Stranger* in the dissonant, angst-ridden style of, who else, Hungarian composer Béla Bartók.

If Eva is appalled by the shabbiness of Willie's apartment, decked out, like Willie and Eddie themselves, in what are clearly thrift store "finds," she never lets on, although at one point she attempts to use a vacuum and at another questions Willy about the source of the ersatz-looking meat in his TV dinner. On the appointed day Eva leaves for Cleveland, and in the second section of the film, helpfully titled "One Year Later," Willie and Eddie set out to find her. *Stranger Than Paradise* maintains its downbeat, deadpan composure until near the end of the third and final "Paradise" section, when a series of lucky and unlucky breaks accelerates the pace and culminates in Willie, Eddie, and Eva each going off in a separate direction. In his attempt to follow Eva, Willie ends up alone on his way to a life that will at least provide a break from his shut-down New York existence. Eva, on the other hand, ends up in the Florida motel room holding the bag, or to be precise, a distinctive hat—a hat that spells trouble—in her lap. The book of photographs that is *Stranger Than Paradise* closes on this image. Every time I picture it in my mind's eye, my blood runs cold.

Two-Lane Blacktop

Monte Hellman, 1971

by Sam Adams

RACING FLAT-OUT ON THE ROAD TO NOWHERE, THE SCRAWNY speed demons of *Two-Lane Blacktop* are caught between a past they've never known and a future they'll never see. The Driver (James Taylor) and the Mechanic (Dennis Wilson) act the part of rebels from a '50s exploitation movie, but their sallow skin and sunken eyes reveal the gnawing uncertainty of a disillusioned age, a longing for a sense of purpose that exists only in the seconds between starting flag and finish line.

Universal, which handed director Monte Hellman nine hundred thousand dollars to make his first (and, as it turned out, only) studio movie, must have hoped for a youth-culture paean in the *Easy Rider* mode. Although neither of the movie's leads had acted before, both were stars in their own right: Wilson was the Beach Boys' drummer and Taylor was a budding soft-rock superstar. (His then-girlfriend, Joni Mitchell, was often spotted on the set.) Two months before the movie's release, *Esquire* proclaimed *Two-Lane Blacktop* "the movie of the year," publishing Rudy Wurlitzer's script in full.

But instead of a carefree ode to easy riding and fast living, Hellman's movie was more like a European art film, with brooding silences and long stretches of empty road. The protagonists are sullen, uncommunicative loners, hardly suited for the role of counterculture icons. And for a car-race movie, it's notably short on tire-burning bravado; the few head-to-head contests are over in seconds, sometimes dispensed with in a single shot. This was evidently not what the studio had signed on for. The movie of the year was dumped into theaters on a holiday weekend with no advance advertising and quickly vanished into myth.

The germ of Wurlitzer's script (taken from a discarded draft by *Gunsmoke* actor Will Corry) is a cross-country race between the Driver's '55 Chevy and a late-model Pontiac GTO, driven by a garrulous dandy (Warren Oates), whose slick patter spills out in bewildering chunks. (The credits call him "G.T.O.," although the characters never address each other by name.) The route (Arizona to DC) is set, the stakes (pink slips) agreed upon, and the cars peel out, intending to drive straight through.

But a series of pit stops and small-town diversions turns their breakneck dash into a roadside odyssey, a travelogue of crumbling towns and crumbled people. With each detour, the movie seems to slip backward in time, searching for a past that has vanished, or perhaps never existed. "I am romantic in the way that Camus is romantic," Hellman once said. "I feel a nostalgia for what can never be." (Ironically, *Blacktop*'s Chevy turned up in 1973 in *American Graffiti*, a movie of distinctly less ambivalent nostalgia.)

Its asphalt milieu notwithstanding, *Blacktop* is a Western in spirit, albeit one whose course purposefully reverses the nation's progress. Manifest Destiny has run its course, but the urge to move forward lingers like the spasms of a twitching corpse. *Blacktop*'s bleak vision is prefigured by Hellman's sand-scarred Westerns *Ride in the Whirlwind* (1965) and *The Shooting* (1967), and it's honed to a bloody point in Wurlitzer's script for Sam Peckinpah's *Pat Garrett & Billy the Kid* (1973). But where Peckinpah's lusty loners are propelled by the imperatives of myth, Hellman's are purely compulsive. They drive because they can't stop.

Like their car, stripped of any creature comfort that might slow it down, the Driver and the Mechanic exist only in relation to the road. They rarely speak to each other, and when they do, their exchanges are terse, almost cryptic: "I think that Plymouth had a hemi"; "She don't seem like she's breathing right." Their primer-gray Chevy, its engine poking through the hood like a bizarre growth, is an eyesore next to the gleaming orange-yellow GTO, with its soft leather seats and state-of-the-art tape deck—not to mention a trunk full of whiskey and pills.

A chance to change course arrives in the form of the Girl (Laurie Bird), a mercurial hitchhiker as forceful as she is enigmatic. Unburdened by the Driver's angst or G.T.O.'s vanity, she acts on instinct, a creature of deeds, not thoughts. After she beds the Mechanic (thus securing herself a place in the Chevy's backseat), a heartsick Driver tries to lay some philosophy on her. At a rural gas station, he muses aloud on the lives of cicadas, the "freaky bugs" who live most of their lives underground, emerging just long enough to mate, breed, and die. It's a bleak view of existence, wholly consistent with the movie's stark existentialism. But the Girl rejects it out of hand, in the simplest way possible, by missing the point: "We've got a better life, haven't we?"

Driven relentlessly forward, *Blacktop* offers few clues to where its characters have been. The Driver and the Mechanic seem to have no past, whereas G.T.O. has too many, a series of varied and incompatible histories he unleashes on a series of dumbstruck hitchhikers. (Among them is Harry Dean Stanton, whose sexual advances are politely but firmly rebuffed. "This is competition," G.T.O. snaps. "I've got no *time*.") The closest the movie comes to externalizing their inner lives is a brief scene where the Driver overhears a middle-aged woman yelling at her henpecked date, "Every time I hit you where it hurts, you withdraw from me!" That act of elementary displacement suggests that beneath his stoic exterior, the Driver nurses wounds unknown, perhaps even to him. In that respect, Taylor's inexperience works in the movie's favor. Shy and withdrawn, he rejects even the camera's intimacy. In close-up, his eyes are downcast, his face turned at an angle. He won't be ignored, but he can't bear to be seen.

The Driver rarely lets his guard down, but in a brief moment of solidarity, he tells G.T.O. that with a few modifications, his assembly-line model could be "a real street-sweeper." But as with the Girl, the Driver's attempt to reach out is misunderstood. "I go fast enough," G.T.O. responds, to which the Driver snaps, "You can never go fast enough."

The Driver's macho maxim has been a rallying cry for generations of gearheads, but in context it sounds more like a petulant outburst, or an admission of defeat. Condemned to a life in the not-fast-enough lane, the Driver and the Mechanic are literally consumed by their need for speed. As the Chevy races off in the final shot, Hellman simulates a breakdown—not the car's, but the movie's. The frame shudders and slows and finally stops, and the image dissolves in a projector-bulb supernova. Instead of riding into the sunset, the Chevy is consumed by the light, leaving nothing and no one behind.

Vanishing Point

Richard C. Sarafian, 1971

by Stephanie Zacharek

IN THE MYTHICAL 1960S—NOT THE ACTUAL DECADE, BUT THE *notion* of the '60s as it's been repackaged in any number of nostalgia compilations—the ideal was to get back in touch with yourself and with nature, to reach that finer part of your character that centuries of civilization and oppression by "the man" had squelched. That's how we got Canned Heat at Woodstock, warbling about "going up the country": "I'm going where the water tastes like wine," they sang, as if enlightenment were a place you could find on a map. The reference is straight from the blues, and from the gospels before that, but the sound has nothing to do with escaping the shackles and misery of this life. It's the sound of hippies noodling, dreaming of idealism without taking the driving lessons you need to steer it.

By 1971, the year of Richard C. Sarafian's *Vanishing Point,* the '60s—the mythical '60s—were nearly over. And the movie's martyr hero, a guy named Kowalski (just one name, no first and no middle), has had it. He's seen the worst of the '60s: Vietnam, oppression by the establishment, Delaney & Bonnie. Now he's decided he's going to stay in the driver's seat, determine his own fate. Kowalski is played by Barry Newman; he's soulful looking, like a Jewish Lord Byron. And he doesn't say much, although he doesn't need to, because it's his driving that tells the story.

Kowalski's job is to drive cars—they may be hot cars—from here to there. He's picked up a white Dodge Challenger—a car with class, one that's inherently, not aggressively, cool—in Denver shortly after midnight on a Saturday. His goal is to deliver it to San Francisco by 3:00 p.m. the next day, driving straight through. He scores—and downs, without water—some speed from a pal, who bets him he can't make the trip in such an unrealistically short time. Kowalski accepts the dare, because it's not really a dare at all. He wants to drive for the same reasons people sometimes want to have sex—to lose himself, to obliterate himself. To *not* drive would surely kill him.

So he drives as if the devil himself were on his tail—or maybe it's just the specter of that demon spawn Richard Nixon, at the time busy betraying his country, although we didn't yet know just how much. Kowalski zips across miles and miles of nondescript highway, perhaps not the prettiest-looking roads, although John A. Alonzo's cinematography captures their generic beauty, the comforting consistency of that dotted white line as it stretches over the horizon and off the edge of the world. There's beauty in the picture, but not much real scenery. Then again, unlike *Easy Rider,* this isn't a movie about finding America, but about trying to survive it in one piece.

Kowalski's Challenger skims and dips through the landscape state by state, always pursued by this or that local law-enforcement official. He's driving fast, but meticulously—he's a former motorcycle racer and demolition-derby driver, so he knows what he's doing. The cops, the sheriffs, the highway patrol all want to get him, not necessarily because he's endangering anyone, but because he's one of those so-called free spirits, and they sure can't stand for that. But no one can catch Kowalski: he eludes his would-be captors by skidding and swerving, by forcing them off the road or into steaming smash-ups. By contemporary standards, the chase scenes in *Vanishing Point* are practically Zenlike: they're not overly screechy; the stunt driving is smooth and controlled, almost balletic. The picture's thrills are measured, almost thoughtful; even its pure B-movie touches—like the sight of a naked lovely running circles on a motorcycle—feel more like crazy poetry than sheer exploitation. (The script is by the renowned Cuban novelist and film critic G. Cabrera Infante, credited as Guillermo Cain, from a story by Malcolm Hart.)

What's Kowalski running from—or running toward? We learn his story in a series of interspersed flashbacks: He's a Vietnam vet. He was once a cop. (He lost his badge, it's suggested, after stopping another cop from roughing up and sexually manhandling a young girl.) He was once in love with a woman; she died in a surfing accident. Kowalski, a mystery at the beginning of the movie, is still something of a cipher at the end. But he's compelling precisely because he's so *unfreakish*—he's somewhat conventional, and definitely principled. He seems to belong nowhere, and other nowhere types gravitate toward him: on the road, he meets a grizzled prospector (played by Dean Jagger, wandering in like a refugee from the old Hollywood that had pretty much given up the ghost by '71) who collects snakes to sell to the local holy rollers—though the holy rollers have decided they don't want snakes anymore, now that they have pseudoreligious pop music to attract the masses. (The singers are the aforementioned and wretched Delaney & Bonnie, enough to drive anyone *into* the arms of Satan.) Kowalski also has a partner in crime he's never even met, a blind DJ named Super Soul (Cleavon Little). Super Soul, who makes a habit of listening in on police-radio frequencies, learns that the cops are after a mysterious and exceedingly capable driver in a Dodge Challenger. Super Soul communicates with Kowalski via the radio waves—and seemingly through a purely psychic connection as well—warning him when the cops are getting too close. He recognizes Kowalski as a folk hero, urging him to keep going at all costs.

The question Kowalski asks himself—and ultimately answers—on this almost meditative road trip is whether or not he wants to keep going. *Vanishing Point* is a blues ballad reimagined as a car-chase movie, the story of a tortured soul (in a very cool car) who's torn between temporal existence and everlasting life. If Kowalski had ever heard Robert Johnson sing, "I feel mistreated and I don't mind dyin,'" he knew the meaning of the words. Forget going up the country: at the end of *Vanishing Point,* Kowalski becomes part of the landscape. The '60s are over, but Kowalski, instead of becoming a casualty of the era, triumphs over it. He doesn't just find the real America; he disappears into it. It's the only place he could possibly call home.

The Big Bus

James Frawley, 1976

by Kevin Thomas

"There have been movies about big earthquakes . . . there have been movies about boats sinking . . . movies about big buildings burning . . . movies about big German balloons busting . . . and now a movie about . . . THE BIG BUS."

THIS IS THE APT AND FUNNY WAY IN WHICH **THE BIG BUS** IS introduced. An appealingly silly spoof of disaster epics written by Fred Freeman and Lawrence J. Cohen, the authors of that inspired send-up of swashbucklers, *Start the Revolution without Me* (1970), *The Big Bus* is a satisfying refresher—not great, maybe, but the kind of picture that's relaxing and a lift to the spirits. In short, it's entertaining.

Even before Cyclops, the world's first nuclear-powered bus, can embark on its maiden nonstop trip from New York to Denver, its inventor, Profesor Baxter (Harold Gould), is wounded in a bomb explosion. The nefarious Ironman (José Ferrer), confined to an iron lung, and his brother (Stuart Margolin) are responsible, having been hired by big oil interests fearing that the vehicle's success could dent their profits.

With Professor Baxter sidelined at least temporarily, it becomes all the more important for his daughter (Stockard Channing) to line up the best possible driver. There's only one man who truly qualifies, and that's her ex-fiancé, Dan Torrance (Joseph Bologna). Actually, he needs the job. Surviving a crash that cost the lives of 110 people, he hasn't been able to live down charges of cannibalism. ("Eat one lousy foot and they call you a cannibal," he wails.)

Soon Cyclops is on its way, headed straight into a series of mishaps and loaded with nutty passengers. First there's the bus's copilot, Shoulders O'Brien (John

Beck), whose nickname refers not to his impressive build but to his tendency to drive off the road. For that matter, he passes out when a vehicle simply starts to move. And then there's Ruth Gordon as a foul-mouthed old lady and Lynn Redgrave as a haughty haute couturiere (who intends to shoot Dan to avenge her father's death). Sally Kellerman and Richard Mulligan play a debonair couple who are constantly fighting yet unable to be apart. René Auberjonois plays a priest who's lost his faith, and Bob Dishy is a veterinarian who's lost his license. ("I'm the only vet who had the courage to put an IUD in a rabbit," he says.) Richard B. Shull plays the obligatory passenger who's only got six months to live, and Mary Wilcox is the quintessential stewardess, Mary Jane Beth Sue. Larry Hagman plays Professor Baxter's inept medico, and Ned Beatty and Howard Hesseman man Cyclops control. Funniest of all is Murphy Dunne as Tommy Joyce, the bus's indomitably cheery, unrelentingly lousy onboard entertainer. When a '53 Chevy pickup carrying some country folks plunges into Cyclops's side, an undaunted Tommy greets them with, "Welcome to the Oriental Lounge!" (Though sleek on the outside, Cyclops is pretty funny on the inside, its décor a triumph of kitschy Americana.)

The Big Bus was directed by James Frawley with an unflagging sense of fun. Bologna and Channing, who in her third film looks like a cross between Elizabeth Taylor and Maureen Stapleton, are nicely teamed, as are Kellerman and the all-too-seldom-seen Mulligan. Still and all, the movie's prime asset is unquestionably Freeman and Cohen's zany, cliché-skewering script.

Part SEVEN: Gunfighter Nation

The Wild Western

NOT ALL REVISIONIST WESTERNS—CHEYENNE AUTUMN, *McCabe & Mrs. Miller, Unforgiven*—are B movies. But most B Westerns are revisionist. It comes with the territory.

Which doesn't answer the key question: What is a revisionist Western? The traditional Western is itself a revision of history and fact; life on the actual frontier was grimier, crazier, more violent, and less glamorous than the golden West portrayed for decades by Hollywood as a combination of bucolic New Eden and he-man shooting gallery. In the real Gunfighter Nation, psychotics were all the rage, and many of the others fit Gene Wilder's description in *Blazing Saddles*: "simple farmers . . . people of the land, the common clay of the new West. You know . . . morons."

In short, the West was a lot more interesting than Hopalong Cassidy's black hat/white hat world. The agile B moviemakers who explored it, among them Anthony Mann, Budd Boetticher, Samuel Fuller, and the unsung Tom Gries, who was mainly a TV director (*Tombstone Territory! Route 66!! Batman!!!*), used a stripped-down palette to paint—and we use that word advisedly—a straightforward, sometimes minimalist, often morally unembellished world.

These auteurs of the Wild West not only re-reinvented the cowboy movie; they revitalized some of Hollywood's most durable stars in the process. Anthony Mann gave James Stewart some of his most psychologically stirring vehicles in the 1950s, just as Randolph Scott and Barbara Stanwyck were extending their talents in new directions via Boetticher and Fuller films. (We admit, however, that when the denizens of *Blazing Saddles* practically genuflect at the mention of Randolph Scott, they probably aren't thinking of the exquisitely sculpted *Seven Men from Now*.)

In old America, the second chance—or the third, or the fifth—might be awaiting you on the frontier. In the movies, the artistic bounty found there has bene-
fited actors, directors, and a country always striving for a vision of itself that has
the vibrancy of life, if not always the ring of truth.

The Naked Spur and Man of the West

Anthony Mann, 1953, 1958

by Jonathan Rosenbaum

Q : *What is the starting point for* The Naked Spur?

A : *We were in magnificent countryside—in Durango—and everything lent itself to improvisation. I never understood why almost all westerns are shot in desert landscapes! John Ford, for example, adores Monument Valley, but I know Monument Valley very well and it's not the whole west. In fact, the desert represents only one part of the American west. I wanted to show the mountains, the waterfalls, the forested areas, the snowy summits—in short to rediscover the whole Daniel Boone atmosphere: the characters emerge more fully from such an environment. In that sense the shooting of* The Naked Spur *gave me some genuine satisfaction.*

—ANTHONY MANN IN A 1967 INTERVIEW

DURING WHAT SEEMED TO BE "LANDSCAPE WEEK" AT Chicago's Gene Siskel Film Center not long ago, you could see Abbas Kiarostami's sublime *Where Is the Friend's Home?* (1987), Jon Jost's mesmerizing *Muri Romani* (2000), and two terrific, eye-filling Anthony Mann Westerns, *The Naked Spur* and *Man of the West*. There are plenty of differences among these offerings. *Muri Romani* consists of nothing but extended overlapping dissolves between various exterior walls in Rome, each one slowly merging into the next, yet it's so beautiful and absorbing that I didn't feel deprived. In fact, all of these films are uncommonly beautiful objects that do more with natural settings than most films do with characters—and to risk a pun, this isn't all they do by a long shot.

All four films collapse the usual distinctions between landscape and architecture, classicism and modernity, and even at times painting and drama—though *Muri Romani* has no landscape in any ordinary sense, and *The Naked Spur*, shot entirely in natural exteriors (apart from a cave where the characters find shelter from the rain), has no architecture. In contrast, *Where Is the Friend's Home?* focuses for long stretches on an ancient village clinging to the side of a mountain, and *Man of the West* features a farmhouse at the bottom of a green valley and a ghost town surrounded by mountains; both movies have a kind of compositional power that's inextricably tied to their views of human behavior and human destiny.

Jean-Luc Godard wrote a review of *Man of the West* when it came out, describing "the delightful farm nestling amid the greenery which George Eliot would have loved." If he'd written his review two years later he might have no less aptly connected the ghost town to the modernism of Michelangelo Antonioni's *L'Avventura* (1960). His view of Mann merged image and idea, classical and modern: "Just as the director of *The Birth of a Nation* [1915] gave one the impression that he was inventing the cinema with every shot, each shot of *Man of the West* gives one the impression that Anthony Mann is reinventing the western, exactly as Matisse's portraits reinvent the features of Piero della Francesca. . . . In other words, he both shows and demonstrates, innovates and copies, criticizes and creates."

Mann (1906–1967) is still cherished today by aficionados of golden-age Hollywood. In *CineAction*, Robin Wood, perhaps the best critic of that cinema, ranks him alongside George Cukor, John Ford, Howard Hawks, Alfred Hitchcock, Leo McCarey, Max Ophuls, Otto Preminger, Nicholas Ray, Douglas Sirk, and Preston Sturges—all of whom, he notes, "retain their amazing freshness and vitality today." If Mann is less known than the others, it may be because his painterly gifts tend to wither on TV screens. Painter-critic Manny Farber first recognized these gifts in the late '40s and early '50s, when Mann still had the "museum space" afforded by 35-millimeter—resurrected today only in special screenings, such as the Film Center's.

The Naked Spur, the most elemental Mann Western, and my favorite of all his pictures, has the most breathtaking scenery, including snowcapped mountains, rock formations, and green forest clearings in the Colorado Rockies near Durango. Yet insofar as Westerns are intrinsically mythological, I suppose one could argue that this one might as well be taking place inside Mann's head.

Part of the elemental lure of that Western mythology today—comparable in some ways to the spell exerted by the Knights of the Round Table in England—is the excitement of an existential context in which characters forge their own personal destinies the moment they encounter or take leave of strangers. You won't catch people in a Western saying "No problem" or "Have a good one" to one another as a ruse for avoiding such challenges. The role of nature in these transactions, as Mann suggests, is to make the characters "emerge more fully"; as critic Donald Phelps once put it, "The great open spaces are sectioned as methodically as a football field."

With the exception of a few nameless Blackfoot Indians killed in a brutal ambush—whom the film lamentably discounts, though the white man responsible for the ambush is no sort of hero—the movie has only five characters. And because it never leaves the spectacular wilderness and everyone's traveling light, no one has a single change of wardrobe—which somehow seems fitting for a landscape film. Moreover, the four male principals, as is typical in Mann Westerns, all develop dialectically.

Howard Kemp (James Stewart), the bounty-hunter hero, starts off as unpleasantly self-centered in relation to a friendly old prospector (Millard Mitchell), a dishonorably discharged yet resourceful cavalry lieutenant (Ralph Meeker), and even the cheerful outlaw (Robert Ryan) whom Kemp captures. Kemp becomes vulnerable when his leg is injured and bits of his tainted past are revealed (physical pain and traumatic backstories are central in Mann's Westerns), and only then do the three other men begin to show their darker natures, sparking an intense psychological war (another Mann specialty). The prospector and ex-officer insist that Kemp make them his partners and split the reward for capturing the outlaw three ways, and the outlaw contrives to unravel the complacencies of all three as they travel through the wilderness toward Abilene. When the prospector, aiming his shotgun at one of the others at a critical juncture, complains, "It's gettin' so I don't know which way to point this no more," he could just as well be speaking for the audience. As usual in such a fluctuating context, the role of the woman—a feisty orphan (Janet Leigh) the outlaw has in tow—is to represent all that's left of civilization, a value that's also prone to change as loyalties and ethical profiles shift.

The settings in *Man of the West*—a western town, a train bound for Fort Worth, a farmhouse in a valley, a desert, and a ghost town (the latter two filmed in California's Red Rock Canyon)—lack the formal purity of those in *The Naked Spur.* As a result, *Man of the West* veers much closer to the grimness of Greek tragedy, its mountains and rock formations often suggesting the silent witness of an ancient amphitheater. (The connection isn't accidental; another of Mann's late interviews is peppered with references to *Oedipus Rex* and *Antigone,* and one of his best early Westerns is titled *The Furies* [1950].)

The hero, Link (Gary Cooper), is headed for Fort Worth to find a schoolteacher for his remote town, but the train is held up by a gang of thieves, stranding him with a card sharp (Arthur O'Connell) and a saloon singer (Julie London). The three go to an abandoned farmhouse, where it emerges that Link used to be a member of the gang, which is led by his half-mad uncle, Dock (Lee J. Cobb); Dock raised him until he ran away in disgust and started a new life. A "link" between the civilization ironically represented by the card sharp and the singer (as well as his offscreen family) and the lawlessness of the gang, Link is welcomed by Dock like a prodigal son returning to the fold, and has to play along to keep his two companions alive.

Scripted by Reginald Rose—a TV dramatist of the '50s, second in prominence only to Paddy Chayefsky; 12 Angry Men is probably his best-known work—Man of the West is shot in CinemaScope, yet it's initially hampered by the shallow dramatic space associated with television. This effect is made worse by the casting, which pairs the stagiest of stage actors (Cobb) with the most cinematic of movie actors (Cooper, at fifty-seven, only three years from retirement). But Mann is canny enough to turn these limitations to his advantage whenever he can, offering sly notations about Link's physical discomfort on the train and using a long, tense scene inside the farmhouse to create claustrophobia before sending the characters outdoors for virtually the remainder of the picture. Once again, the hero is a dialectical contradiction, both regressing toward an unbearable past and making an anguished effort to break free from it—the struggle ultimately engendering hatred, violence, pain, and humiliation, and revealing boundless evil.

Classical tragedy is evoked in both of these Westerns as all of the characters apart from the hero and heroine are gradually killed off. In The Naked Spur, three white men and several Blackfoot Indians die. In Man of the West, the entire gang and one captive are killed, and the penultimate shoot-out in the ghost town is an appropriately eerie split-level confrontation between two wounded, supine men—one stretched out on a porch at screen left, the other stretched out underneath the porch at screen right, as if he were already buried. It's a key example of the way that landscape and architecture, people and settings, painting and drama, image and idea, classicism and modernism all merge on Mann's monumental canvases.

POSTSCRIPT:

The above essay first appeared in the Chicago Reader *on July 5, 2002. Writing about* Road to Perdition *in the Reader the following week, I concluded: "What bothers me is the compulsive reliance on revenge in movies, not only as a dramatic staple but as an embodiment of this country's sense of ethics. It's seldom examined in detail; instead it's usually glamorized, with the avenger most often seen (as he is in* Road to Perdition*) as a model of grim stoicism, driven by some sense of a higher purpose, not simply getting his rocks off. Vengeance is a notion that tastes sweet mainly to the powerless, which often means members of minorities, including the Irish in this story—and that makes it a fantasy of compensation, much as PC language seems most vital to people without the power to change their lives in other respects. As a result, revenge plots have surefire commercial appeal almost everywhere, which is why commercial filmmakers rely on them. But the moment they go beyond a simple desire to entertain and profess to teach us some form of wisdom is the moment I start to gag.*

"A good counterexample is provided by the two Anthony Mann westerns I wrote about last week. Both incorporate some notion of an avenging hero resorting to violence, though not at all stoically, and both heroes' loss of emotional control shows their vulnerability, not their power. James Stewart actually bursts into tears in the final scene of The Naked Spur *(1953), and Gary Cooper in* Man of the West *(1958) comes close to doing the same when he punishes an outlaw, who forced Julie London at knifepoint to strip, by tearing off the man's clothes. In both cases the impulse toward revenge is clearly and honestly marked as a form of regression toward childhood or more recent traumas, not as any sort of catharsis or adult achievement of justice. Perhaps if [director] Sam Mendes looks for scripts worthy of Anthony Mann, we may get something better than double standards and Oscar bait."*

Will Penny

Tom Gries, 1968

by David Sterritt

EVEN A HARD-CORE AUTEUR CRITIC WOULD HAVE TROUBLE pinpointing the "author" of *Will Penny,* a Western that made a beautiful case for traditional genre storytelling one short year before *The Wild Bunch* turned the stagecoach in a very different direction. The director and writer, Tom Gries, made dozens of movies and TV dramas over twenty-three years without developing much in the way of personal themes or characteristic styles. The star, Charlton Heston, played lots of Westerners but is better remembered for historical roles like Moses and Ben-Hur, not to mention his notorious National Rifle Association ads. And while cinematographer Lucien Ballard did a superb job of capturing the rugged California terrain where the picture was shot, he's more renowned for the anamorphic framing he mastered so brilliantly a few months later in, you guessed it, *The Wild Bunch.*

So the best bet is to praise all three of these artists, along with composer David Raksin, whose mood-setting music has the energy and edginess that were his trademarks. Together they made this mostly conventional Western as enjoyable as any of its period. It was also something of a trailblazer, since its realism helped spark a trend that revitalized the genre during the 1970s, '80s, and '90s, from *The Wild Bunch* to Clint Eastwood's admired *Unforgiven* (1992), where hero William Munny's kids are named Will and Penny.

Gries developed *Will Penny* from an episode he'd written for Sam Peckinpah's television series *The Westerner* in 1960. The title character is an aging cowpoke (back then you got called Grandpa if you were over fifty) who finds himself out of work after giving up a job to a young fella who needs it more. Riding north with a couple of friends, he gets tangled in a quarrel with a weird guy called Preacher Quint, resulting in a shoot-out that kills one of the preacher's sons. A peaceable man at heart, Will continues his journey and finds employment as a watchman on an enormous ranch, responsible for keeping travelers from stopping or squatting on the place. But no sooner does he start "riding the line" than trouble comes his way. When he gets to the cabin where he'll be living, he finds a young woman and her little boy living there. And far worse, Preacher Quint tracks him down, getting the drop on him and inflicting serious injuries.

The woman tends Will's wounds, so he decides to let her and the child stay on for the harsh winter that's about to hit. As time passes, he feels more and more affectionate toward them, but it's unlikely they'll live happily ever after. Preacher Quint is still skulking around, and Will's boss is going to be mighty mad when he finds his new employee squatting with the very squatters he's supposed to chase away. Sure enough, the ending puts a bittersweet twist on the old convention of cowboy and cowgirl riding into the sunset. This was risky, as Heston candidly observed when he wrote *In the Arena*, his autobiography. He recalled people saying to him, "That's maybe the best movie you ever made, Chuck, but if you'd taken the girl with you at the end, it would've made a ton of money, too."

The actor also wrote candidly about director Gries, calling him "a gifted, mercurial, oddly unpredictable and somewhat childlike man," who was not "a good captain, which a great director must be," but rose to the occasion when he had "the right material." *Will Penny* was terrific material, and Heston regarded it as one of the best films he ever appeared in. It was also his personal favorite, thanks partly to its themes—loyalty, fatherhood, the challenges of aging—and partly to the enthusiastic reviews it brought him, which were arguably the best of his entire career. The rest of the cast is also impressive: Joan Hackett as the woman in Will's life; Gries's eight-year-old son, Jon Francis, as her child; the great British actor Donald Pleasence as the evil preacher; Bruce Dern as his craziest son; Anthony Zerbe and Lee Majors as Will's best buddies; Slim Pickens as another cowpoke; Ben Johnson as the straight-shooting ranch foreman; Clifton James as a greedy saloon keeper; and William Schallert as a doctor who sees all cattlemen as irresponsible children at heart.

Will Penny was a fairly modest production, with Heston's big-star salary the largest single expense. Things didn't always go smoothly—both Lee Remick and Eva Marie Saint turned down the role that Hackett eventually accepted—but there were few major problems. Still, the movie earned only $1.3 million at the box office. Along with its downbeat finale, Heston blamed apathy by a new management team at Paramount Pictures, who "more or less buried the release of films made under the previous regime, preferring to press forward with their own plans." And it didn't help that Heston was competing with himself—his legendary science-fiction adventure *Planet of the Apes* had been released one short week earlier. *Will Penny* had healthy TV, home video, and cable revenues in later years, though, and its reputation is still rising.

Ballard photographed all kinds of films during a career lasting half a century, and if a large number of Westerns show up on the list of his most respected pictures, one reason is that he shot important ones for such gifted directors as Peckinpah, the great Budd Boetticher, and Henry Hathaway, not to mention the ungifted Howard Hughes, who hired Ballard as second-unit cinematographer on *The Outlaw,* his 1943 ode to Jane Russell's cleavage. *Variety* praised *Will Penny* for its "topnotch technical crew headed by Lucien Ballard with his color cameras," and even with movies like *Buchanan Rides Alone* (1958), *Ride the High Country* (1962), and *True Grit* (1969) to his credit, it's safe to say Ballard never shot a more visually evocative Western. In a movie where atmosphere really counts—the sprawl of the ranch, the mountains in the distance, the chill of the winter—his contribution is a key reason for its success.

Seven Men from Now

Budd Boetticher, 1956

by Richard T. Jameson

THE MAKING OF **SEVEN MEN FROM NOW** WAS A MODEST enterprise. John Wayne's old Batjac production company had a B-movie arm in addition to the main unit, which set up A-class vehicles for producer-star Wayne, and *Seven Men from Now,* which clocks in at a second-feature length of just under an hour and twenty minutes, was produced under its auspices for release by Warner Bros.

The screenwriter, Burt Kennedy, was a newcomer who'd been scribbling for radio; the director, Budd Boetticher, was a colorful fellow who'd started as a bullfighter in Mexico, made some trim B movies in the '40s—and one distinctive, highly personal film, *The Bullfighter and the Lady* (produced by Wayne, as it happens) in 1951—and then reverted to only slightly more upscale Bs later in the decade. At the time when *Seven Men from Now* went into production, Wayne was busy giving his finest performance ever in John Ford's Western *The Searchers,* so the leading role fell to Randolph Scott, a fading star who'd been working in mostly unremarkable Westerns since the mid '40s.

No one at Batjac or at Warners was expecting more from *Seven Men from Now* than reasonable profitability. Yet the three men's talents blended uncannily, producing the best movie by far ever to sport the Batjac label. It's not just a terrific Western, it's a cinema masterpiece—an ironical, beautifully spare bit of storytelling that became the ideal showcase for Scott's sandy reticence.

You don't want anybody synopsizing the plot for you; there's little of it, really, yet how it's told makes it complex and compelling. We know from a memorable first scene that Scott is hunting down seven men who did something terrible; we soon gather that he's also seeking to assuage a nameless guilt of his own. He will be thrown together with several other characters, including Lee Marvin as an affable but deadly rascal with whom he shares some history. Everybody has private reasons to be traveling through Apache country. Savor every syllable of the laconic dialogue, what people say, what they don't quite say. And what they think they understand about one another's motives, except that the understanding keeps getting rearranged.

The dandy screenplay keeps taking surprising turns and disclosing new layers of complexity in the journeys and interrelationships of its characters. There's a wry, persuasively frontier ring to the dialogue, especially as delivered by Marvin (who improbably sports an elegant, overlong green scarf). He owns the movie's best scene, in which he and Scott seek shelter in a covered wagon belonging to the Greers, a married couple played by Gail Russell and Walter Reed. By the light of a single lantern, as the rain pours down outside, Marvin begins to make love to Russell without laying a hand on her—simply talking about another woman he once knew, whose hair and eyes "were nothing like yours, Mrs. Greer." Scott and the husband have to sit and take it. But only up to a point. Lee Marvin never played a slyer scene (and Boetticher would repeat the gambit in 1960's *Comanche Station*). The coda of the scene has Russell and Scott bedding down for the night—she in the wagon, he underneath it, and the two of them acutely aware of lying parallel to each other.

Boetticher's setups are never fancy or pretentious, but there's always something tensile about the point of view—the disposition of people within the frame and within the spare, mostly desert-rock landscape—and the way shots cut together as the action turns brusquely lethal. It would be nice to report that 1950s audiences embraced the movie as a singular event in American cinema history, but in fact it took the French—notably the influential critic André Bazin—to recognize its distinction and praise it for working narrative miracles without ever breaking a sweat or breaking faith with the unassuming requirements of its genre.

Make no mistake, Scott and Boetticher knew they'd hit on a good thing. Reuniting with his longtime producing partner Harry Joe Brown, Scott kept Boetticher on to make five more low-budget Westerns over the next half decade. *The Tall T* (1957), *Decision at Sundown* (1957), *Buchanan Rides Alone* (1958), *Ride Lonesome* (1959), and *Comanche Station* (1960)—the Ranown cycle, as they came to be known, from RANdolph Scott and Harry Joe BrOWN—were all good pictures, and *The Tall T, Ride Lonesome,* and *Comanche Station* are better than good. Perhaps not coincidentally, those three are also from scripts credited to Kennedy, though the disappointing fact is that none of Kennedy's own films (he became a writer-director in 1961) ever came near the highs of the Boetticher collaborations. Ironically—and Boetticher always relished irony—the Ranown pictures, which were released through Columbia, would remain more or less constantly available over the years, on TV and through film societies, while the movie whose success inspired them was nowhere to be seen for more than twenty years after John Wayne's death in 1979, which threw the Batjac library into limbo.

It saw the light of day again in 2000, when a UCLA restoration was showcased at the New York Film Festival to the ecstatic reception of press and audiences. Budd Boetticher was there for it—a happy, gallant gentleman—and Burt Kennedy knew about it. Both men would die the following year. But their film lives. God, does it live. And we'll never lose it again.

Forty Guns

Samuel Fuller, 1957

by Peter Travers

FOR ME, THE BEST B MOVIES ALWAYS REFLECT THE JOY A gifted filmmaker takes in busting loose from the shackles of realism, restraint, and good taste. And you can feel Samuel Fuller's creative glee all over the screen in *Forty Guns,* a Freudian hellzapoppin' disguised as a Western. Just so you know what you're in for, Fuller starts off at full gallop with Barbara Stanwyck—a woman with a whip astride a white stallion—leading forty engorged penises (disguised as mounted cowboys) across a widescreen canvas filmed in Rorschach black and white by the great Joseph Biroc. Attention, cineastes who enjoy the hard labor of digging out phallic symbols: your work here is done.

Stanwyck was pushing fifty when she took on the role of Jessica Drummond, but the femme-fatale allure she exuded in such 1940s classics as *Ball of Fire* (1941) and *Double Indemnity* (1944) hadn't aged a bit. She even aced out Marilyn Monroe for the role. And you can see Fuller's point; taming Monroe hardly seems the interesting challenge posed by Stanwyck, who did her own stunts. Hard, tight-lipped Griff Bonnell (Barry Sullivan), riding in a sissy buckboard with his brothers, Wes (Gene Barry) and Chico (Robert Dix), can only sit open-mouthed as this high-ridin' prefeminist in black leather makes him choke on her dust.

You may choke, too, at the sheer outrageousness of it all. But Fuller, a poet with the soul of a tabloid journalist (he'd specialized in crime and war reporting), would never settle for being just a camp tease. Like his other most flamboyant B movies, *Shock Corridor* (1963) and *The Naked Kiss* (1964), *Forty Guns* comes fully loaded with subconscious obsessions about sex, violence, fate, the conflicted nature of manhood, and the increasingly thin line separating civilization from chaos.

The time is 1881, and the place is Tombstone, Arizona, where Wyatt Earp would shoot it out with the Clantons at the O.K. Corral. Here it's the Bonnell brothers facing off with their worst nightmare: a woman who wears the pants. Leave it to Fuller to set up the conflict with a song. As men sit naked and vulnerable in outdoor bathtubs, pop singer Jidge Carroll (Barney Cashman) shows up carrying water and a tune. The song, by Harold Adamson and Harry Sukman, is called "High Ridin' Woman," and includes this provocation:

She's a woman that all men desire
She commands and men obey
She has eyes full of life, full of fire
But if someone could break her and take her whip away
Someone big, someone strong, someone tall
You may find that the woman with a whip . . .
Is only a woman after all.

Gloria Steinem had barely hit puberty when that song was written, but I can imagine she was spoiling for a fight even then.

Griff, a hired killer turned lawman, is in town to bring in one of Jessica's forty guns on a mail-robbery charge. Fuller has a high old time setting up Griff's machismo, using close-ups of his boots, his eyes, and the gun bulging above his belt buckle as he strides down the street to confront Jessica's psycho brother, Brockie (a bugfuck John Ericson in a tour de force of Oedipal emotions). "There's only one man walks like that," says Brockie's henchman with an awe clearly shared by Sergio Leone, who would later embellish that walk in his spaghetti Westerns. As Griff pistol-whips Brockie, who enjoys killing and raping and drinking, in that order, and hauls him off to jail, there's no doubt a battle is brewing.

Jessica isn't tamed, but she's impressed enough to offer Griff a job running her Dragoon ranch: "I need a strong man to carry out my orders." To which he replies, "And a weak man to take them."

Ouch. Things stay frosty between them until a dust storm kicks up and they take shelter together. Jessica tells Griff that the frontier is finished and that it's time for him to "start to break yourself. You don't want the only evidence of your life to be bullet holes in men."

As always in Fuller, men have intimacy issues that need deflecting. For Griff, the method is the job at hand. For his brother Wes, given a lewd smirk by Barry, it's the bravado he uses to size up pretty gunsmith Louvenia (Eve Brent) through the barrel of a rifle. (Jean-Luc Godard borrowed the shot in 1960 for *Breathless*, just as Clint Eastwood copied Fuller's use of a corpse in an undertaker's window for his 1992 *Unforgiven*.) It's then that Fuller cuts to them in a heavy clinch. "I've never kissed a gunsmith before," says Wes as Louvenia plays Bacall to his Bogie. "Any recoil?" she responds.

The erotic gun imagery becomes almost pornographic when Jessica asks Griff if she can stroke his pistol. "Watch out," he says, "it might go off in your face." Talk about cum shots. Oh, to have been a fly on the wall when Fuller and the actors filmed that still-notorious scene.

With moments like these, you hardly miss the action, which is just when it comes. For a movie produced in the space of ten days, *Forty Guns* is loaded with tracking shots and complex camera movements. There's a long, beautifully nuanced sequence with Griff in an alley unaware of the assassin waiting in a room above and the assassin unaware that Griff's brother Chico is stalking him.

Fuller is a master of surprise as punctuation. On the day Wes marries Louvenia, a shot goes off and the bride and groom fall on top of each other, leaving us wondering which one has been felled by Brockie's bullet. In another groundbreaking scene, the weak, corrupt sheriff Ned Logan (the great Dean Jagger) interrupts a romantic moment between Griff and Jessica to confess his love for the woman with a whip. She cuts him dead, a Stanwyck specialty. Later, a thumping sound is heard outside, leaving Griff and Jessica to discover that Logan has hanged himself, his swaying boots thumping against the wall in a lifeless rebuke.

This is the stuff of Greek tragedy stuffed into a B movie so full of nutso inspiration it seems amazing that critics of the time shrugged it off. Near the end, Brockie uses his sister as a shield against an armed and dangerous Griff, who is seeking vengeance for the murder of his brother. In a split second, Griff shoots the woman he loves and then her brother. Brockie's dying words—"I'm killed, Mr. Bonnell, I'm killed"—is pure Fuller. It's impossible not to savor the absurd, haunting formality of the "Mr."

Sadly and predictably, the studio pressured Fuller to soften the ending. But his intentions remain impervious to compromise. Any movie that comes with the label, "written, produced and directed by Samuel Fuller" is going to spit in the eye of convention. And *Forty Guns* does so with a B-movie energy that can still floor you. Fuller died in 1997 at the age of eighty-six, and nothing, least of all Hollywood, ever fenced him in.

Part EIGHT: Up Against the Wall!

Political Pictures

THIS CATEGORY IS AS SCHIZOID AS ANY IN THIS BOOK, because nobody has ever pinned down a definition of political cinema. For Jean-Luc Godard, it could be a choice of camera movements; for Don Siegel, an allegorical plot; for John Waters, a well-timed gross-out aimed at the bourgeoisie; for the Warren Beatty of *Reds,* a heroic, star-studded, witness-laden treatise on the early twentieth-century left. The genre's domain is oceanic, churning, angry, tumultuous, and constantly in flux. Charlie Chaplin's *Modern Times* is political; so is *Hostel.* What *isn't* political?

Current events are a different story, and in American film it's always been the norm to avoid smoldering issues until they become moldering issues. Sometimes it's worth the wait: *Platoon,* the landmark Vietnam parable by Oliver Stone, didn't appear until 1986, long after the war had ended. And sometimes it isn't: *Sands of Iwo Jima,* released in 1949, has been treasured mainly by the neocon right, who've adopted it as their pet psychodrama.

The fact is that big studio movies can't tackle hot political topics without fear of alienating part of their audience; but B pictures, and larger productions with the fighting B spirit, have often not given a damn. *Salvador,* another by Stone, hit the screen when the Reagan-Bushies were still slicing and dicing Central America. *Heroes for Sale,* with its Bolsheviks and striking workers and strikebreaking cops and Depression-era resentments, was in theaters by 1933. *Man on a String,* a fact-based cold-war drama starring Ernest Borgnine, was out by 1960 (before the Cuban missile crisis!), and *The President's Analyst*—whose star, James Coburn, prefigured the entire age of irony of the '70s, '80s, and '90s—appeared in 1967. It is a satire of Swiftian proportions, as topical today as when it was new. And very, very prescient about the Nixonian paranoia to come.

Many pictures pretend to be political but don't have the spine to stand up for anything. It took years of Bush and Iraq for mainstream movies to adopt an attitude of resistance to the politics of fear, the drumbeat of perpetual war, and the futility of shock-doctrine foreign policy. History may repeat itself regardless of what the cinema comes up with, but today's issue-oriented films could certainly take some tips from the movies discussed in the following pages.

Platoon

Oliver Stone, 1986

by Eleanor Ringel Cater

BASED ON WRITER-DIRECTOR OLIVER STONE'S OWN EXPERIENCES in Vietnam in the late 1960s, *Platoon* takes us to hell and back and back again. This was the first war movie made about the Vietnam War. That is, it was the first nonpolitical film made about a tragedy that had hitherto been treated within a politicized prowar/antiwar context.

Stone comes not to bury Vietnam or to praise it. He isn't interested in the extraordinary hallucinations of Francis Ford Coppola's *Apocalypse Now* (1979) or the "Give Peace a Chance" posturing of *Coming Home* (1978). Nor does he indulge in the insulting and absurdly retro-macho fantasies of the Rambo films. *Platoon* is, quite simply, about the way it was—one day at a time, over there—when the only thing a grunt worried about was getting back to base camp alive.

True, the movie has its share of heroics and adrenalin-pumping scenes of jungle warfare, but the film is less a battle hymn than a battle dirge for a battered republic. Appropriately, it begins with a lament—Samuel Barber's "Adagio for Strings"—as some impossibly baby-faced recruits are disgorged from the yawning maw of a transport carrier. "You're gonna love 'Nam," mutters a passing vet as they stare wide-eyed at the massed body bags waiting to take their place on board. Those bags hold the remains of last year's new recruits—or perhaps last week's.

Stone's autobiographical stand-in, Taylor, is played with skill and sensitivity by Charlie Sheen. (Who could've guessed back then that he'd end up in TV's *Two and a Half Men?*) Taylor is a middle-class white kid who enlisted because he wanted to serve his country and because he thought it was wrong that the privileged found ways to get out of the draft while the poor did not. When he relates his egalitarian rationale to a comrade in arms, the man laughs, "You gotta be rich in the first place to think like that."

With Taylor as our guide, we're plunged into the tropical hell of this war. First, there's the jungle itself, where everything bites or stings or blows up.

Then there's the enemy—silent, deadly, evoking every flag-waving American's clichéd dread of the inscrutable Oriental, with ways to torture and kill not known to more "civilized" enemies (those orderly Nazis, say).

Finally, there are the men themselves—an all-too-human mix of heroes and horrors, heads and hoochers. Some, like Sergeant Elias (an exceptional Willem Dafoe), have found themselves in this war. Elias is a saintlike symbol of the very good soldier—a veritable Hector in army fatigues who truly understands that the only glory of war is survival. He becomes the movie's Red Badge of Conscience. Others, like Sergeant Barnes (Tom Berenger), have lost themselves to the war. With his theatrically scarred profile, Barnes is Ares, the bloodthirsty god of war, merciless and invincible.

There isn't much in the way of narrative structure in *Platoon*, but that's part of what Stone is telling us—that there wasn't much in the way of a narrative structure in Vietnam; that there was a numbing sameness to the senselessness, and that acts of courage had no more weight than acts of brutality. Fear is a given, a constant. Even the soul-dead, like Barnes, feel the fear. Only for them it is an aphrodisiac, a delicate bouquet of butchery. The climactic battle (superbly shot by Robert Richardson and edited by Claire Simpson) is a crazed nightmare of death in the dark, illuminated by lightning-like flashes of artillery and rockets.

Back at base camp for a few days, the squad breaks down into the smokers and the drinkers. The two factions are eerily similar to their home-front correlatives. The boozers play "Okie from Muskogee" and indulge in good-ol'-boy horseplay. The dopers, meanwhile, have created their own crash pad in hell, with candles and Grace Slick and marijuana being smoked through anything that's hollow. (You've never seen shotgunning like this before.)

Yet even in these scenes of R&R, Stone never entirely lets up. He uses them to emphasize the inherent divisions and tensions among the men—the us-versus-them mentality (endemic to any group) that eats away at the platoon's effectiveness. He also uses them as a subtle mirror of America-the-Not-So-Beautiful in the late '60s, divided against itself and caught in the hopeless quagmire of a war that it could neither fully commit itself to winning nor fully reconcile itself to losing.

Taylor writes to his grandmother, "Someone once said that Hell is the impossibility of reason. This place is Hell." That's what Stone shows us in *Platoon*—not just the old chestnut that war is hell, but the very specific hell that was Vietnam.

At the center of the film is the insane unreasonableness of it all. Not the rights or wrongs of American involvement but how a thousand-year-old village could be destroyed because it happened to be in the way the day the soldiers discovered one of their number had been tortured and murdered by the Cong.

You could almost say Stone made the Vietnam War movie that John Wayne would've wanted to make (rather than his excruciatingly simpleminded 1968 picture, *The Green Berets*). But the Duke came from a simpler time, and the movie wars he was accustomed to fighting sprang from a simpler outlook. Influenced by the Greatest Generation valor of World War II, Wayne couldn't possibly comprehend the combination of psychedelic bravado and purple-hearted futility that made Vietnam the first rock 'n' roll war.

Platoon gives us the quick, the dead, and the stoned. It's an "All Queasy on the Eastern Front," showing the stomach-churning realities of an unpopular war that allowed napalm to be dropped on children but left American GIs stranded and unsupported by the full force of their country's techno-military expertise. "You ever get caught in a mistake you just couldn't get out of?" Taylor asks in one of his letters home. Vietnam was that kind of mistake for the nation. It snuck up in the early '60s and snuck away (or, more accurately, was swept under the rug) in the middle '70s. Stone shows us what it was like to be caught in the middle. He doesn't judge. He doesn't say it was right or wrong to be there. He just says, Some of us were there and here's what it was like. He wants us to look and look and look and finally see beyond the political platitudes and pop-culture clichés that have shrouded Vietnam and made it a conceptualized symbol rather than a heart-rending matter of torn flesh and spilt blood.

Coppola wants us to look into the heart of darkness. Stone wants us to look into these boys' faces. Coppola shows us a nation's loss of innocence. Stone shows us a nation's lost lives.

Salvador

Oliver Stone, 1986

by John Powers

THE FIRST TIME I WROTE ABOUT OLIVER STONE, BACK WHEN he coscripted *Year of the Dragon* (1985), I called him a hack and a bigot. But a few minutes into *Salvador* I knew I'd been wrong. The film is no polished work of art—it's too messy and rambunctious for that—but it restores to American movies the genius of pulp: its passion, its visceral pull, its willingness to dive headlong into life's muddy waters even at the risk of coming out dirty. By comparison, all other movies about journalists in the Third World feel sanitized and tame—mere Hollywood fictions.

Loosely based on the experiences of photojournalist Richard Boyle, who wrote the script with director Stone, *Salvador* has the plot of a redemption melodrama: its hero loses everything but saves his soul. But it doesn't play like anything nearly so idealistic. Even at its slackest, this swaggering tale has the jitteriness of real experience, and when things get cooking, events unfold like an acid trip or a nightmare—the speedy rush is almost hallucinatory. Welcome to Gonzo Time.

When we first see him, Boyle (James Woods) seems an unlikely hero. Broke, jobless, marriage on the skids, he looks like a ferret dipped in motor oil. Normal life has whipped him, and he's trying to survive on his rep as the last journalist to leave Cambodia: "While Schanberg was collecting his fucking Pulitzer Prize, I was getting my ass shot off." (Boyle's exploitation of this story is one of the movie's running gags.) Hoping to escape the shambles of his life, he tries to borrow money from his friend Dr. Rock (Jim Belushi), an unemployed DJ who looks "like a walking museum of the '60s." But Rock's life is also a mess. Crying good-bye to the "fucking yuppies," Boyle and Rock follow America's great tradition and hit the road, joyriding down to Central America, smoking reefer, passing bottles, chomping pills, while Boyle chortles out the virtues of El Salvador: "You can drive drunk, get anybody killed for fifty bucks . . . the best pussy in the world. Where else can you get a virgin to sit on your face for seven bucks? Two virgins for twelve." Of course, the road sign to San Salvador has a vulture sitting on it, and corpses burn black on the highway.

Salvador's madness throws Dr. Rock into a full-body tailspin—he's not used to this shit!—and he bounces between drunkenness, the trots, and sputtering rage. Boyle, though, feeds on the chaos. He immediately sets up house with his ex-girlfriend, a *campesina* named Maria (Elpedia Carrillo), then beetles around Salvador scouting out work, cadging money, and linking up with an assortment of American types. There's the Dick Tracy–jawed functionary, the meat-headed military adviser, the preppie social worker (Cynthia Gibb), and the U.S. ambassador, Thomas Kelly (Michael Murphy), whose liberal hands ache from all that wringing. Boyle also connects with his peers, a journalistic menagerie ranging from "the blowjob queen of New York" (a network correspondent who parrots the official line) to saintly John Cassady (John Savage), a photographer who gets high on danger and wants to show the "dignity of human suffering." There's plenty such dignity to be shown in '80s El Salvador, where *campesinos* are shot in the streets for lacking the proper ID. This place is scary: neighborhood bars teem with death-squad hulks whose shoulders start above their ears.

As Boyle bombs around the countryside, pissing off the government and trying to wangle papers for Maria—the term "grifter" would not be out of place here—*Salvador* maintains a startling level of immediate intensity. Part of its wallop comes from Bruno Rubeo's harrowing production design, its rat-trap plazas littered with rotting fruit and turds, its improvised soup kitchens where the burned and crippled line up for food. (No designer rubble *here*.) San Salvador is dirty and hellish and crowded—yet it's heaven compared to El Playon, a body drop for the death squads where corpses lie strewn by the hundreds in various stages of rot and dismemberment.

Here, as elsewhere, Stone's direction goes straight for your gut. From the opening credits on, he's on top of you, showing you the swooning brutality of murder and rape, filling your ears with the bloody gurgle of a battlefield tracheotomy, accentuating the transcendent horror of mass death. While a movie like *Under Fire* (1983) keeps the viewer at a safe distance from the ghastliness, *Salvador*— brilliantly shot by Robert Richardson—flings you into the action with huge close-ups, busy handheld camera, and editing rhythms that are deliberately disorienting. The story leaps from scene to nervous scene, shattering our relaxation, forcing us to regain our bearings. Fast paced, jumpy, and pregnant with violence, it captures the amoral exhilaration of Third World horror, the amphetamine thrill of chaos.

Stone has, of course, jacked things up. With an artistic license bordering on the brazen, *Salvador* throws Boyle into that phantasmagoric land known as Fictionalized History, in which every moment is supercharged, guerrillas engage in John Ford cavalry charges, and the hero is always exactly where the action is. Sometimes this gets pretty hokey: although I can believe that Boyle knew the nuns who were raped and murdered by the death squads, I'm skeptical that he was actually chewing his communion wafer when the guy next to him assassinated Archbishop Romero.

But I don't doubt for a second that Boyle is *real.* James Woods has always been a ferocious screen presence (he seizes the screen like a coyote snatching up a cat), and he brings this scruffo character to life with a dazzling full-court press of a performance, gesticulating wildly, laughing till he spits, juking in pleasure and dismay, bobbing his upper body like a perpetual-motion duck. He wheedles, he cajoles, he talks out of both sides of his mouth. With his Hawaiian shirts, his manic glee, and his eyes scouring the cosmos for the next angle, Woods's Boyle is a screen classic, a vision of the hero as a "fuckin' weasel" (to use his own self-description). War gets Boyle all juiced up, and *Salvador* takes its fire and its fun from his runaway tongue and desperation, from all the crazy-assed complexity that lets him find salvation in El Salvador (hence the title) yet still lets him goof on "this redemption thing."

In telling Boyle's story, *Salvador* adds to a constantly growing subgenre: movies about journalists. It says a lot about late twentieth-century culture that they have become heroes, especially the ones who cover the madness of modern history—the wars, the revolutions, the purges. These days, when the literal frontiers seem to have vanished, a *nostalgia for experience* has settled on the land. Movies about reporters in the Third World offer a vicarious outlet for an emotional intensity we can't find or express in daily life. After all, foreign correspondents are surrounded by Life Writ Large. In their work, other people's history becomes *our* spectacle—the fall of Ferdinand Marcos is "a good story"—and journalists experience its drama for us. They become our surrogates.

Though I can never get enough of reporter movies (hey, my life's dull, too), they're usually shallow and square. They tend to offer us heroes who are handsome, hardworking, likable, and painfully sane. At their giddiest heights—in, say, *The Year of Living Dangerously* (1982)—they capture the thrill of crashing a roadblock or racing through a burning city. Neat stuff, but they don't push far enough. They don't show the sickness skulking through the glamour. *Salvador* does. Although it, too, turns history into melodrama, it offers an unprecedented look at those journalists who flock to Beirut, San Salvador, Darfur, or wherever people are slaughtering one another this year. Stone and Boyle know these people's motives aren't pure, intelligent, or even sane.

No, there's a lurking madness in these folks, a psychic disarray that lets them feel most comfortable amid social chaos. The inner and outer world mirror each other: Boyle's psychological wreckage at the beginning of *Salvador* finds a pacifying reflection in the bloody tumult of Central America. He's nothing without the action, the adrenalin jolt that he never seems to find in the ordinary world, the nonstop drama that means he never has to face his own inner anarchy. A person can grow addicted to this kind of stimulation, and *Salvador* captures its buzz far better than any other movie.

Predictably, the movie has taken all sorts of abuse, not least from those who are unhappy with Stone's cavalier treatment of the facts. Those on the left have squawked that he isn't clear enough about the United States' villainy in El Salvador and the nobility of the rebels. Those on the right (including the *New York Times*) have accused Stone of twisting reality to suit his anti-interventionism. Both sides have agreed in thumping its lack of political lucidity.

All of these objections are ways of saying that *Salvador* is romantic and melodramatic, not analytical and factual. And frankly, such complaints don't matter. The movie succeeds *as a movie* just because of the things people are objecting to. *Salvador* may lack a classic narrative, but it has an intensity and immediacy that few films even dare dream of. Its detractors have beefed about the very things that keep it from being just another soul-withering documentary about Central America. It has a tonic effect on viewers precisely because it feels honest—it doesn't suffer from the usual leftist piety. (Say what you will about Stone, he's unsullied by liberalism.) The movie shows that even a fuckin' weasel can learn what our diplomats and TV newsmen never do: that the Salvadoran government is filled with crooks and killers, that U.S. officials either suppress this fact or don't give a damn, that American involvement ensures that innocent *campesinos* will die by the thousands, that the rebels *are* nobler than the government—but that they, too, commit cold-blooded murder far too easily.

Granted, *Salvador* occasionally goes a bit bonkers in showing Boyle's transformation from rampaging sleazeball to Man with a Conscience. This is most egregious in the heavy-handed scene where Boyle lectures to U.S. officials about patriotism and human rights. (This speech is probably the political version of l'esprit d'escalier—things that the real-life Boyle always wanted to say and never did.) Yet even here Stone and Woods almost pull the scene off with their absolute conviction, with the total absence of self-consciousness that is the essence of great pulp. It is this hell-bent honesty, not the progressive politics, that I respond to in *Salvador*. I love its down-and-dirty romanticism, its shameless willingness to tell a redemption story, its sweating and drinking and contempt for good manners, its bristling contradictions that make its hero an asshole and every scene surprising. I even like the bollixed scenes when Woods and Belushi aim for lunatic heights and land on their keisters.

Seen in retrospect, *Salvador* injected American filmmaking with a badly needed emotional explosiveness. And it established Stone as the heir to Samuel Fuller—an American barbarian with more up his sleeve than muscle and lewd tattoos. Like Fuller, he's attracted to obsessive, contradictory, unlikable characters; like Fuller, he's fascinated by destructive impulses; like Fuller, he's hostile to authority in all forms; like Fuller, he tells stories that are unbelievably lurid; like Fuller, he deftly skewers admired social types; like Fuller, his dialogue sometimes floors you with its awfulness; like Fuller, his mother/whore vision of women would shame Mike Hammer. Because of all this, like Fuller, Stone can achieve a power that more civilized directors cannot.

Never is this truer than in *Salvador,* which remains his greatest work. Mangy and flawed though it sometimes is, it still burns hotter, much hotter, than other movies we've been enduring over the last few years. Watching it again, I was reminded of Fuller's great line in Jean-Luc Godard's *Pierrot le fou* (1965): "The film is like a battlefield: love, hate, action, death . . . in one word, EMOTION."

The President's Analyst

Theodore J. Flicker, 1967

by James Verniere

A SATIRIC-PSYCHEDELIC VARIATION ON A THEME OF ALFRED Hitchcock's *North by Northwest* (1959), Theodore J. Flicker's *The President's Analyst* springs from the fertile Kennedy-assassination-conspiracy-theory mind-set, which also gave birth to such subsequent films as *The Parallax View* (1974) and *JFK* (1991). Although Flicker's flickery work will always stand in the shadow of the master's 1959 original, and the more substantial paranoid fables to follow, it's still more fun, stylish, accomplished, and marvelously cast than any mere copycat movie.

Meet Dr. Sidney Schaefer (James Coburn in a Cary Grant-ish riff on his 007-knockoff persona, Derek Flint), a debonair psychiatrist with a stunning Manhattan bachelor pad, an even more stunning girlfriend (the fetching Joan Delaney), and, after moving to Washington, only one patient: the president of the United States. (The film was made at the height of the Vietnam War, and the faceless president is clearly the tragic Lyndon Baines Johnson.)

When shadowy figures with secret government ties determine Schaefer a national security risk, he finds himself a target of assassins from both the CEA and the FBR. Arte Johnson of *Rowan & Martin's Laugh-In* fame plays one FBR agent, and all of them appear to be less than five feet tall. (The FBI and CIA were identified by name during filming, but the names were altered in postproduction overdubbing.)

As a ruse, Schaefer, whose paranoia grows by comic leaps and bounds, hitches a ride from DC to Seaside Heights, New Jersey, with an all-American family of gun-toting "liberals" headed by amiable, Ward Cleaver-ish Wynn Quantrill (William Daniels). The ensuing hijinks involve government-sanctioned murder, a drug-induced orgy, and a separate peace between an African American CEA hit man (Godfrey Cambridge) and an amiable Soviet secret agent (a delightful Severn Darden). The score is by the hipster's Bernard Herrmann, Lalo Schifrin (*Mission: Impossible* [1996]). One sequence combines animation with live action, and an American corporation is the film's true villain.

Though predated by such efforts as John Frankenheimer's *The Manchurian Candidate,* the classic 1962 anti-McCarthy fable (also produced by Howard W. Koch), *The President's Analyst* is surprisingly barbed. One cannot say this sort of film would not be made today, only that it would be bowdlerized in the manner of an Austin Powers movie or have Will Ferrell in the lead and more gay jokes. The David Mamet–scripted *Wag the Dog* (1997) explores many of the same issues of government-sponsored lies and distortions and the government sanctioned, if not encouraged, corporate subversion of the U.S. Constitution. And even super-spy Derek Flint poked fun at Washington. The most memorable line in the *Our Man Flint* (1966) sequel, *In Like Flint,* which was released in March 1967 (*The President's Analyst* was a 1967 holiday release), is spoken when Flint realizes that a double has taken the place of the kidnapped U.S. president. "An actor? As president?" Flint muses incredulously, more than a decade before the election of Ronald Reagan.

Taking a cue from Hitchcock and *North by Northwest* scribe Ernest Lehman, writer-director Flicker uses such landmarks as the Whitney Museum, where Schaefer admires abstract sculpture; the Lincoln Memorial; the Washington Monument; and the Statue of Liberty as visual cues, giving his cartoonish political satire psychic and symbolic weight. (Reportedly, during the filming of a foot chase in Lower Manhattan, Coburn was mistakenly struck in the head by a real uniformed NYPD police officer with his nightstick.)

Produced by Koch (*Robin and the Seven Hoods* [1964], etc.) and Stanley Rubin (*Francis in the Navy* [1955], *Oh Dad, Poor Dad, Mama's Hung You in the Closet and I'm Feeling So Sad* [1967], etc.) and featuring excellent camera work by legendary William A. Fraker (*Rosemary's Baby* [1968], *Bullitt* [1968], etc.), *The President's Analyst* is an Austin Powers movie with teeth, and owes a huge debt to *Mad* magazine's trademark spoofs of hit movies. While considerably less scabrous and alienating than Luis Buñuel's indictments of modern Europe or Jean-Luc Godard's *Weekend* (1967), *The President's Analyst* has moments of genuinely offbeat power. Posing as one of Dr. Schaefer's patients in an early scene, Cambridge beautifully relates a haunting, even heartbreaking childhood anecdote involving racism, an anecdote that later turns out to be perhaps a fabrication. Also in the cast are Pat Harrington Jr., as a game-show-hostlike phone company spokesman, and future

Waltons patriarch Will Geer, as Sidney's Mark Twain-like mentor. And watch for Dyanne Thorne, of *Ilsa, She Wolf of the SS* (1975) fame, as a cocktail waitress.

If you'd like to see how uninspired this sort of thing can be when not well handled, take a look at Irvin Kershner's 1974 romp *S*P*Y*S,* an attempt to cash in on Elliott Gould and Donald Sutherland's success in Robert Altman's surprise 1970 hit *MASH.* Flicker's previous credits included TV's *I Dream of Jeannie* [1965–1970], *The Andy Griffith Show* [1960–1968], and, natch, *The Man from U.N.C.L.E.* [1964–1968], and he also cowrote the Elvis Presley outing *Spinout* (1966). He returned to television after *The President's Analyst,* where he cocreated the long-running hit series *Barney Miller* [1975–1982], a show that brought an unprecedented number of adult male minority faces to network TV.

Lanky six-foot-two leading man Coburn, a Nebraska native, was already a counterculture hero by the time he made *The President's Analyst* due to the manic individualism he'd brought to roles in John Sturges's *The Magnificent Seven* (1960) and *The Great Escape* (1963), Don Siegel's *Hell Is for Heroes* (1962), and the aforementioned Flint films. (*The President's Analyst* was produced by Coburn's company, Panpiper Productions.) In the Marlon Brando–James Dean–Lee Marvin–Jack Nicholson mold, Coburn was one of the most notable and talented embodiments of the American actor-as-rebel. Like several of them, he possessed an unforgettable voice and killer smile.

A martial-arts enthusiast, Coburn served as a pallbearer at Bruce Lee's funeral along with Steve McQueen. Coburn also notably appeared in Sergio Leone's *Giù la testa* (*Duck, You Sucker,* 1971); Sam Peckinpah's *Major Dundee* (1965), *Pat Garrett & Billy the Kid* (1973), and *Cross of Iron* (1977); and Walter Hill's *Hard Times* (1975). Coburn capped his career by winning the Academy Award for best supporting actor opposite Nick Nolte in *Affliction* (1997). He died in November 2002. *The President's Analyst,* a paranoid pop fable for the Warren Commission Report–*Dr. Strangelove* generation, is a memorable part of his enduring screen legacy.

Man on a String

André de Toth, 1960

by David Sterritt

ANTI-COMMUNIST MOVIES ARE OUT OF STYLE—THERE'S BEEN less Communism to be anti since the Soviet Union went out of business—but after World War II there were lots of them. Some, like the 1954 animation *Animal Farm,* presented their messages as allegories or fables. Others, like the 1952 melodrama *My Son John* and the mid–1950s television show *I Led Three Lives,* tackled the Communist menace head-on, making up in moral indignation what they lacked in common sense.

Man on a String, a spy thriller starring Ernest Borgnine, is too eccentric to fit either of those categories. Its dark atmosphere disqualifies it as diverting entertainment, while its ambivalence about Soviet life—just how menacing *is* the Communist menace?—hurts its credentials as Commie-hating propaganda. Yet the movie's ambiguity is one of the things that make it interesting.

Borgnine plays Boris Mitrov, a character based directly on Boris Morros, a real-life double agent who published a memoir called *My Ten Years as a Counterspy* a year before the movie premiered. Morros was born in Russia but immigrated to the United States when he was in his early thirties. A dozen years later the Soviets recruited him to spy for them, and a dozen years after that—following a tip-off to J. Edgar Hoover about him—the FBI shipped him to the USSR as an American counterspy. All this was the last thing you would have expected from a Paramount music director and independent film producer with features like *The Flying Deuces* (1939), starring Stan Laurel and Oliver Hardy, among his credits. With all that scooting around the world to dig up secrets for the Soviets, the Americans, or both, it's no wonder his *life* has been compared to a Laurel and Hardy comedy, if a complicated and sometimes scary one.

Although it's clearly a dramatized account of Morros's exploits, *Man on a String* has a quasi-documentary look that was probably inspired by producer Louis de Rochement, who specialized in nonfiction films as well as war pictures and, in the middle 1950s, innovative wide-screen extravaganzas. Portions were filmed in four international cities—Los Angeles, New York, Berlin, and Moscow—by four different cinematographers. Why did the Communist Soviets open their doors for an anti-Communist movie? It seems the authorities trusted de Rochement from earlier documentary projects, but after *Man on a String* his welcome immediately (and unsurprisingly) wore out.

Borgnine's performance also contributes to the picture's realism, despite his recognizability as a movie and TV star. Defending his casting of Borgnine, director André de Toth described Morros as "a flat and dull nobody" who cleverly used his nondescript manner as a survival tool in the espionage game. Borgnine was the ideal actor to play him, de Toth said, not because he resembled Morros physically ("I didn't care if [he] looked like Boris Morros or Alfred Hitchcock") but because he "blended in with [the] drapes as if they weren't dry-cleaned," capturing the "quality of a stray dog" that Morros had in real life. Although not everyone agreed with the director, *New York Times* reviewer Howard Thompson called Borgnine's acting "completely persuasive." Borgnine had made his career breakthrough as the sadistic sergeant in the 1953 army drama *From Here to Eternity,* but he'd earned an Oscar for the title role in *Marty* (1955), playing another guy who blended in with the drapes. His portrayal of Mitrov can be seen as a variation on the award-winning *Marty* theme.

The nonfiction feel of *Man on a String* also benefits from the clipped narration by Clete Roberts, a war correspondent who later became a groundbreaking reporter on Los Angeles television. And a large share of the credit goes to de Toth, for casting Borgnine and then filming his exploits in a no-nonsense style that rarely allows visual flourishes or narrative irrelevancies to slow the action's momentum. The story of Morros/Mitrov was completely in tune with the creative personality of a director who, in Andrew Sarris's words, understood "the instability and outright treachery of human relationships" and found antisocial behaviors "more like the natural order of things than like mere contrivances of melodrama." The central theme of de Toth's cinema is betrayal, and as critic Fred Camper observes, his interest is "not single betrayals by individuals but networks of betrayal that implicate most of his characters." This certainly applies to *Man on a*

String, which surrounds Mitrov with self-seeking manipulators, sunshine patriots, and a tangled web of bad faith and broken promises, not to mention offers he can't refuse. One is the Soviets' promise that his father and brothers can leave Russia if he'll just risk his life for Communism; another is the counteroffer he accepts from the Americans, but only after learning that—contrary to everything the Soviets have told him—his brothers are already dead and gone.

Some critics have faulted *Man on a String* on two amusingly contradictory grounds—that its anti-Communist theme is now irrelevant, and that it's not really anti-Communist, because it doesn't make the Soviets look miserable. De Toth answered both arguments well. Told by critic Anthony Slide that the movie's politics are dated, the director noted that it still contains a true picture of its era, including "its problems, its *modus vivendi* and [its] slogans," adding that what's bothering the critic may be "today's incomprehension of a ridiculous period." As for those contented-looking Soviet citizens, de Toth stated that "Russians, generally happy people, were happy with Communism. The West wasn't. According to [this] criticism, the Russians should've been asked to be unhappy because some jackass wanted to spread anti-Communist propaganda." Enough said.

Today's responses to *Man on a String* depend largely on how curious moviegoers are about a recent historical period whose paranoid notions have much to teach us, and how convinced they are by Borgnine's portrayal of Morros, the "bizarre character" whose psychology intrigued de Toth more than any other aspect of the project. It's also fascinating to speculate on what filming important parts of this story in cold-war Moscow must have been like. According to de Toth, playing dumb was a key part of the secret. "The lesson is . . . if you're smart, you keep your big mouth shut."

Heroes for Sale

William A. Wellman, 1933

by Jay Carr

IN AMERICAN POP CULTURE, ERUPTIONS OF SOCIAL UNREST, SO inexplicably AWOL today, sizzled off movie screens in the 1930s. *Heroes for Sale,* filmed with raw, gritty immediacy by the no-nonsense William A. Wellman, covers all the Depression-era bases. Perhaps even a few too many. It's crammed with plot, and the joinery lurches from casual to nonexistent. But while it's ungainly, it's also unfailingly urgent and never boring, even when the characters stop talking in anything resembling human speech and start sounding like placards proclaiming a tacked-on message—specifically, Franklin Delano Roosevelt's inaugural address punch line, that we have nothing to fear but fear itself.

Actually, the characters have plenty to fear. They just don't fear it, especially Richard Barthelmess's World War I veteran. After taking a shellacking from life, he's still upright at the end when he says, "It takes more than one sock on the jaw to lick a hundred and twenty million people." Barthelmess, who came to fame as Lillian Gish's leading man for D. W. Griffith, was one of the handful of silent-movie stars who enjoyed a career in the sound era. His Frank Merriwell grit gets quite a workout, starting in a scene of trench warfare, where he's painfully wounded and left for dead, another soldier gets credited for his act of heroism, and he's taken prisoner by the Germans. His wounds are treated, but as a result, he returns a morphine addict.

In contrast to the heated war propaganda of the World War I era, the film, while not going so far as to portray Germans sympathetically, does at least portray the German doctor as a humane and honorable man. Nor does it stigmatize Barthelmess's addict, Tom Holmes. When his addiction becomes apparent, he's sentenced to a state facility, goes cold turkey, and subsequently proves he's a man of character, several times over. The film reserves its contempt for the doughboy, a banker's son, who spinelessly appropriated Barthelmess's heroic act and returned home medal-bedecked. For keeping silent about what really happened, the real hero is rewarded with a job in the bank of the false hero's father. When the old man finds out about Tom's addiction, he sanctimoniously dismisses him. He epitomizes the film's perception of capitalist bosses failing America.

The tough matter-of-factness with which the war sequences are filmed stems in part from Wellman's own experience, although he fought from the cockpit of a primitive plane (only four controls, no parachute) as a member of the Lafayette Flying Squad. Later, of course, came the first best-picture Oscar winner, *Wings* (1927), based on Wellman's war experiences. It invented the airplane-movie genre and still has flying sequences that have never been surpassed. Wellman's image as a Hollywood wild man was fed by his practice of landing his plane on the polo field of his friend Douglas Fairbanks, who got Wellman his first Hollywood jobs. Only a man who had experienced combat could open *Heroes for Sale* with a throwaway scene, as Wellman does, in which an officer sends ten men on a suicide mission because "that's all I can afford to lose."

Heroes for Sale is an odd mix of tough-mindedness and populist verve. The rehabbed Tom goes to Chicago, rents a room above a free soup kitchen run by kind-hearted Aline McMahon, meets (and marries) fellow roomer Loretta Young, gets a job at the commercial laundry where she works, and loses no time proving himself a go-getter. He also deflects the comes-the-revolution ravings of another roomer, a self-declared Communist (Robert Barrat). The film easily, if not quite naturally, reflects its Depression-era realities. Life is stark. And there's lots of class anger to go around. But Wellman and screenwriters Robert Lord and Wilson Mizner aren't about to buy into any isms. The Communist is depicted as a buffoon. Later, when he gets rich from an invention that automates operations at the laundry, and Tom gets rich with him, the Communist turns fervent capitalist, declaring that money is all, now that he has a lot of it. Thus the film avoids confronting seriously any arguments for change by ridiculing the character who had advocated it, painting him as shallow and easily separated from his professed ideals.

But as Tom begins to climb the ladder, he's slammed by a new set of circumstances. The kindly capitalist owner of the laundry dies. The machines they all thought would ease the workers' lot are used by the new owners to downsize the labor force. When the now unemployed workers march (in suits, collars, ties, and hats!) on the laundry to smash the machines, Luddite-fashion, they're met by cops, thinly disguised minions of the owners of the means of production, who identify the interests of the bosses with the public good. Violence erupts. Tom's wife is killed, struck down by a cop's nightstick (leaving their son motherless), and Tom is jailed as a trouble-fomenting Red. Although his young son is cared for by the soup-kitchen saint, with Tom pumping his share of the laundry-machine royalties into the soup kitchen's upkeep, his troubles don't end.

No sooner is he released from prison than he's run out of town by the local Red Squad. He rides the rails and lives in hobo jungles, even though he's roughed up at first by the other hoboes in this film, which simultaneously romanticizes and takes a dim view of them. Squaring his jaw one last time, presumably motivated by something between penance and an urge to canonization, Barthelmess's classy everyman embraces life on the road. Refusing to succumb to cynicism, and anything but a broken man (one cynically remembers that Barthelmess was the name above the film's title, and the one used to sell tickets), he proclaims his (well, FDR's) upbeat message, anticipating Tom Joad in *The Grapes of Wrath* (1940, based on the 1939 novel).

If that ringingly pro-proletarian work, and soul mates like the stage musical *The Cradle Will Rock,* seem more boldly contoured and proclamatory, films such as *Heroes for Sale,* half-digested as they are, ring more true, more powerful, strike a deeper chord precisely because they are less self-consciously message films and more like daily newspapers being slammed out under deadline pressure. They simmer with tabloid vigor, fielding the realities as they unfolded in America's collective experience, with no time to digest them or reflect upon them. It's very much reactive cinema, not reflective cinema. As such, it avoids the pitfalls of message-mongering, letting texture and details—not speeches—carry the message.

It's material well suited to the muscular style of Wellman, who used real hoboes in the hobo scenes and real laundry workers in the laundry scenes, and told an interviewer in *Film Comment* that he never shot a scene more than twice. Later in 1933 he followed *Heroes for Sale* with *Wild Boys of the Road,* another film steeped in the realities of the Depression, again ending with a voice of hope (Barrat, the buffoon caricature of Communism in *Heroes for Sale,* this time as a judge who gives four wayward boys another chance). This may have been rooted in Wellman's admiring view of the lifelong work of his beloved mother, a probation officer in Massachusetts. (She gave him his enduring nickname, Wild Bill, saying that she could bring any boy into line but her own son!) Both of these Depression-era films are about hanging in there until a new day dawns on a new deal. Or, rather, New Deal. Pungent, richly textured, and strongly felt, *Heroes for Sale,* about a hero who is not for sale, deserves to be better known.

Part NINE: Whole Lotta Shakin'

Rock, Pop, and Beyond

WITH DUE RESPECT TO LENNON AND MCCARTNEY, JAGGER and Richards, Townsend, Prince, Patti Smith, and Thom Yorke, rock 'n' roll is a quintessentially B art form. Its potency, even the bulk of its charm, has always been about *no respect* for artistic authority, musical elegance, refinement of taste, or virtuosity. Born of an anti-aesthetic, it gets into trouble only when its aspirations exceed themselves, like a '57 Chevy overdriving its headlights. Bad things can happen. Like rock operas. Or King Crimson.

If Beethoven is a '61 Mouton Rothschild, rock 'n' roll is a cold beer, which makes the movie translation of rock energy something like Pabst Blue Ribbon. But not always; occasionally the music and the screen have collided in a shower of bright light and gold dust. *Woodstock* is epic; *A Hard Day's Night* is neo–Marx Brothers without Zeppo singing; *Sid and Nancy* is the nourishing meat byproduct of unbridled hedonism, a rock 'n' roll quality if ever there was one. *School of Rock,* while hilarious, thinks rock can be taught first, felt later—it's a boomer movie, and boomer, although beginning with B, has never fully understood the smashing of Les Paul Customs on the stage of Madison Square Garden circa 1974 with Keith Moon on drums.

Which is to say that translating rock to the screen is mostly about attitude, and the killer Bs we address here boast a surfeit of same. Long before he became the albino assassin of *Lethal Weapon* (1987) and lent his talent to *The Gingerdead Man* (2005), Gary Busey gave a memorable performance as the doomed pop pioneer Buddy Holly in a film that captures the smiling-surly innocence of early rock. Elvis Presley, alive and well to this very day (although he hasn't shown up for a National Society of Film Critics meeting since 2003—remind him when you see him, okay?), gives what's probably the finest performance of his woeful, Colonel

Tom Parker–orchestrated film career in *King Creole,* a movie that screams unful-
filled potential. And trusty Jayne Mansfield, the girl who can't help it? She's the
front-loaded idolette of infant rock 'n' roll in one of Frank Tashlin's most outlandish social satires.

B sides, R & B, B-tles, "B My Baby"—see the connections? The B pop movie is
not the perfect visual manifestation of rock, but it's better than the music video,
which because of its time constraints is a very nervous tiger in a very small tank.
Rock 'n' roll needs to stretch, like a cat, or an unemployed vinyl salesman on a
rainy Sunday afternoon watching *American Hot Wax* on his stolen cable hookup.
Like the rock movie, he needs to not fall off the couch into carpeted complacency
and inertia. He needs to be perfectly in tune. Like the movies we talk about here.

The Buddy Holly Story

Steve Rash, 1978

by David Ansen

THE BUDDY HOLLY STORY WAS RELEASED AT A TIME WHEN many musical con jobs were masquerading as movies (*Thank God It's Friday,* anyone?), so audiences had every right to be suspicious of it. But they could easily lower their guard: this unpretentious, affectionate biography of the horn-rimmed Southern boy who changed the course of rock 'n' roll is a real movie, with a firm grasp on its characters, an honest-to-God plot, and an old-fashioned heart. The filmmakers approach Holly (Gary Busey) with a respect that mercifully falls short of idolatry—you don't feel hyped, but you do feel a genuine pang of regret for the man himself, who died at twenty-two in a 1959 plane crash that also took the lives of Ritchie Valens and The Big Bopper.

Along with Elvis Presley, it was Holly who broke down the color lines in popular music. A gangly Texas kid, he turned his back on hillbilly music for a harddriving black beat, outraging his fundamentalist hometown in the process. In the film's funniest, most rousing sequence, Holly and his trio, the Crickets, arrive in New York to sign a contract with Coral Records and are booked into Harlem's Apollo Theater by a manager who has assumed they're black. The shock of the crowd at their white faces gives way to foot-stomping joy as the band rocks out.

The music in this movie is hot, thanks to the producers' decision to record all the numbers live, with Busey, Don Stroud, and Charles Martin Smith doing their own singing and playing on such Holly hits as "Peggy Sue," "That'll Be the Day," "Oh Boy," and "Maybe Baby." The climactic version of "Not Fade Away," building to an exhilarating crescendo of heavy metal, beautifully stands up to the Holly original. No mean feat.

Above all, it's Busey's stubborn honesty as Holly that elevates the film well above sentimental musical biographies such as *The Glenn Miller Story.* As Busey plays him, you understand why Holly got as far as he did—he has the driven, slightly fanatical perfectionism of a real artist. With his riveted stare, canine grin, and abrupt manner, Busey doesn't waste time ingratiating himself with the audience. But he wins us over anyway with his ardent, wolfish charm. It's a brilliant job of acting, and like the best scenes in this lower-case movie, it suggests both the exhilaration and the cost of Holly's musical success.

Stroud is particularly effective as the Crickets' drummer, whose ego is bruised by Holly's stardom. The film bogs down a bit in its depiction of Holly's marriage to Maria Elena (Maria Richwine), his Puerto Rican wife. Her attractive performance suggests complexities of character that the script fails to explore. But as a portrait of the young, obsessive artist, Busey and director Steve Rash have given us a full-bodied chunk of rock 'n' roll history. They suggest that Holly rocketed to the top because of his precocious talent—and also because he pushed himself harder than anyone around him.

Superficially, the burly, blond, straight-haired Busey seems an unlikely choice to play skinny, curly-haired Holly. Dig a little further, though, and the casting seems made in heaven. Born in Goose Creek, Texas, in 1944, Busey grew up on the music of Elvis, Roy Orbison, and Holly, and when he was approached to play the part, he says, he already "knew the songs frontwards and backwards." Actually, Busey had been cast a few years earlier as Holly's drummer in the aborted movie biography *Not Fade Away.* A drummer since his high school days in Tulsa, Oklahoma, Busey has kept his musical and acting careers running side by side, sitting in with friends Leon Russell, Willie Nelson, and Kris Kristofferson under his nom de drum, Teddy Jack Eddy, while playing supporting roles in movies and television features such as *Blood Sport, The Law, The Execution of Private Slovik,* and *A Star Is Born.*

"My wife, Judy, thinks I'm multiphrenic," he says. "I got so involved in making *Straight Time* [in which he gave a faultless performance as a hapless junkie] that she didn't know who she was living with." Total immersion is the Busey style. To prepare for *Big Wednesday,* a summer release about surfing, the heavy-set Busey worked out with trainer Vince Gironda to get in shape: "I lost 35 pounds and my waist went from 37 to 31." In Hawaii he rode the waves for the first time, surfing eight hours a day for three weeks. "That kind of stuff changes life—getting out in 25-foot surf. I've never been frightened like that in my life." At the same time, he was brushing up on acoustic guitar, learning to play Holly's songs. "For four months I was a complete surfing Nazi zealot, then all of a sudden I was immersed in Buddy."

Busey may be one of the most natural actors of his time, but his gift for losing himself in a role has kept him from becoming a household word. Moreover, Hollywood stardom does not seem to be his burning desire. "I've got outlaw blood in me," he says in his Okie drawl, pointing out that his uncle was the famous train robber "Black Jack" Ketchum. His ambition has been to make music that's true to his world and "makes you dance and makes you feel sexy." He hopes anthropologists can look at movies like *The Buddy Holly Story* years from now "and see a slice of true American culture."

King Creole

Michael Curtiz, 1958

by Gerald Peary

ADAPTED FROM HAROLD ROBBINS'S NOVEL **A STONE FOR DANNY**
Fisher, King Creole is probably Elvis Presley's best picture of all time: a rock-solid
B crime drama sugared with Elvis musical numbers. It's got a sassy script by
Herbert Baker and Michael Vincent Gazzo (and, uncredited, playwright Clifford
Odets), effective New Orleans locales, and Presley smashingly cast as the tor-
mented juvenile, Danny, a kid growing up fast (too fast?) in the French Quarter.

Elvis actually made decent movies?

In his later Hollywood years, he was spoiled, tanned, porky, oily, his beach
pictures—girls! girls! girls!—lazy gigolo romps in the sand. It's a mistake to lump
these with early Elvis flicks. Presley's directors in the '50s praised the young per-
former, the evanescent voice of "Hound Dog" and "Don't Be Cruel," as unfailingly
polite and, on the set, very hard working. Among his fans was *King Creole*'s veteran helmer, Michael Curtiz, whose long career at Warner Brothers included such
classics as *Angels with Dirty Faces* (1938), *Yankee Doodle Dandy* (1942), and
Mildred Pierce (1945). Curtiz, seventy, was at home at Paramount Pictures
enlivening *King Creole*'s Bourbon Street nightclub milieu: here was the man who'd
animated Rick's Place when he directed *Casablanca* (1942).

Elvis's three pre–*King Creole* movies showed the rocker turned thespian exper-
imenting, trying on and discarding disparate filmic personas. He was a callow,
mercurial cub in the post–Civil War *Love Me Tender* (1956), wrongly married to
his older brother's ex-girlfriend, too young and egocentric to understand the complexities of the adults around him. He was a sweet-tempered, ingenuous country
lad in *Loving You* (1957), bashful about the successes of a fledgling singing career

and happily in love with a simple country girl. In *Jailhouse Rock* (1957) he was an ex-convict who, hardened in prison, became a cynical singer for the monetary awards and the brassy broads.

By the time of *King Creole*, Presley had made enough movies to get comfortable on screen, yet he wasn't past an appealing rawness: that non-Hollywood Southern-boy regionalism, the blue-collar Tupelo, Mississippi, slur and drawl. With Curtiz's guidance, he stretched beyond the functional two-dimensional characterizations of his first films. If anything, Elvis's Danny Fisher might have too many facets, a wildly contradictory personality.

He's divided between loathing his weak-willed father (Dean Jagger) and wanting his dad's respect. He's caught between a desire to succeed by following the rules and hard-to-control impulses toward criminal behavior and self-destructive sexual passion. Schizoid in romance, Danny scrambles between the virginal girl (Dolores Hart), who is surprisingly agreeable to degrading herself to please him, and the experienced coquette (Carolyn Jones), who discovers a hidden heart when they rub bodies.

Danny's nemesis, a degenerate street punk, is played by Vic Morrow, who brought to bear his iconic JD bad attitude from *Blackboard Jungle* (1955). But the major filmic inspiration for *King Creole* was obviously *Rebel Without a Cause* (1955), starting with Elvis's moody, wounded, James Dean–influenced performance. Surely the movie Danny is based, uncredited, on *Rebel's* Jim Stark, Dean's pained high-schooler. Danny's love/hate feelings for his pushed-about father, who writes out notes for what he wants to say to Danny, parallels Jim's ambivalent relationship to his henpecked dad, who wears an apron doing housework and makes lists of good and bad points to advise his son. Both films subscribe to a seminal 1950s belief about "manhood": ninny patriarchs are disastrous role models for their male progeny, causing good boys to stumble blindly into trouble.

Both *King Creole* and *Rebel Without a Cause* are hopeful in the first act (though there's a nervous feeling in the air), with the protagonists off for high school. In both works, the day goes awry with adolescent violence. The good intentions of Jim and Danny are trampled on and defeated, almost with a Fritz Langian inevitability. "Everything's been fixed," Danny says, fatalistically, "like a crooked fight."

About *King Creole's* song-and-dance numbers: Curtiz conceived the film to operate as a credible drama, so Elvis can't break into tunes whenever, in the way of many fanciful musicals. It's only the first number, in which Danny leans out of his French Quarter balcony and sings "Crawfish!" back and forth with an African American woman in the street below, that realism is, quite delightfully, broken.

After that, Elvis's singing must be justified by character motivation: i.e., someone orders Danny to do a song, Danny performs onstage in a nightclub.

In truth, the Jerry Lieber–Mike Stoller score for *King Creole,* the buoyant title cut the exception, isn't their strongest material. "Crawfish," "You're the Cutest," "Danny Is My Name," and others are not even close in quality to their rowdy classic title song for *Jailhouse Rock* or, also from that earlier movie, "I Want to Be Free" and "Young and Beautiful." And if there's an absurdity in *King Creole,* it's the Jordanaires, Presley's guitar-based backup country band, standing on stage with unplayed saxes and clarinets in their hands, feigning that they are Dixieland musicians. Elvis's best number is neither rock nor New Orleans jazz, but a traditional, bragging-cocksman blues work—in the Willie Dixon vein—"I'm evil, don't you mess with me!"

Why was *King Creole* that rare Elvis picture to fail at the box office? I'd venture that it was deeper, and a lot darker, than what the casual Elvis fan wanted. And it was far more complex in generic structure, going from a serious dramatic musical, already an odd form, into, at one key point, pure 1940s drive-by-night film noir. That's when Danny and the bad-good chick Ronnie (Jones, with a Lee Krasner haircut) go on the run from the mob. There's an astonishing prototype "noir" shot—because you simply don't expect to see Elvis Presley in the middle of it—with Ronnie too long at the car wheel and an exhausted, troubled Danny asleep in the shotgun seat. The lighting is low key, and there's a harsh spot on Ronnie's anxious face. Where have we seen it before? To start, Sylvia Sidney and Henry Fonda, bouncing along the dark highway in Fritz Lang's *You Only Live Once* (1937).

There's a sad end here for the heart-of-gold slut, Ronnie, and a kind of benign conclusion for Elvis, who had suffered major fan complaints when his character was killed in *Love Me Tender.* But Elvis goes Hollywood-happy-ending only a bit in *King Creole:* his final love song, "As Long as I Have You," can be regarded skeptically, ironically, since he's just told nice girl Nellie (ever-faithful Hart) to back off. To chill. His nightclub crooning is to nobody: "You're not my only love, but my last." It's like when loner heartbreaker Marlene Dietrich concluded *The Blue Angel* (1930) by singing that she's "Falling in Love Again."

Sure, Marlene. Sure, Elvis the Pelvis.

American Hot Wax

Floyd Mutrux, 1978

by Charles Taylor

IT'S 1959 AND IN FLOYD MUTRUX'S FILM **AMERICAN HOT WAX** the legendary disc jockey Alan Freed is staging his big rock 'n' roll show at Brooklyn's Paramount Theatre. It will be his last—only Freed doesn't know it yet. In the movie's B-melodrama terms, the forces of repression, aka the DA's office, suspicious of kids letting loose, and more specifically, of white kids and black kids letting loose together, are closing in for the kill. And Freed goes down fighting, telling them, "You can stop me. But you can never stop rock 'n' roll."

The real story isn't so pretty. Driven off the air by the payola scandal, hounded by the government for tax evasion, Freed died, an alcoholic, in 1965 at the age of forty-three—two years longer than Tim McIntire, the actor who plays him here, would live to be.

But amid the teeming life of *American Hot Wax*—an urban pop paradise where neon street life beckons outside the windows of homey living rooms; where hucksters hustle people who turn out to have real talent; where songs that will still sound great nearly fifty years later are tossed off as an afternoon's work; where LaVern Baker's hits come effortlessly and a downer like Connie Francis doesn't stand a chance; where every broadcast Alan Freed makes reaches down into teenage bedrooms like messages from the Resistance; where the boundaries that have defined American life, keeping black from white, girls from boys, and dreamers from their dreams, are about to crack wide open—Freed is a hero. In his hipster's checked sport coats and bow ties, his hair slicked back, one hand keeping rhythm to the records he plays while the other alternates between puffs on a Chesterfield and swigs from the fifth that's his on-air companion, Freed is the snap and jive of the music incarnate.

Yet Tim McIntire brings a big man's sadness to the role. His baby-soft jowls make him look remarkably like the man who has long been rumored to be his father, Orson Welles, and his dark-circled eyes hint at the melancholy that he seems to stave off only for the duration of a three-minute pop song. That's the quandary he shares with his listeners. In *American Hot Wax,* the right song at the right moment can wipe away the dross, make the world make sense. But how do you keep that feeling? Freed's sign-off—"It's not good-bye. It's just good night"—is a plea to his listeners to be strong, to keep the faith. "Could they really take all this away, boss?" asks Freed's driver, Mookie (played by a young Jay Leno).

With rock 'n' roll a permanent fixture of our culture, pop having even replaced the Muzak that used to play in supermarkets, it may seem quaint to think of it as any threat to the established order. The squares in the movie who are scandalized by Chuck Berry were comical when the picture was released in 1978. But the film realized that the fissures opened by rock 'n' roll, the country's second civil war, have never been smoothed over; it says that the freedom and release and pleasure rock 'n' roll represents can always be taken away. And by making that pleasure synonymous with the very fabric of life, Mutrux made it seem ineffably precious. At times, the movie invokes the title of a song by Fairport Convention, a band whose versions of English folk music would have been unthinkable as rock 'n' roll in 1959: "Now Be Thankful."

The joy of *American Hot Wax* is that it accomplishes all this with the verve and energy and spontaneity of B movies. Mutrux had already shown himself to be a genre whiz with his previous picture, *Aloha, Bobby and Rose,* a young-lovers-on-the-lam movie that had real emotional pull and the kind of craft you can barely find in today's A movies. Popular art is the art of appropriation, and as *American Hot Wax* cuts from one narrative thread to another, as the characters and their talk crisscross the screen, you think this is what Robert Altman might have done if he'd made drive-in movies. Both life and art are improv here. When a doo-wop group assembled for a recording session is beating the life out of "Come Go with Me" with their funereal style, their producer (played by real-life record producer Richard Perry, whose long face and lantern jaw make him look like a tough-guy version of the Muppet game-show host Guy Smiley) drags everyone he can find into the studio, from the sandwich-delivery boy to the janitor ("You look like you got big hands," he tells the guy) to clap and sing along. Then he turns to the lead singer. "Okay," he says, thinking fast, "we need something here. Give me a dom,

dom, dom, dom . . . *dom*. Five doms, and a dom-be-doobie." And presto—doo-wop nirvana.

That scene is about the transformation at the heart of *American Hot Wax*. Those three nice, clean-cut kids we see practicing close harmony in a stairwell at the Paramount turn out to be the Fleetwoods, whose aching songs may express the purest longing in all of rock 'n' roll. The ditties that Teenage Louise (Laraine Newman in her moment of screen glory as the young Carole King) composes on her family's neglected upright piano turn out to be perfect for the four young black guys who've formed a street-corner doo-wop quartet (is there any other kind?).

If Mutrux's direction suggests a B Altman, the screenplay, by John Kaye, suggests another American master: Preston Sturges. Kaye loves, as Sturges did, the glint in the eye that reveals the obsessiveness of ordinary Americans, just as he loves the mixture of wised-up cynicism and openhearted belief in the patter of everyday speech. Kaye had demonstrated this in his screenplay for the lovely and overlooked 1975 road movie *Rafferty and the Gold Dust Twins*. (He also showed an altogether darker grasp of American myth in his indelible diptych of novels, *Stars Screaming* [1997] and *The Dead Circus* [2002]. As portraits of Los Angeles, they can be mentioned in the same breath as those by Raymond Chandler and Ross Macdonald.) All the folks in this movie—the hip ones, at least—are both streetwise and moonstruck. And Kaye's comedy gets a pair of terrific mouthpieces in Leno's Mookie and Fran Drescher's Sheryl, Freed's secretary. Drescher was twenty-one when the movie was made, and her grating nasal whine hadn't yet become shtick. Here her voice could stand for the abrasiveness and charm of New York City itself (she could be Selma Diamond's daughter). She's never funnier than when the screeching brake sounds emanating from her vocal chords are affecting propriety as she fends off another of Mookie's klutzy advances. Leno, with that curling mumble-mouth in the midst of an absurdly oversized jaw, like a mini-bow lost on a box containing a vast Christmas present, looks as if the name Mookie might have been invented for him.

In *American Hot Wax* rock 'n' roll is a pixilated version of democratic pluralism, the only thing that could draw all of these disparate people together—even as it draws lines in the dirt between them and others. But if rock 'n' roll provides a home for people who feel homeless elsewhere, like the twelve-year-old president of the Buddy Holly Fan Club (Moosie Drier, who shines in the movie's most touching scene), Mutrux and Kaye never let us forget what these folks look like to the movie's arbiters of morality and law. For the DA and his thugs backstage at the Brooklyn Paramount, Chuck Berry, doing the incomparably salacious

"Reelin' and Rockin'," is a purveyor of smut. Jerry Lee Lewis, treating the piano as his trampoline, is the most depraved hillbilly. Screamin' Jay Hawkins? Jesus! A goddamn cannibal, for crissakes, as Nixon is reported to have said of Idi Amin.

And then there's the guy out front.

Unnoticed by anyone else, a homeless black man sits out in front of the Paramount, oblivious to the excited kids, and then to the marauding cops, intent on banging the cans he's upturned on the sidewalk to use as percussion for his versions of "Lucille" and whatever other tune catches his fancy. What would Freed's teen fans see if they noticed him? Some strange colored guy, providing a little preshow entertainment. What would the movie's defenders of decency see? A tramp, a bum, that nigger in the alley, a phrase Curtis Mayfield had sung in another context a few years earlier. But to Mutrux he looks like the spirit of rock 'n' roll itself, making the noise there always is to be made by anyone who wants to say, "I'm here!" A frightened parent's worst nightmare of what will happen to their kids if they listen to rock 'n' roll, he's right out in the open and yet a secret agent. He's the spirit that will sneak its way into crevices and open windows, that will survive Frankie Avalon (or, we hope, John Mayer), a termite artist, in Manny Farber's phrase. When the DA brings down the curtain, the DA thinks he's won. What that crazy guy in the street knows is that the fighting is in rounds.

The Girl Can't Help It

Frank Tashlin, 1956

by Carrie Rickey

LONDON, 1956: RICHARD HAMILTON'S COLLAGE JUST WHAT IS *It That Makes Today's Homes So Different, So Appealing?* rocks the British art world. Resembling a full-page ad from a slick magazine, Hamilton's satirical image of a male physical-culture specimen and a female pinup posing in a modern apartment among products such as a canned ham and a TV set challenges the prevailing modernist esthetic of abstraction. This representation of consumer culture and fetishized sexuality is a progenitor of pop art. Now, "pop" is generally understood as shorthand for "popular." But another, covert, source of its etymology is inscribed in the collage. Hamilton underlines the male model's sexuality by having him extend a tennis racket at pelvis level, like a phallus. The racket sheath is emblazoned with the letters "P O P," cartoony shorthand for ejaculation.

Hollywood, 1956: Frank Tashlin's movie *The Girl Can't Help It* rocks America. Essentially a live-action Looney Tune, Tashlin's spoof of the seismic impact of rock 'n' roll on the culture stars Jayne Mansfield as Jerri, a perambulating peroxide-blonde pinup. Her mobster beau, Marty (Edmond O'Brien), hires milquetoast agent Tom (Tom Ewell) to make her a star.

Both figuratively and literally a jukebox musical, the film features one-dimensional characters, shiny as new Cadillacs, who do little more than sashay or simper across the screen while the narrative is carried by a Greek chorus of rock sensations. They include Little Richard (the title number), Gene Vincent ("Be-Bop-A-Lula"), the Platters ("You'll Never Know"), and the splendiferous Abbey Lincoln ("Spread the Gospel"). Tashlin frames the movie so that we hear the singers but look at Mansfield, her epic breasts emphasized in sight gags, most

175

famously the one where Jerri enters Tom's apartment with a jug of milk under each jug. When the milkman (Phil Silvers) sees Jerri, his own milk-bottle rocket bursts in cartoon ejaculation.

To one revisiting these cultural events of 1956, Hamilton's England and Tashlin's America are eroticized lands of plenty cluttered with gleaming consumer products and overdeveloped pinups. In content, their messages are identical: sex sells. In form, both the high-art salvo and the mass-entertainment missile are self-referential works that draw attention to, and poke fun at, the tropes of the trade.

From the opening sequence of *The Girl Can't Help It,* cartoonist turned filmmaker Tashlin tweaks the conventions of movies that, like all popular entertainment, had to be bigger, louder, and more garish to command attention in the cultural supermarketplace. Breaking the fourth wall to directly address the movie audience, Ewell introduces the picture and announces, while opening wider the curtains at either side of the film's squarish frame, that it will be in panoramic CinemaScope, a self-referential bit of pop modernism. As is the film's narrative about an agent's efforts to transform a no-talent into a star, reinforcing the public perception of Mansfield, a Big Blonde famous for being famous and without apparent talent other than what an architect might call her frontal elevation.

Mobster Marty, famous in his sphere for rigging slot machines and jukeboxes, wants statuesque Jerri to become a celeb before they marry. Tom, broke and heartbroken since the departure of girlfriend/client Julie London (haunting his dreams while singing her hit "Cry Me a River"), takes the job even though buxom Jerri has no obvious talent. (Tom and Jerri, the names of the leads, refer to the cartoon tomcat and mouse—though with the live-action pair, who are just as two-dimensional as their cartoon namesakes, it's Jerri who's chasing Tom rather than vice versa.) The movie exploits the twin cultures of celebrity and hype even as it satirizes them. Tom promotes Jerri as the film promotes its teen musical sensations. Is there a pithier document of American pop music, circa 1956? I think not.

It's easy to describe the gloss and pop of *The Girl Can't Help It*—for instance, how Mansfield, with those eye-popping headlights, moves like a twin-finned Cadillac. It's easier still to invoke the snap and crackle of the jukebox hits. What's hard to express is why this cheerfully vulgar artifact is so entertaining—much more pleasurable, I submit, than perhaps any other cinematic article of pop art, with the possible exception of *Gentlemen Prefer Blondes* (1953), another contender in the race for Bigger! Better! Blonder!

Greendale

Neil Young, 2003

by Sam Adams

AS HE MOVES INTO HIS FIFTH DECADE AS A SONGWRITER, even Neil Young's characters are starting to wonder if he's run out of gas. The fabric of his songs has grown so thin that half a verse into his album *Greendale*, porch-sitting crank Grandpa Green sees right through it: "See that guy singin' this song, been doin' it for a long time. Is there anything he knows that he ain't said?"

Grandpa's fourth-wall breaking isn't just a playful acknowledgment of Young's age. It's a vital question, a challenge posed by Young to himself: What have you got, old-timer? *Greendale* provides an answer. Conceived as a "musical novel" about an American small town in turmoil—Young's answer to *Winesburg, Ohio*—the project blossomed into a mythology too expansive to be contained by any single medium. Young was so eager to welcome audiences to his fictitious coastal town that he took to playing *Greendale* in its entirety on the road, months before the album's release, with performers acting out the story line in front of makeshift sets. As the audience streamed out of the auditorium, you could hear them muttering, "When did Neil Young get so *weird?*"

In fact, Young's back catalog is full of such odd digressions, like the robotic *Trans* and *Everybody's Rockin'*, a rockabilly history of a fictitious band called the Shocking Pinks (conceptually, at least, *Greendale's* closest precursor). After his famously erratic 1980s, a period during which he was sued by his record label for, in essence, not sounding enough like himself, Young reclaimed the mantle of guitar hero in the 1990s, stretching his shaggy-dog jams to the point of self-parody. (In concert, a single song could last over half an hour.)

With *Greendale,* Young did his best to wipe the slate clean. In a musical echo of the Dogme 95 manifesto, he further streamlined the bare-bones Crazy Horse, leaving out rhythm guitarist Frank Sampedro, and scrambled his studio crew, bumping each member up a notch so that he'd be too busy learning the ropes to develop any bad habits.

The result, unfortunately, still sounded like a prototypical Neil Young album, with Young's worn-out maxims thrown into stark relief by the stripped-down production. Young's before-the-fall vision of small-town life was comically anachronistic, and the final image of a town rising up to fight corporate evil felt like a holdover from Young's hippie days. The irony of Young's performing such songs on a tour booked largely in Clear Channel venues was a killer, and the use of actors to re-create scenes from the songs was merely laughable as they flailed their arms in an attempt to be seen "talking" hundreds of rows away.

But on film, *Greendale* finds its ideal form. The stage actors were Young's puppets, but onscreen the same performers seem to think for themselves, even though they're only lip-synching Young's vocals. When a song breaks in the middle of a line of dialogue, you can actually see the actors thinking, as if they're coming up with what to say next—an astonishing feat, given that the actors are nonprofessionals, mostly Young's friends and neighbors. When Captain Green (Gary Burden) tells the fishermen on his boat that the devil walks the streets of Greendale, you can see them rolling their eyes and thinking, "Yeah, right," a reaction Young's weakness for rhetoric is bound to prompt sooner or later.

Although the movie upgrades the stage show's rickety sets, it has touches of ostentatious falsehood, like the haphazardly pasted-on headlines in Grandpa's newspaper. But its gloriously grainy Super–8, shot by Young and producer L. A. Johnson, is a far more apt analogue for the rough-hewn beauty of Young's music. Unlike the desaturated DV of Lars von Trier's dour *Dogville* (2003), *Greendale's* photography positively aches with love for the landscape it depicts, golf-ball grain and all.

Evocative as its visual fuzziness is, *Greendale's* lack of focus serves Young less well when it comes to the plot. Greendale is home to three generations of the Green family: Grandpa and Grandma (Ben and Elizabeth Keith); their son, Earl, and his wife, Edith (James Mazzeo and Young's wife, Pegi); and their two children, Jed (Eric Johnson) and Sun (Sarah White). The story starts rolling when wayward Jed murders Officer Carmichael (Paul Supplee) and the media descend on Grandpa's house like the proverbial plague of locusts. As the news copters circle overhead, Grandpa comes out on the porch, where he's met by an unfazed TV reporter who starts to pump him with questions about his son's crime. The old fellow can't take it; he keels over face-first and dies right there on the porch.

The lyrics to "Grandpa's Interview" paint him as a hero who "died fighting for freedom of silence—trying to stop the media, trying to be anonymous." But as Grandpa breathes his last, it's not the media's cameras he fixes with an accusatory glare, but the one (at least metaphorically) in Young's hands. It's a moment of startling, unexpected confrontation, the most powerful *Greendale* has to offer, suggesting that authors, like Young's media bugaboo, deprive people of the right to write their own stories.

After Grandpa's death, *Greendale* settles into a straightforward eco-fable. Granddaughter Sun, who's already developed an obsession with the Alaskan wilderness, leaves town and chains herself to a statue in the lobby of Powerco, whose Haliburton-ish government connections are hinted at by the CNN-style crawl that accompanies the TV reports of her deed. Flowing from "Sun Green" into "Be the Rain," the movie's images become steadily more apocalyptic, with footage of falling trees and land-ravaging bulldozers. Here both movie and songs become incoherent, not least because *Greendale*'s budget obviously didn't include funds for location shooting in Alaska. But Sun apparently assembles some sort of revolution-cum-theater production, with the fist-pumping cry to "save the planet for another day."

It's goofy, if inarguable, stuff, the kind of hollow anthem that's been paying Young's bills for years. More complex is this exhortation in the fisherman's lecture to his skeptical crew: "'One thing I can tell you, you got to be free.' John Lennon said that, and 'I believe in love.' I believe in action when push comes to shove." There's no question of distance here: it's Young speaking through his character, transmuting Lennon's abstract sentiment into a call to arms.

If *Greendale*'s climax reveals Young's failure to conceive "action" outside the terms of 1960s counterculture, it's also the product of a bold rethinking of the Manichean scenario of "Let's Roll." Osama bin Laden makes it into *Greendale*'s rogues' gallery, but so do Tom Ridge and John Ashcroft. The enveloping 3-D mix of the album's sound puts Young's vocals front and center when he's singing dialogue, but it sometimes kicks his narratorial comments into the rear speakers. Coming from behind and above, Young's interjections might suggest the voice of God, but they also inspire an equal, more worldly desire to keep looking over your shoulder. No doubt Grandpa Green would approve.

Part TEN: Provocation and Perversity

Cult Classics

SOME MOVIES ARE BORN CULTISH; SOME ACHIEVE CULTDOM; and some have culthood thrust upon them. But how a movie becomes a cult film is a less pressing question these days than whether one can actually exist in an entertainment universe that has made cult appeal into a commodity. By definition, a cult film has to appeal in a very major way to a very narrow band of acolytes, movie freaks who will find in it some quality that is deeply personal, winningly flawed, perhaps charmingly wrong, but something, somehow, somewhere, that appeals to their particular point of view, however warped and woofed it may perhaps be. While we consumers may still be cogs in the Establishment's machine, the machine has learned to stroke our individualities via iPods, blogs, Web polls, interactive television, and a never-ending rat race toward niche-marketed achievement. What's culty now? Chopin? Montaigne? Ingmar Bergman? It certainly wouldn't be one of George Kuchar's demented films, even if the underground giant himself still warrants cult enshrinement.

So let's face it, from time to time the fringe becomes the mainstream—commerce starts catering to the odd, the weird, and the perverse—and then what have we got? When the provocations of a John Waters become the norm, the idea of *being* John Waters becomes obsolete. When the culture loses its moral recoil, the very idea of a cult movie becomes quaint. When the cultural midsection implodes like an ungirdled Divine, may he rest in peace, ugly things can happen.

That's not what this chapter has in mind, however. There are directors like Edward D. Wood Jr. and William Beaudine whose unique creations are against-the-grain curiosities and hence attract a devoted fan base. But there are others who, through unstinting control of their tools and their medium—an extraordinary phenomenon, given the constraints of the B picture—have digested the world and coughed it back up in a shape recognizable but new. They knew exactly what they were doing, understood the conventions of the pictures they were making, recognized that the essence of their movies would be the revelation of their struggles within the genre boxes they entered, and yet produced pictures that were extraordinary in personal expression and in their take on the world we live in. The following are this book's most eclectic assortment of films, and their unbridled heterogeneity is, ultimately, the point.

Videodrome

David Cronenberg, 1983

by Dennis Lim

THE CENTRAL IMAGE OF **VIDEODROME**—A GOOEY, THROBBING VHS cassette, bearer of hallucinogenic nightmares, plunged into an abdominal slit—remains the wittiest illustration of how David Cronenberg's movies affect the viewer. Head trips and mind expanders, they are also, in the most literal sense, visceral, as likely to reverberate in the entrails as the nervous system.

Cronenberg's sixth feature, released in 1983, just a few years into the home-video revolution, ingeniously pairs the gross-out body horror of his earlier films with the techno-poetic musings of media guru (and fellow Torontonian) Marshall McLuhan. A droll, chilling riff on McLuhan's view of media as "extensions of man," *Videodrome* is a supremely trippy meditation on the transformative power of images, on the fraught relationship between what we watch and who we are.

The film's hero, Max Renn (James Woods), is a sleazy cable-TV entrepreneur, always on the hunt for kinkier programming. When he discovers a pirate transmission of a show called *Videodrome* that specializes in S-M torture-chamber porn, he's gripped by the snufflike realism and tries to track down its source. His new flame, Nicki Brand (Deborah Harry), a masochistic therapist and radio personality given to stubbing out postcoital cigarettes on her chest, is so hooked that she attempts to audition.

It soon transpires that exposure to the *Videodrome* signal results in psychic turmoil and even bodily transfiguration. Just as the heroine of Cronenberg's 1977 *Rabid* sprouts a retractable blood-sucking phallus under her arm, Max here grows an unmistakably vaginal opening in his stomach. Stumbling through an Escher maze of altered states, he finds himself a pawn in a deepening conspiracy involving

Barry Convex, leader of the shadowy Spectacular Optical Corporation, and Brian O'Blivion, a disembodied McLuhanesque talking head who exists only as a library of videotapes overseen by his daughter, Bianca.

In its own elusive fashion, *Videodrome* addresses one of the hot-button issues of the culture wars: the effects on the viewer of exposure to violent imagery. The film revels in Max and Nicki's voyeuristic desires, even while apparently supporting the idea that graphic images can affect us in ways we don't immediately understand. Convex speaks in punitive terms of the decision to implant the brain-warping signal in debased pornographic material, but the point that it could have been embedded in any telecast echoes McLuhan's assertion that the medium is the message.

The ambiguity in Cronenberg's films has led to charges of conservatism, but he is more a satirist than a moralist, and his films are above all philosophical. It's perhaps best to view the *Videodrome* virus as a technological variant on the epidemics of his earlier films, in which extravagantly repulsive diseases are reimagined as revolutionary agents of change. In both *They Came from Within* (aka *Shivers,* 1975) and *Rabid,* the plagues attack repression and bourgeois norms, ultimately purging bland, dehumanized communities. Whether or not Cronenberg is fully on the side of the infection, he gravitates toward characters who are poised to escape their corporeal prison or otherwise cast off the shackles of self, even if the emancipation eventually proves untenable.

Thanks in large part to Rick Baker's prosthetic effects (very slick, considering the period and the relatively low budget), *Videodrome* amply showcases Cronenberg's distinctive talent for gruesomely literalizing a metaphor. Biotechnology, in the Cronenberg sense, tends to involve an actual merging of man and machine. There are several vivid examples in his oeuvre—the violent meldings of smoking metal and bruised flesh in *Crash* (1996), the sphincterlike spinal "bioports" for game downloading in *eXistenZ* (1999)—but the "new flesh" of *Videodrome,* a deliriously somatic symptom of a media-blasted consciousness, is perhaps the mutation that most pertains to our information-age existence.

It may be less meaningful to speak of the movie's influence than of its continuing—or perhaps growing—relevance. Cronenberg updated it for a video-game paradigm in *eXistenZ.* Olivier Assayas borrowed from it for his shape-shifting Web-porn cyber-thriller *demonlover* (2002). In Japan, where *Videodrome* has a sizable cult following, its traces can be seen in *Tetsuo: The Iron Man* (1989) and the *Ring* movies (2002, 2005), which are likewise premised on the infectious malignancy of a video signal.

Sometimes termed "prophetic," *Videodrome* is prescient in much the same way as its cyber-punk kin, William Gibson's 1984 novel *Neuromancer.* It grasped the cultural and existential implications of emerging technologies at an early stage, and its "sci-fi" extrapolations have come to seem less far-fetched as those technologies have extended their reach. We may not have developed video-ready orifices just yet, but *Videodrome* can only resonate more profoundly as our dependence on—and communion with—technology continues to reach unprecedented levels and as the gratification promised by virtual worlds becomes ever more immediate.

There is also the matter of content. Lightweight cameras and Internet video have made it easier than ever before to capture and disseminate footage of real sex and real death. In the early twenty-first century, extreme imagery is not something that might drift into your living room in the middle of the night from a wayward cable broadcast—often enough it's on CNN, and for anyone with an Internet connection, the hard stuff is just a couple of clicks away. "Long live the new flesh," goes *Videodrome's* indelible mantra. In the age of new media, the new flesh, for better or worse, looks more robust than ever.

Vampire's Kiss

Robert Bierman, 1989

by Rob Nelson

CHEWING A LIVE COCKROACH ON CAMERA HARDLY BEATS swallowing a hot lump of dog shit on location in Baltimore—in drag, yet. Still, among low-budget movie stunts performed by hungry actors in lieu of star power, television ads, and special effects, it makes a helluva money shot. "I saw it as a business decision," recalls Nicolas Cage on the DVD commentary track of *Vampire's Kiss*. "When people see that cockroach go in my mouth, it's like the bus blowing up in *Speed* [1994]." But a lot cheaper. Indeed, Cage earned just forty grand for his wildly unhinged turn as literary agent–cum–bloodsucker Peter Loew. He was twenty-four at the time and used his salary to buy a car—a '67 Corvette Stingray 427.

Likewise driven to extremes, as its title suggests, *Vampire's Kiss* was produced in New York City for a mere $2 million by Hemdale Film Corporation—a "major independent," as the company billed itself at the time. Riding high on back-to-back best-picture Oscars for *Platoon* (1986) and *The Last Emperor* (1987), Hemdale put its black-comic *Dracula* up against *Batman* in the summer of 1989 (winged creatures of the night went for broke in those days) and declared bankruptcy just three years later. The movie, too, is up and down—hysterically funny one moment and deeply disturbing the next. Cage told *American Film* that seeing Jerry Lewis on TV at the age of six is what made him want to be in movies, and it's no wonder. *Vampire's Kiss* is Cage's *Nutty Professor* (1963)—an aptly mood-swinging vehicle for its actor's Method bipolarity and a fearless declaration of the philosophy that true humor is horror.

"I got a little upset at the office," Loew tells his shrink (Elizabeth Ashley) in a rare display of understatement. A monster even before his fateful run-ins with a stray bat and a sharp-toothed one-night stand (Jennifer Beals), Cage's control-freak yuppie berates and otherwise abuses his secretary (Maria Conchita Alonso), repeatedly blows off a would-be girlfriend (Kasi Lemmons), and speaks in a maddeningly pretentious accent—"continental bullshit," according to the actor, who claims he borrowed it from his Comp. Lit. professor dad. Developing a strong aversion to sunlight, using an overturned couch as a coffin, trolling Manhattan discotheques for hot young blood (and, yes, snacking on a long, plump, wriggling cockroach), Loew eventually becomes just another weird, lonely New Yorker roaming the streets and talking to himself—but with a wooden stake and a three-dollar pair of plastic fangs.

Nothing in 1989, with the possible exception of a Wall Street trading floor, looked vaguely like *Vampire's Kiss*. Treating the manic, bloodthirsty, confession-prone capitalist as everyman, the movie beat the publication of *American Psycho* by two years and *The Sopranos'* debut episode by a decade. Critic Stuart Klawans got it right away. Writing in the *Village Voice*, Klawans pegged *Kiss* as being about the "infantilism that lurks behind romantic love and corporate swinishness alike." Other reviewers, alas, weren't nearly as appreciative or insightful. In the *New Yorker*, Pauline Kael faulted the movie for failing to "distinguish Loew's fantasies from his actual life," as if a delusional character demands clinical treatment. And the *New York Times's* Caryn James—who likened Cage's bug-eyed fiend not to Lewis's Buddy Love or Max Schreck's Nosferatu but to Martin Short's Ed Grimley(!)—found the film "dominated and destroyed by Mr. Cage's chaotic, self-indulgent performance."

Self-indulgent? How else for an actor to satirize extreme narcissism than to embody it? If Cage couldn't possibly have gone further in the role, neither could director Robert Bierman have done more to ground his utter prick of a protagonist in the concrete jungle. Bierman's frequent images of New York skyscrapers—gorgeously photographed at sunset by Stefan Czapsky, who went on to capture an even darker Gotham cityscape for *Batman Returns* in 1992—effectively point the middle finger at late-twentieth-century American capitalism and make Loew look like one more phallic symbol. The movie's mock-gothic expressionist style—modeled, Bierman has said, on Jean Cocteau's *Orphée* (1950) and Orson Welles's *The Trial* (1962)—never remotely jells with the actor's inventively hyperactive mugging. Hell, no two of Cage's own takes match each other. But taken by itself, this guilt-inducingly pleasurable depiction of male pathological vanity is among the great underrated American performances—rivaled in recent years only by Robert Downey Jr. in *Two Girls and a Guy* (1997) and Vincent Gallo in *The Brown Bunny* (2003), give or take Harvey Keitel in *Bad Lieutenant* (1992).

Comedy is one thing, and indeed, the moment when Loew excitedly tears off his *own* shirt during foreplay, bouncing like a toddler, remains hysterical even on tenth viewing. But Cage's ultimate gamble in *Vampire's Kiss* is whether he can make his sexist creep appear pitiful if not sympathetic. As sunlight pierces a once marvelously nocturnal New York bachelor pad, Cage's dying vampire meets the dawn with arms outstretched. He could be asking the audience for mercy.

The Core

Jon Amiel, 2003

by Charles Taylor

SOMETHING'S OFF WHEN A MOVIE THAT COST $85 MILLION can be included in a book on B movies. But the reality of Hollywood in the zips is that the sort of schlock once made on the cheap to rake in quick bucks from the drive-in circuit is now budgeted at hundreds of millions of dollars and made with A-list stars. Disaster movies of the 1970s like *The Poseidon Adventure* (1972) and *The Towering Inferno* (1974) were an early indication of where Hollywood would be thirty years later, with spectacle having almost completely overtaken narrative. But even those pictures, their formula derived from *Grand Hotel* (1932) and *The High and the Mighty* (1954)—the drama of a diverse group of people who find themselves thrown together in a dire situation—made an attempt to be *movies*. And that's the very thing that could make them seem talky and dull to contemporary audiences who no longer demand that movies make sense—who can make a hit of a picture like Michael Bay's *Armageddon* (1998), a picture so visually incoherent that there is no way to tell, in the action sequences, where the characters are in physical relation to one another.

All this may suggest why Jon Amiel's *The Core,* a sci-fi adventure that in any sane time would be a modest good night out at the movies, seems almost like a return to principles. It's an end-of-the-world movie, made to capitalize on the success of *Armageddon* and the offensive *Deep Impact* (1998) with its whorish faux spirituality. It came too late to ride those movies' box-office coattails. But you can't help wondering whether, even if its release had been timed to take better advantage of those precedents, the things that make *The Core* so good would have seemed alien to fans of Michael Bay's idiot apocalypse demolition derby.

The premise of *The Core* is that Earth's core has stopped rotating, generating killer lightning storms and weakening the shield that protects us from the incinerating rays of the sun. A group of academics, scientists, and military are sent on a mission aboard a super-duper ship that will drill through to the center of the earth, where they'll detonate a nuclear charge whose shock waves will get the core spinning once again.

What distinguishes the movie from the usual high-concept CGI pap is that Amiel and the screenwriters, Cooper Layne and John Rogers, are actually concerned with story and character. (Did anyone ever think that would be an almost radical approach for a mainstream movie?) With the exception of two expendable sequences involving the destruction of Rome and San Francisco, which feel like a sop to audiences' appetite for destruction, the special effects in *The Core* are pretty much confined to establishing shots of the ship moving through the meat of the planet, and to the computerized rendering of their surroundings that the pilots see on computer screens. Amiel and cinematographer John Lindley instead pull off shots that are trickier than CGI but feel simpler and, because of that, are more unnerving. In the opening sequence, the camera travels in an unbroken pan from an executive collapsing in a glass-walled boardroom (a sudden elecromagnetic pulse has shorted his pacemaker) to the chaos of the city street outside, where failed traffic signals have sent cars careering into one another. The shot is a good example of how impersonality can work for an action movie: we take in the confusion and fright without being made to linger on the pain of anyone who's been hurt.

The Core accomplishes what Richard Lester, during the vogue for disaster movies, accomplished with *Juggernaut* (1974), a beautifully made picture that put the rest of the entries in its debased genre to shame. Lester used a cold aloofness to undercut the melodrama of disaster films. Since the focus of special-effects extravaganzas isn't people at all, Amiel doesn't have to be cold.

The Core gives us a stake in the ship's crew. Inevitably in a movie of this sort, part of the suspense comes from our knowledge that some of the characters won't make it. It's a testament to Amiel's taste and humanity that the deaths, when they come, are handled quickly and quietly, in a way that allows these departing characters, of whom we've grown fond, their dignity. This is a movie where eccentricity and wit are the same thing as braininess. Good lines are tossed off as if this type of cleverness were no big deal, just what smart people are able to do.

In the role of the scruffy, shambling academic (whose template was set by Jeff Bridges in John Guillerman's lovely 1976 remake of *King Kong,* still the best version of that material), Aaron Eckhart proves himself a casual, offhand leading man. As the hotshot young pilot who has never faced a situation she couldn't think her way out of, Hillary Swank makes her rawboned face stand for the kid's largely untested confidence. (When Eckhart asks her if there's anything she can't do and she answers, "If there is, I don't know," it's an unconscious echo of the moment in *Saratoga Trunk* [1945] when Ingrid Bergman is told she's very beautiful and answers, laughingly, "Yes, isn't it lucky?")

As the weapons specialist who's also Eckhart's buddy, the wonderful Tchéky Karyo plays up the advantages of possessing one of those faces that wins an audience immediately to his side. Delroy Lindo and Stanley Tucci take, respectively, the stock roles of nerdy scientific genius and arrogant scientific genius, and come to seem as if they're a hipster comedy team. Tucci, in particular, does a wicked parody of privileged arrogance. He keeps us laughing, and in his exit, his character earns our affection by showing he knows how to laugh at himself. There are also good bits from the slope-nosed character actor DJ Qualls, as the hotshot computer hacker helping the team from the safety of the planet's surface, and Richard Jenkins, as the general in charge of the mission. Jenkins's hangdog face brings a human touch that distinguishes him from the professional dullards usually cast in military brass roles.

Most of the movie is shot close in, within the cocooned spaces of the ship and Mission Control. But Amiel and Lindley don't miss the opportunity for beauty, as in the lovely shot of whales swimming with the ship as it makes its way through the ocean depths; they might be familiars come to wish the crew bon voyage. And the focus on story and character, the refusal to OD on special effects, all of it lends the enterprise a becomingly modest air.

The Core isn't a big deal, but its mix of decency and craft make you remember it with affection and gratitude. Karyo's character says he's not out to save the human race, just three members of it, his wife and kids. *The Core* isn't out to save mainstream movies. But it brings some humanity back.

Beat the Devil

John Huston, 1953

by Roger Ebert

THE VILLAGE BAND POUNDS OUT AN OOM-PA-PA TUNE, AND police march four disreputable characters across the square. Already we're smiling. One is tall and round, one is tall and cadaverous, one is short and round, and the fourth is a little rat-face with a bristling mustache. On the sound track, Humphrey Bogart tells us they are all criminals, but we know that; they were born looking guilty.

John Huston's *Beat the Devil* shows how much Hollywood has lost by devaluing its character actors. In an age when a $20 million star must be on the screen every second, this picture could not be made. Huston has stars, too: Bogart, Jennifer Jones, Gina Lollobrigida, but his movie is so funny because he throws them into the pot with a seedy gang of charlatans. "We have to beware of them," the Jones character warns her husband. "They're desperate characters. Not one of them looked at my legs."

Beat the Devil went straight from box-office flop to cult classic; it has been called the first camp movie, although Bogart, who sank his own money into it, said "only phonies like it." It's a movie that was made up on the spot. Huston tore up the original screenplay on the first day of filming, flew the young Truman Capote to Ravello, Italy, to crank out new scenes against a daily deadline, and allowed his supporting stars, especially Robert Morley and Peter Lorre, to create dialogue for their own characters. (Capote spoke daily by telephone with his pet raven, and one day when the raven refused to answer, he flew to Rome to console it, further delaying the production.)

The story involves a crowd of raffish misfits killing time in the little Italian seaport until repairs are completed on the rust-bucket ship that will take them to British East Africa. They all have secret schemes to stake a claim to a uranium find. Bogart and Lollobrigida play Billy and Maria Dannreuther; he once owned a local villa, but has been reduced to having his hotel bills paid by Peterson (Robert Morley), a crook in a magnificent ice-cream suit, his tie laid out like a Dover sole on the upper reaches of his belly. Peterson's other associates include a man named O'Hara (Peter Lorre), who has a German accent and says, suspiciously, that there are a lot of O'Haras in Chile; the rat-faced little Major Ross (Ivor Bernard), who observes approvingly, "Hitler knew how to put women in their place"; and the gaunt, mournful, hawk-nosed Ravello (Marco Tulli). Also waiting for the boat to sail are Gwendolen and Harry Chelm (Jennifer Jones and Edward Underdown), who claim to be from the landed gentry of Gloucestershire.

These characters are imported, more or less, from an original novel by "James Helvick," actually the left-wing British critic Claud Cockburn (whose son Alexander named his column in the *Nation* magazine after the movie). The film was originally set in a French town, and was intended to be a halfway-serious thriller about the evils of colonial exploitation. When Bogart signed aboard, that's what he thought it would be, but at some point in the transfer to Italian locations Huston decided to make it a comedy, and hired the twenty-eight-year-old Capote on the advice of Jones's husband, the tireless memo writer David O. Selznick.

There are times during the movie when you can sense Capote chuckling to himself as he supplies improbable dialogue for his characters. Lollobrigida, the Italian sex star, was making her first English-language movie, but Capote has her explain, "Emotionally, I am English." She claims to take tea and crumpets every afternoon, and quotes the writer George Moore, whom I believe has not been quoted before or since in any movie. Bogart describes his character's early upbringing: "I was an orphan until I was twenty. Then a rich and beautiful lady adopted me." And Peter Lorre of course has his famous observation about time, which deserves comparison with Orson Welles's "cuckoo clock" speech in *The Third Man* (1949). "Time . . . time," Lorre says. "What is time? Swiss manufacture it. French hoard it. Italians squander it. Americans say it is money. Hindus say it does not exist. Do you know what I say? I say time is a crook."

The plot is an afterthought; this is a movie about eccentric behavior. Underdown, as Jones's husband, affects British upper-class manners, travels with his hot water bottle, takes to his bed with "a shocking chill on my liver," and seems not to notice that his wife has fallen in love with the Bogart character. For that matter, Bogart's wife (Lollobrigida) has fallen in love with Chelm, and he seems oblivious to that as well. It is a measure of the movie that we are never quite sure if the Dannreuthers are both committing adultery, or simply trying to discover the Chelms' secret plans for the uranium; when Hollywood censors questioned the adultery in the original story, Huston and Capote simply made it enigmatic.

Much of the humor is generated by the two women. Jones plays a busybody, one of those women who accidentally blurt out exactly what they intend to say. Lollobrigida wears a series of similarly low-cut, cinched-waist evening dresses at all times of the day. And Morley's gang turns up inappropriately dressed for the hot weather, sweating and squirming, all except for the imperturbable Lorre, who has died his hair platinum and sucks continuously on a cigarette in a holder that he holds like a flute.

Even the third-team supporting characters are entertaining. When the two couples drive out for dinner, Bogart hires an antique open-topped Hispano-Suiza automobile he claims to have gotten from a bullfighter and given to the driver (Juan de Landa). Later, when the car is lost through hilarious miscalculation, the driver wants compensation. "Why, you thief, *I* gave you that car!" Bogart roars. "How I came into possession of it is beside the point," the driver insists.

Other bit players include the ship's purser (Mario Perrone), who has the knack of materializing instantly when anything goes wrong and knowing exactly what has happened. And the captain (Saro Urzi), continuously drunk. And Ahmed (Manuel Serano), the Arab leader who arrests them after they're shipwrecked in Africa and pumps Bogart for details about Rita Hayworth. When he asks Bogart to betray Morley, Bogart wants to be paid. "Your demands are very great, under the circumstances," the official tells him. "Why shouldn't they be?" says Bogart. "Fat Gut's my best friend, and I will not betray him cheaply."

One of Huston's running jokes through the film involves the composition of his shots of Morley and his three associates. They are so different in appearance, height, and manner that they hardly seem able to fit into the same frame, and Huston uses a system of rotation to bring each one forward as he speaks, mournfully framed by the others. Despite their differences, they form a unit, and when it appears that Morley may have been killed in the auto mishap, the rat-faced major is distraught: "Mussolini, Hitler—and now, Peterson!"

If *Beat the Devil* puzzled audiences on its first release, it has charmed them since. Jones told the critic Charles Champlin that Huston promised her, "Jennifer, they'll remember you longer for *Beat the Devil* than for *Song of Bernadette*" (1943).

True, but could Huston have guessed that they would remember him more for *Beat the Devil* than for the picture he made next, *Moby Dick* (1956)?

The movie has, above all, effortless charm. Once we catch on that nothing much is going to happen, we can relax and share the amusement of the actors, who are essentially being asked to share their playfulness. There is a scene on a veranda overlooking the sea, where Bogart and Jones play out their first flirtation, and by the end of their dialogue you can see they're all but cracking up; Bogart grins during the dissolve. The whole picture feels that way. Now that movies have become fearsome engines designed to hammer us with entertainment, it's nice to recall those that simply wanted to be witty company.

Mona

Michael Benveniste and Howard Ziehm, 1970

by Richard Corliss

IMAGINE THAT THERE WAS NO FEATURE FILM BEFORE *The Birth of a Nation* in 1915; no Western before *Stagecoach* in 1939; no musical, on stage or screen, before *42nd Street* in 1933. Imagine that D. W. Griffith, John Ford, and the Lloyd Bacon–Busby Berkeley tandem had to invent, rather than perfect, the conventions that made their movies work. That, to overstate the case just slightly, was the challenge facing the makers of *Mona,* the first known feature-length film that integrated explicit sex into a fictional plot.

For a few years at the end of the Vietnam era, hard-core sex movies enjoyed a vogue that attracted the rich, the hip, and the curious. In those days of porno chic, seeing a hard-core film or two was de rigueur for trendy urbanites, a rite of passage for college kids. After the 1972 comedy *Deep Throat* earned many millions for its gangland sponsors, porn directors got ambitious. The form soon appropriated a handful of genres—musicals (*Alice in Wonderland,* 1976), science fiction (*Flesh Gordon,* 1974), and Bergmanesque drama (*The Devil in Miss Jones,* 1973)—before fading out later in the decade.

And before them all was *Mona,* aka *Mona the Virgin Nymph,* produced by porn pioneer Bill Osco (scion of the nationwide drugstore chain), written by Bucky Searles (who, according to the Internet Movie Database, was credited with writing an episode of the Diahann Carroll sitcom *Julia* the same year), and codirected by Michael Benveniste (the dialogue scenes) and Howard Ziehm (the sexy stuff). No names appeared on the film, to protect the perps. Whatever artistic daring *Mona* required of its makers, the legal bravado was greater; they could all be arrested. But this scuzzy little fable, made in three days for five thousand dollars, had two unique achievements: it played in major U.S. cities without being shut down by the police; and, for the very first of its kind, the movie was pretty good.

Our rambunctious heroine (Fifi Watson) is engaged to Tim (Ric Lutze) but won't have intercourse with him, because she's promised her widowed mom (Judy Angel) that she'd be a virgin on her wedding day. Figuring that her vow leaves plenty of options for recreation, Mona agrees to fellate Tim in a public park. The activity agrees with her, and she's soon pleasuring strangers in back alleys and movie theaters. Meanwhile, Tim drops by the family manse, where Mom lures him into some vigorous sex. When Tim learns of Mona's escapades, he insists she have a simultaneous assignation with all four of her tricks, and her every orifice is plundered en masse. Returning home, Mona tearfully says, "Mother, I have something to tell you." Mom replies, "I have something to tell you, too, dear." They hug. Fade out on this sadder-but-wiser mother-daughter sisterhood.

Mona was a natural blending of two bastard genres: the soft-core sexploitation film, which was basically a low-budget fiction feature with heavy-breathing innuendo, simulated lovemaking, and the occasional exposure of skin; and the stag film, a silent, black-and-white, one- or two-reel depiction of explicit sex. Putting the two forms together—making a feature-length hard-core narrative talkie in color—was almost a historical inevitability, especially as the laws against showing eroticism in movies were gradually relaxed in the late 1960s. But *Mona* was the first to do it, and show It.

The movie packs plenty of weirdness, and not a few stabs at artistry, into its sixty-nine minutes. When Mona goes to the movie house, the dialogue she hears is pertinent sexual badinage from Shakespeare's *The Taming of the Shrew.* The score is an ambitious mix of jug-band tunes, sentimental ballads from the 1920s, baroque stylings on a harpsichord, and, during some of the sex scenes, a kind of aleatory, found-sound symphony in the fashion of John Cage and Walter Carlos. These aural experiments are more distracting than erotic, but they sure beat the disco music that wallpapered every porn soundtrack in later years.

There were also hints the filmmakers had read Freud, or at least Krafft-Ebing. In a black-and-white flashback early in the film, the child Mona is seen being approached sexually by her father, and she is forced into the act she will later perform with such obsessive gusto. Later, when Tim visits Mona's mom, she tells him he reminds her of her late husband and promptly seduces him. The father is a shadow presence, but his depredations haunt, and may have helped form, the sexual compulsions of both Mona and Mom. I wouldn't praise the film's psychology as highly as Kenneth Turan and Stephen Zito did in their 1974 sex-film history *Sinema*—they describe the relationships as "clear and credible," the motivations "fully developed," and Angel's acting "remarkable"—but it's worlds more sophisticated than an early porn feature had any need or right to be.

And the sex? It's energetic in Watson's scenes, and, when Angel and Lutze go at it, volcanically passionate. The performers weren't the most gorgeous people around, but considering that the available talent pool for a hard-core feature must have been on the shallow side, they do fine. They are the lower-rung kin to actors in off-off-Broadway theater or indie films of the '60s: what they lack in charisma they make up for in authenticity. Besides, what's the point of a porn movie that's pretty? It's got to be dirty, and make its viewers feel that way, too.

I didn't see *Mona* until 2005, when the release of the documentary *Inside Deep Throat* prodded me to do some research for a Time.com essay on porno chic. After the piece appeared, I heard from Ziehm, the codirector, who kindly entertained a few film-historical questions. The people in the movie, for example: Were they actors who agreed to be photographed having sex, or swingers who tried to act? The answer was the latter. "Rarely had anyone learned their lines before the day of the shoot," Ziehm wrote. "They were sexual people, not thespians, although some kidded themselves into believing otherwise. It would be like trying to pretend that a defensive end could play cornerback. The idea of writing a complex script for people who were going to come to the set without even looking at the script was absurd."

As for going incognito, Ziehm wrote: "I used a pseudonym for most of my work because I was busted so many times I didn't want to give them a map where to get me next. . . . In all, I had a court battle over my head for almost 11 years." In 1974 he, Osco, and Benveniste made the soft-core fantasy *Flesh Gordon* at one hundred times the budget of *Mona,* employing the effects expertise of Oscar nominee Jim Danforth and future Oscar winners Dennis Muren, Joe Viskocil, and Rick Baker. Ziehm said that in 1980, when porn went to video and everything became cheap again, "I dropped out. The legal and other problems just weren't worth it." A few years ago he published a collection he'd compiled, *Golf in the Comic Strips,* with an introduction by Bob Hope.

Today, *Mona* and its progeny seem as distant as *Flesh Gordon*'s Planet Porno. Hard-core is just another corporate assembly line; it lacks not only the lovely old sense of the forbidden but also the artistic boldness, the zizz and the zazz. As for the film that started it all, *Mona* can be found in the catalog of Something Weird Video, the Criterion Collection of sleaze, under the title *Bucky Beaver's Stags, Loops and Peeps Vol. 050.* Which is probably where the *Birth of a Nation* of porn belongs.

Part ELEVEN: Transgressive Chic

The World of Midnight Movies

THE MIDNIGHT-MOVIE PHENOMENON REFLECTS A LOT OF WHAT'S
happened in American culture over the last few decades: what began as a desperate
last resort has become a marketing bonanza. The concept began with a certain tendency of the TV networks to relegate their semi-disreputable B movies to late-late
showings in the dead of night and wee hours of the dawn, hosted by the likes of
Zacherley and Vampira; later it was developed as a theatrical hook for fare deemed
uncommercial, from *El Topo* and *Night of the Living Dead* to *Targets* and *The Rocky
Horror Picture Show,* the most legendary of them all. Today the "midnight movie"
label is a status symbol, signifying outsider cachet and transgressive chic. Which is
all right with us, even if it puts the MM brand in danger of becoming a banality.

The specimens discussed here are messages from the golden age of midnight
shows, extracted from some overlooked time capsule buried under the Waverly
in Greenwich Village, or maybe it was the Roxy in San Francisco, or perhaps the
Orson Welles in Cambridge, or one of the other venues adventurous enough to
light up their projectors when respectable citizens were safe in slumberland. The
psycho-socio-sexo-political perversities of *Rocky Horror* and *Pink Flamingos* have
long been absorbed into prime-time culture, and *Night of the Living Dead* is a
Disney flick compared with a French *bain de sang* like *Frontière(s)* or the like-minded
Hostel and *Saw* franchises. In their day, however, these were true Killer Bs that
shocked the gentry down to their pretzel-twisted knickers.

And then there's David Lynch, still a beacon of insanity in a world that values
fever-dream aesthetics far less than it ought to. As radical in his tenth feature, the
deliriously inventive *Inland Empire,* as in his first, the quintessentially midnight-
esque *Eraserhead,* he's a living embodiment of the midnight-movie ethos. The film
that launched his fame is an ideal no-budget vision to close this volume.

Pink Flamingos

John Waters, 1972

by Roger Ebert

JOHN WATERS'S **PINK FLAMINGOS** WAS RESTORED FOR ITS twenty-fifth anniversary revival, and with any luck at all that means I won't have to see it again for another twenty-five years. If I haven't retired by then, I will. How do you review a movie like this? I am reminded of an interview I once did with a man who ran a carnival sideshow. His star was a geek who bit off the heads of live chickens and drank their blood. "He's the best geek in the business," this man assured me. "What is the difference between a good geek and a bad geek?" I asked. "You wanna examine the chickens?"

Pink Flamingos was filmed with genuine geeks, and that's the appeal of the film, to those who find it appealing: what seems to happen in the movie really does happen. That is its redeeming quality, you might say. If the events in this film were only simulated, it would merely be depraved and disgusting. But since they are actually performed by real people, the film gains a weird kind of documentary stature. There is a temptation to praise the film, however grudgingly, just to show you have a strong enough stomach to take it. It is a temptation I can resist.

The plot involves a rivalry between two competing factions for the title of Filthiest People Alive. In one corner: a transvestite named Divine (who dresses like a combination of a showgirl, a dominatrix, and Bozo); her mentally ill mother (sits in a crib eating eggs and making messes); her son (likes to involve chickens in his sex life with strange women); and her lover (likes to watch son with strange women and chickens). In the other corner: Mr. and Mrs. Marble, who kidnap hippies, chain them in a dungeon, and force their butler to impregnate them so that after they die in childbirth their babies can be sold to lesbian couples.

All the details of these events are shown in the film—oh, and more, including the notorious scene in which Divine actually ingests that least appetizing residue of the canine. And not only do we see genitalia in this movie—they do exercises.

Pink Flamingos appeals to that part of our psyches in which we are horny teenagers at the county fair with fresh dollar bills in our pockets and a desire to see the geek show with a bunch of buddies so that we can brag about it at school on Monday. (And also because of an intriguing rumor that the Bearded Lady proves she is bearded all over.) As extras with the restored version, director John Waters hosts and narrates a series of outtakes, which (not surprisingly) are less disgusting than what stayed in the film. We see long-lost scenes in which Divine cooks the chicken that starred in an earlier scene; Divine receives the ears of Cookie, the character who costarred in the scene with her son and the chicken; and Divine, Cookie, and her son sing "We Are the Filthiest People Alive" in pig latin.

Waters is a charming man whose later films (like *Polyester* in 1981 and *Hairspray* in 1988) take advantage of his bemused take on pop culture. His early films, made on infinitesimal budgets and starring his friends, used shock as a way to attract audiences, and that is understandable. He jump-started his career, and in the movie business, you do what you gotta do. Waters's talent has grown; in this film, which he photographed, the visual style resembles a home movie, right down to the overuse of the zoom lens. (Amusingly, his zooms reveal he knows how long the characters will speak; he zooms in, stays, and then starts zooming out before speech ends so that he can pan to another character and zoom in again.)

After the outtakes, Waters shows the original trailer for the film, in which, not amazingly, not a single scene from the movie is shown. Instead, the trailer features interviews with people who have just seen *Pink Flamingos* and are a little dazed by the experience. The trailer cleverly positions the film as an event: Hey, you may like the movie or hate it, but at least you'll be able to say you saw it! Then blurbs flash on the screen, including one comparing *Pink Flamingos* to Luis Buñuel's *Un Chien Andalou* (1929), in which a pig's eyeball is sliced. Yes, but the pig was dead, while the audience for this movie is still alive.

FOOTNOTE: *I do not give a star rating to* Pink Flamingos, *because stars seem not to apply. It should be considered not as a film but as a fact. Or perhaps as an object.*

The Rocky Horror Picture Show

Jim Sharman, 1975

by Kevin Thomas

AN OLD CAGE ELEVATOR DESCENDS INTO A POP-ARTISH ballroom and deposits a figure in garish makeup, spangles vest and elbow-length gloves, black bikini, black opera hose, and steep ankle-strap wedgies. No, it's not Raquel Welch. It's Tim Curry as Dr. Frank-N-Furter, making his grand entrance in *The Rocky Horror Picture Show,* an outrageous camp musical based on Richard O'Brien's stage hit *The Rocky Horror Show.*

Dr. Frank-N-Furter is really from another planet, Transsexual, in another galaxy, Transylvania, and he's kicking off the Annual Transylvanian Convention being held in his moldy Gothic castle, where the creepy delegates are doing a new dance, the Time Warp. Just before his arrival a couple of square kids, Brad Majors (Barry Bostwick) and his fiancée, Janet Weiss (Susan Sarandon), have come to the castle seeking shelter during a violent storm. (In the time-honored fashion, they've had a flat tire—but while listening to President Nixon's resignation speech on the radio!) The highlight of the convention is to be the unveiling—more precisely the unwrapping—of Dr. Frank-N-Furter's creation, a blond and blue-eyed Adonis (Peter Hinwood) dubbed Rocky Horror. He, alas, seems to have more of a yen for Janet than for his creator, who, in turn, has a yen apiece for Brad *and* Janet.

All this plays less depraved than it sounds, but *The Rocky Horror Picture Show* is unquestionably consenting-adult fare. *Young Frankenstein* (1974) it isn't, but then again it also isn't the morbid Grand Guignol-gory outing that *Andy Warhol's Frankenstein* (1973) and *Andy Warhol's Dracula* (1974) were. O'Brien's musical is simply too exuberant and funny to be seriously decadent. Indeed, there's an underlying quality of tenderness and even innocence in this loving send-up of horror and sci-fi flicks and celebration of postgraduate sexuality.

One big musical number follows another, climaxed by an extravaganza that features Curry wondering, in song, whatever happened to Fay Wray as he stands before a stage set re-creating the old RKO logo. Rocky, Brad, and Janet, having been temporarily zapped into statuary—the easier to dress them in outfits identical to Dr. Frank-N-Furter's—reawaken to form a chorus with him before diving into a pool decorated on its bottom with the section of Michelangelo's Sistine Chapel ceiling that depicts the creation of Adam—a bottoming-out of taste, as it were. Our now happy quartet, however, has not reckoned with Dr. Frank-N-Furter's jealous servant, the cadaverous Riff Raff (O'Brien) and his sexy sister, Magenta (Patricia Quinn).

Adapted for the screen by its original stage director, Jim Sharman, and designed by Brian Thomson, who also created the settings for the stage version, *The Rocky Horror Picture Show* moves fast and looks slick. The performances are amusing, including that of Curry, who created Dr. Frank-N-Furter on the stage and is husky and deep-voiced beneath his sequined elegance. Among other excellent principals is Charles Gray, the film's smirky, insinuating narrator. No wonder this flamboyant film became the midnight-movie hit, complete with audience participation, par excellence.

Targets

Peter Bogdanovich, 1968

by David Sterritt

ONE REASON WHY MOVIE CRITICS LOVE **TARGETS** IS THE PROOF
it offered that American critics could do what the cinephiles of the French New
Wave had already pulled off: start your career as a film critic and historian, then
move into directing and screenwriting projects that take full advantage of what
you've learned from writing about pictures you love. Peter Bogdanovich was the
first American to manage this trick, and *Targets*—his first feature, and arguably
the best he's ever made—manifests his immersion in cinema lore every bit as
much as his criticism does. Better still, the movie traditions that Bogdanovich
loves aren't tacked onto the main story like DVD extras or Brian De Palma's less
successful in-jokes and homages. They're woven into the fabric of the narrative
with an ingenuity that adds additional levels of meaning without slowing the picture's full-throttle momentum for an instant.

The story begins in a Hollywood screening room, where a small group of
insiders are watching the climax of the movie they've just made—a Roger
Corman–type horror yarn, with Jack Nicholson chasing Boris Karloff through a
creaky old castle full of cobwebs, corpses, and creepiness. This introduces the
film-reference side of *Targets,* since the movie-within-the-movie is *The Terror,* an
American International Pictures quickie that Corman directed (with uncredited
help from Francis Ford Coppola and others) immediately after *The Raven* on an
astonishingly tight schedule in 1963. Even more to the point, *The Terror* played
a key role in allowing Bogdanovich to make *Targets,* since Karloff still owed
Corman a few days of work, and Corman agreed to greenlight a Bogdanovich
production if the first-time director would give Karloff a significant part.

Knowing that he'd have limited use of Karloff's talent, Bogdanovich cleverly designed a narrative (with Polly Platt, who receives co-credit for the story) that could be filmed in separate stages, one featuring the Karloff plotline and another focusing on a second protagonist.

When the screening is over, the lights come on and we meet two of our main characters. One is Sammy Michaels, the (fictional) writer and director of the movie-within-the-movie, played by Bogdanovich, the (real-life) writer and director of *Targets* itself. The other is Byron Orlok, the (fictional) star of the movie-within-the-movie, played by Karloff, the (real-life) star of both *The Terror* and *Targets* itself. We quickly learn that something important is on Orlok's mind: he's decided to retire, even though this will end his long career and hurt his friend Sammy by ruining the prospects for Sammy's next project, a contemporary drama he's written for Orlok to star in. Everyone is upset by Orlok's decision, but he doesn't waver. The only concession he finally makes is to go through with an in-person appearance at a local drive-in theater, which he agreed to before anyone knew it would mark his farewell to the film business. Back at the hotel where he's staying in Los Angeles, he has a healthy number of good stiff drinks while pacifying his secretary and trying to soothe Sammy, who pays a drunken and argumentative visit in hopes of changing Orlok's mind.

By this time we've also met the movie's other main character. Bobby Thompson, neatly played by Tim O'Kelly, is a clean-cut Californian who lives with his pretty wife and respectable parents in a neat suburban home. The first time we see him is in a gun shop, where he's checking a rifle's telescopic sight by leveling the crosshairs on Orlok, who happens to be standing across the street. After completing his purchase, Bobby opens the trunk of his car to stow the new gun away, and we observe with a shudder that this is just the latest addition to a hefty arsenal he's already stockpiled. At home with his family, he's well behaved and upright to a fault, saying "Amen" after grace, calling his father "Sir," and all the rest. But these are people who don't examine life too closely, and when Bobby confesses to his wife that he has . . . well, troubling thoughts from time to time, she says she's late for work and scurries off. Little does she know how troubling those thoughts have become.

For most of its eighty-nine-minute running time, *Targets* cuts between these two story lines as Orlok moves closer to his last public appearance and Bobby moves closer to some kind of breaking point. Bobby's big moment comes first. The following day he greets his wife and mother by shooting them dead. Then he drives to a nearby oil refinery, lugs a bagful of pistols and rifles to the top, kills a worker who comes to investigate the ruckus, and starts sniping at speeding cars on the freeway as if they were plastic ducks in a carnival shooting gallery. Fleeing the cops who eventually arrive, he races back to his car, pushes the pedal to the metal, and zips into an excellent hiding place he finds—namely, a drive-in theater that's just opened up for early arrivals.

And you guessed it, this is the very same drive-in where Orlok is slated to appear that night. Not knowing or caring about this, Bobby finds a parking place, climbs onto the scaffolding behind the screen, locates a peephole with a good view of the cars pouring in as dusk approaches, and recommences shooting at the unprotected vehicles and their unsuspecting inhabitants. This is among the eeriest scenes of violence ever filmed, and also one of the most piquant commentaries on both California car culture and American moviegoing habits. As the killing spree goes on and on, Bobby's sitting ducks gaze obliviously at the silver screen that conceals him, making out and munching popcorn in their isolated automobiles as if life's only terrors were make-believe ones concocted for nothing more serious than our momentary amusement. By escaping into Hollywood fantasies— even "scary" ones like *The Terror,* which the drive-in crowd is watching—today's conformists and consumers have managed to escape from a meaningful awareness of what their lives and their society are all about. Making this message all the more remarkable is Bogdanovich's success in conveying it via the same kind of entertainment fare he's implicitly disparaging, up to and including his use of *The Terror* as a prime specimen of this dismaying breed.

It's impossible to discuss the climax of *Targets* without a spoiler or two, so consider yourself cautioned. The drive-in moviegoers eventually realize that something ghastly is going on. Cries of "Someone's shooting!" and "There's a sniper here!" start moving from car to car, and before long a walloping traffic jam develops as too many drivers cram their vehicles into the narrow exit driveways. Soon word of the panic gets to the limousine where Orlok is waiting for his moment in the spotlight, and elderly as he is, he decides to take action, walking toward the screen just as Bobby climbs down from his hidden perch to retrieve some weaponry he's dropped. Coming into the light, the psychotic sniper faces an awe-inspiring sight: Byron Orlok, the very embodiment of horror, is striding toward him from both the left and right, in flesh-and-blood on the pavement and in living color on the screen. Trapped between these twin terrors in a nightmare come true, Bobby collapses in quivering fear like the regressive psychopath he is. And now Orlok utters a key line of the film, revealing in a few simple words the motivation for his courageous action, the real reason for his retirement from horror films, and his sudden realization—sparked by the sight of how puny and pathetic his adversary turns out to be—that those films aren't really as pernicious as he's come to imagine. "Is *that* what I was afraid of?" he rhetorically asks after slapping the psycho around. Horror movies may be self-fulfilling symptoms of a culture gone astray, but to react too strongly against them is to give them a power they neither need nor deserve.

Although its ideas remain as socially and culturally relevant as they were in 1968, *Targets* is intimately tied to the period that produced it. The character of Bobby is plainly modeled on Charles Whitman, a mentally ill young man who'd killed his wife and mother before sniping at cars from an observation tower at the University of Texas in Austin two years earlier, giving Americans an early (and largely unheeded) warning about escalating gun fetishism across the land. In an ominous coincidence, moreover, the film's release on August 15, 1968, came in the immediate wake of two political assassinations—of Martin Luther King Jr. in April and Robert F. Kennedy two months later—that had renewed the sense of dread provoked by John F. Kennedy's murder late in 1963. And the film indirectly hints that Bobby is a Vietnam veteran who learned his killing skills in the Southeast Asian killing fields. Considered in these contexts, *Targets* is all the more chilling; and considered in the additional context of events like the Columbine and Virginia Tech shootings, it's almost too prescient for comfort.

Returning to the film's cinematic merits, its style has more quiet sophistication than you'd expect from a filmmaker with far more experience than Bogdanovich had. During the scenes centering on Bobby, the camera often moves in his tracks as if it were a stalker with motives as sinister as his. The scenes revolving around Orlok have a different look, less sneaky and more straightforward. Even the movie's humor plays subtly into the themes it's exploring. After their hotel-room spat, Sammy and Orlok fall drunkenly into Orlok's bed, and when Sammy awakens in the morning, he gives a sudden start of alarm; when Orlok asks what jolted him, he says it was a shock to open his eyes and find Byron Orlok right next to him! Leaving the room a moment later, Orlok walks past a mirror, catches a glimpse of himself, and has a momentary jolt of his own. The superstar of horror is so scary that he even frightens himself! No wonder he's reassessing the foundations on which he's built his long career. (It's also worth noting a novel interpretation of *Targets* that says the whole movie after this scene is an enactment of Sammy's unproduced script, which Sammy has described as a contemporary drama in which Orlok would show a whole new side of himself; substitute Peter for Sammy and Karloff for Orlok, and entertain the possibility that Orlok now stands in for Sammy's father, who's never seen or mentioned again.)

The movie references in *Targets* are also fascinating if you have sharp enough eyes to spot them. You can't help noticing the clip from Howard Hawks's 1931 classic *The Criminal Code,* reverently watched by impatient Orlok and boozed-up Sammy just before their quarrel in Orlok's living room; it's truly poignant to see Karloff at eighty-one years old viewing himself at half that age in a time-worn print on a tiny TV screen. Also unmistakable is the resemblance between Bobby's position on the refinery tank and the last stand of Cody Jarrett, indelibly played by James Cagney, at the climax of *White Heat,* the Raoul Walsh masterpiece of 1949. Bogdanovich's treatment is far cooler and crisper than Walsh's, however, evoking the detachment from reality of the radically depersonalized killer.

I'll leave readers to find more movie references on their own, but I want to close by saluting the moment in *Targets* that most movingly sums up Bogdanovich's reverence for the living history of film. It comes when Orlok is conferring with Sammy on how to prevent his drive-in appearance from becoming just another snoozefest with a near-decrepit actor who's all but irrelevant to the younger generation. Sammy suggests that Orlok tell a story, and Orlok likes the idea so much that he rehearses one from memory there and then: "An Appointment in Samarra," the W. Somerset Maugham tale about a long-ago servant who fears that Death is coming for him in Baghdad, and flees to distant Samarra for safety, not knowing that Death's rendezvous with him has been slated for Samarra all along. The tale is a microcosm of *Targets* as a whole, which begins with Bobby sighting Orlok through his crosshairs and ends with their fateful confrontation in a very different place. But more important, the story of *Targets* stops in its tracks during this scene, allowing Karloff to recite the grim fable with all the artistry he's acquired over a lifetime of dedicated creative work; it's clearly a moment of tribute by a filmmaker who, out of profound respect for the actor and all he represents, records the recitation as both a sign of personal affection and a cinematic time capsule for ages to come.

Bogdanovich acted not a moment too soon. Although it doesn't show on screen, Karloff was very sick with emphysema when *Targets* went before the camera—he rested in a wheelchair between takes, breathing oxygen from a tank—and this was the last feature he completed before his death the following year. Bogdanovich went on to a long and checkered career, but he never outdid his debut picture for originality or inspiration. And a key factor in its brilliance is the heartfelt participation of an elderly icon who'd be keeping his own appointment in Samarra all too soon.

Night of the Living Dead

George A. Romero, 1968

by Desson Thomson

FOR AN OBJECT LESSON IN TURNING LIMITATIONS TO MAGNIFICENT advantage, look no further than George A. Romero's *Night of the Living Dead*. With only $114,000 and a modest circle of actors and crew, the Pittsburgh filmmaker created a zombie flick with surprisingly epic dimension and in-your-face menace. It not only broke the frontiers of convention, but its no-frills artistry set a precedent for generations of other exploitation-horror movies, from John Carpenter's *Halloween* (1978) to Danny Boyle's *28 Days Later* . . . (2002). Romero's robotic zombies became the paradigm for such pictures' own flesh-eating shufflers or psychotic killers, as well as metaphors for anything from mass consumption to video-game slackerism.

The secret behind Romero's alchemy? A creative resourcefulness born of empty pockets—the same formula artists have used in every low-budget art form, from punk rock to graffiti spray-painting. Instead of being beset by his low-end production values, which included chocolate syrup for blood and mortician's wax for zombie makeup, Romero repurposed them as aesthetic assets.

What would the movie's edgy atmosphere be, for instance, without that washed-out, black-and-white look, a sense that this particular world is deteriorating into monochromatic oblivion? The film's stark, almost documentary imagery imbues it with spooky gravitas as a plague of zombies emerges from the grave to devour every living being in sight. And its freewheeling camera movement, decades before the self-consciously fidgety camera of *The Blair Witch Project* (1999), gives us the queasy sensation that the cinematographers are jumpy newsmen doing their nervous best to follow the action.

Budgetary issues forced Romero to assemble a motley collection of actors, some of them from the Pittsburgh stage but most of them amateurs, friends, and eleventh-hour walk-ins. In a story about a world gone nightmarishly wrong, the resulting performances—undisciplined, quirky, uneven—worked in the movie's favor. (Romero also understood the B-movie ethos: audiences are conditioned to accept the bizarre, the weird, and the insane in these films, so what's a clumsy acting turn or two?)

Ironically, the hammiest turn comes from Judith O'Dea, a professional, who plays Barbra, one of the traumatized victims huddling in terror. Her ham-fisted descent into Ophelia-style madness is initially a campy distraction, but it's also apropos, given the slow-moving, laconic cannibals around her and the zombie state she's all but guaranteed to assume.

Romero's bargain-basement casting paid off especially well in the case of Duane Jones, an unknown African American stage actor, and Karl Hardman, a producing partner on the film who was deputized for a role. As two of Barbra's fellow survivors who increasingly bump heads about the best way to defend themselves, they create an intriguing racial atmosphere that becomes the movie's most stirring element. Their increasingly frenzied histrionics (as much a mark of the actors' inexperience as a considered artistic choice) further the film's purposes and even deepen it. Here's a black man—in a movie made during the contentious civil-rights struggle of the 1960s—winning the day in scene after scene. And when he meets his ultimate destiny with a zombie vigilante mob, the undertones of lynching are impossible to ignore, lending *Night of the Living Dead* an extraordinarily powerful extra dimension.

As if artistic and cultural success weren't enough for the Little Film That Could, it proved to be enormously lucrative, reaping $12 million in North America and $30 million abroad. On top of this, the Library of Congress would later enshrine it in the United States National Film Registry of "historically, culturally or aesthetically important" works. In the spirit of his reanimated dead, Romero had created a self-perpetuating phenomenon whose profitability and significance never seem to stop coming.

Not bad for a shoestring flick.

Eraserhead

David Lynch, 1977

by David Sterritt

ERASERHEAD DIDN'T INVENT THE MIDNIGHT MOVIE SHOW. That honor goes to Alejandro Jodorowsky's savage *El Topo* and George A. Romero's chillers *Night of the Living Dead* and *Martin,* which pioneered the field in the early to middle 1970s. Nor did David Lynch's genre-bending melodramedy skyrocket to success when it did make its witching-hour debut, courtesy of an enterprising Greenwich Village theater that took a chance with it in 1977. Lynch later recalled an opening-night crowd of twenty-five people, and reviews were lukewarm at best.

But momentum grew as word-of-mouth enthusiasm spread—complete with rumors that the sound track emitted an inaudible drone that tapped into the audience's unconscious, as if only subliminal trickery could account for the picture's uncanny power. By the end of the '70s it had scored a midnight hit in San Francisco and started a Los Angeles run that lasted into 1981; by 1983 it had played everywhere from Mexico and England to Germany and Japan.

Today the movie that took Lynch five years to complete remains a cult phenomenon par excellence, decades old but still able to burrow insidiously under the skin. And the filmmaker himself has become a major figure in world cinema without sacrificing a shred of his ornery, uncompromising vision. Lynch was a student at the American Film Institute when he began *Eraserhead,* shooting most of it on ramshackle sets knocked together in an old stable on the AFI grounds. Now respected stars lobby him for parts, Cannes gives him world premieres, and even Hollywood honors the outlandish likes of *Mulholland Dr.* and *Blue Velvet* with Oscar nominations. As career stories go, it's as curious as . . . well, a David Lynch movie.

Eraserhead centers on Henry Spencer, a young man with an introverted nature, a stand-up hairstyle, and an uncertain relationship with his girlfriend, Mary X, who's been staying away from him lately. Invited for dinner at her parents' house, he learns he's the father of a baby she's just had. Or something like that. At the hospital where she gave birth, Mary blurts out, they're not sure it *is* a baby.

Be that as it may, the next scene finds Henry and Mary caring for the newborn in their apartment. And it's quite a newborn—armless, legless, shrouded in bandage from the neck down, and emitting plaintive cries from the gaping mouth in its turtle-like face. Stressed beyond endurance, Mary goes back to her parents, leaving Henry to tend the little one. When the infant pushes him over the edge as well, he resorts to self-protective violence.

That's the basic story of *Eraserhead,* but the film's most interesting elements are less easily described. When we first see Henry, for instance, he's adrift in the heavens, floating translucently among the stars while an unnervingly anomalous creature—part worm, part fetus, part whatever—slides gracefully out of his mouth. We also visit a grungy-looking planet, inhabited by a grotesquely damaged man whose rust-covered industrial levers affect Henry's fortunes in some unknown, unknowable way. Back on Earth, we meet a chipmunk-cheeked chanteuse who lives in Henry's radiator, filling his reveries as he listens to music (Fats Waller at the pipe organ) on his run-down phonograph.

And then there's the nightmare Henry has after a weirded-out tryst with the Beautiful Girl Across the Hall, who seduces him while Mary is away. Henry dreams that he's visiting the Lady in the Radiator on the little stage where she sings and dances. Suddenly a bizarre stalk shoots out of his neck and knocks off his head, which is promptly replaced by the baby's cranium poking out from his empty collar. Henry's disembodied head bleeds copiously, then sinks through the floor and falls to the street below. There it's grabbed by a street urchin, who sells it to a factory that uses the brain as raw material for pencil erasers. Only then does Henry awaken, more disgruntled and perplexed than ever.

What's going on here? Critics of every kind have taken a crack at *Eraserhead,* explaining how it liberates repressed thoughts, probes the collective unconscious, questions the concept of meaning, gives new life to ancient gnostic doctrines, and—take your pick—rejects traditional morality or promotes reactionary ideas. Like most Lynch movies, this one contains more than enough inspired ambiguity to sustain all such interpretations, plus others that haven't been dreamed up yet. But one reliable entryway is Lynch's connection to surrealism, which he got acquainted with during his years as an art student and painter.

Cinema and surrealism are an odd couple. Surrealism thrives on images from the world of dreams, while cameras can only film physical objects; even digital techniques usually aim at making the unreal look as real as possible. Still, a handful of innovators (Luis Buñuel, Maya Deren) have brought surrealism to the screen, and its spirit lives on vibrantly in Lynch, who described *Eraserhead* as "a dream of dark and troubling things." Every aspect of the film, from its spacey performances and grim cinematography to its jagged editing and nerve-jangling sound design, contributes to its restlessly off-kilter atmosphere.

In this context, the actual dream sequence has to be super-dreamlike if it's going to seem dreamlike at all. Lynch pulls this off by using the nightmare scene to substantiate the movie's title, rendering Henry's "eraser-head" as an (in)apposite link in the narrative chain. The result is an additional layer of mystery, wrenched (like the baby from Mary's body or the brain from Henry's skull) from the most spectral depths of Henry's being. For me, this scene marks the transition from feeling involved in somebody's dream to feeling caged in somebody's delirium. Few moments match it for pure hallucinatory power, although several other segments of *Eraserhead* come close.

The first time I saw *Eraserhead* was in the late 1970s, at a dilapidated theater near the Long Island town where I lived. I'd been told by a French filmmaker of my acquaintance that the movie was "very advanced cinema," so I opted for an afternoon showing in the suburbs rather than a midnight one in Manhattan, where the late hour might render me less than totally alert.

Not a problem, it turned out. The film grabbed me instantly and never let go, hurling more novel ideas at my (totally alert) eyes and ears than I normally found in a score of movies. I noted a few missteps along the way—moments when the first-time filmmaker pushed too hard, miscalculated an effect, or bit off more than he could cinematically chew. (I still think the twitching "man-made chicken" is kind of silly.) But most of Lynch's feverish creation struck me as utterly original, hugely audacious, and fearlessly strange.

Especially the ending, which hit me like a revelation—the ideal conclusion to a film so bravely idiosyncratic that the only suitable finale would be a courageous leap beyond the boundaries of cinema itself. I watched as Henry's attack on the "baby" pushed the film into a seizure of stuttering, nonlinear montage, culminating in a new encounter with the Lady in the Radiator, who rushed up to embrace him in a shot so intensely bathed in blinding ultra-white light that the image all but disappeared, becoming a barely detectable trace of indecipherable motion and shade. Following the film's hero, I felt I'd transcended the realm of coherent sights, sounds, and perceptions, entering an undefined new dimension where time and space no longer follow their familiar laws.

I was wrong, of course. Catching the film again at a better movie house, I saw that while Henry and the Lady are indeed swathed in dazzling radiance, they're unmistakably visible as they cling to each other in a ghostly variation on Hollywood's conventional end-of-story clinch. What a surprise—this stunningly outlandish film was actually less outlandish than my imagination, assisted by a rotten projection system, had made it out to be!

I was compensated for this disappointment, though, since overall the film was even more impressive on the second viewing that it had been on the first. Since then my interest in "cult classics" has diminished, but my respect for *Eraserhead* remains high. Its idiosyncrasies bespeak the courage and tenacity of a screen artist exquisitely attuned to inner voices the rest of us may never hear, and eager to share their darkling echoes despite the likelihood that the conundrums, para-doxes, and enigmas they raise will be sounded by almost nobody and fathomed by fewer still. In this sense at least, Lynch's mission is generous and optimistic to its core.

Looking back on *Eraserhead* some twenty years after its release, Lynch observed that his debut film was made from profoundly personal motives and has a clear set of meanings for him. Yet in all that time, he continued, not one critic, scholar, or enthusiast has interpreted it the same way he does. I'll add that there's no reason why we should. *Eraserhead* is at once a movie on the screen, a vibra-tion in the air, and an apparition in the phantasmal space between Lynch's mind and ours. Invite it to tunnel beneath your psychological skin, if you haven't already. It's an ideal introduction to Lynch's universe, and perhaps to unexplored shadowlands of your own inner cosmos as well.

Notes on Contributors

Sam Adams is a contributing editor at *Philadelphia City Paper*. His writing has appeared in the *Los Angeles Times, Entertainment Weekly,* the *Hollywood Reporter,* the *Philadelphia Inquirer,* and *Film Comment.*

John Anderson's reviews and features appear regularly in *Variety,* the *New York Times, Newsday,* the *Guardian* (London), and *Screen International.* He has also contributed to the *Los Angeles Times,* the *Los Angeles Times Magazine,* the *Nation, Film Comment, LA Weekly, Schizophrenia Digest,* and the *Washington Post.* He is a past member of the New York Film Festival selection committee and the author of *Sundancing* (Avon, 2000), *Edward Yang* (University of Illinois Press, 2004), and, with Laura Kim, *I Wake Up Screening* (Billboard, 2006). He is a member and two-time past chair of the New York Film Critics Circle.

David Ansen is the movie critic for *Newsweek* magazine.

Sheila Benson, who lives in Seattle, Washington, began reviewing for *Seattle Weekly* seven years ago and thanks her lucky stars every day that she's no longer the *Los Angeles Times*'s chief film critic.

Jami Bernard is a film critic, columnist, and media consultant, and a past chair of the New York Film Critics Circle. Her most recent book is *The Incredible Shrinking Critic* (Avery, 2006). For further information, visit www.jamibernard.com.

Ty Burr has been a film critic for the *Boston Globe* since 2002. For ten years prior to that he was chief video critic for *Entertainment Weekly,* also covering film, music, theater, books, and the Internet. He is author of *The Best Old Movies for*

Families: A Guide to Watching Together (Anchor Books, 2007) and two earlier books, *The Hundred Greatest Movies of All Time* (Time-Life Books, 1999) and *The Hundred Greatest Stars of All Time* (Time-Life Books, 1998). He has written on film and other subjects for the *New York Times, Spin,* the *Boston Phoenix,* and other publications.

Jay Carr, longtime *Boston Globe* film critic, now reviews films for Turner Classic Movies and New England Cable News. He is a recipient of the George Jean Nathan Award for Dramatic Criticism and was named Chevalier, Ordre des Arts et Lettres (France), for writings on French film. He serves on the Library of Congress's National Film Preservation Board. He edited and wrote six essays for the National Society of Film Critics anthology *The A List* (Da Capo Press, 2002).

Eleanor Ringel Cater was the lead movie critic for the *Atlanta Journal Constitution* for twenty-nine years and has been a regular contributor to CNN, MSNBC, *Entertainment Weekly,* Headline News, and *TV Guide.* The author of *Stargazing,* Ringel Cater currently covers film and DVDs for ALM Syndicate and *Pink* magazine. She is a multiple Pulitzer Prize nominee and has been honored by Women in Film (with Sir James Ivory!) and the IMAGE Film & Video Center (with Michael Stipe!). And her face was on an Atlanta city bus, just like Carrie in *Sex and the City.*

Richard Corliss has written on film and show business for *Time* since 1980 and is a prolific contributor to Time.com. From 1970 to 1990 he was editor of *Film Comment.* His books include *Talking Pictures: Screenwriters in the American Cinema* (Overlook Press, 1974), *Greta Garbo* (Pyramid Publications, 1974), and for the BFI Film Classics series, *Lolita* (British Film Institute, 1994). He lives in Manhattan with his wife, Mary Corliss, who for thirty-four years ran the Film Stills Archive at the Museum of Modern Art, New York.

Roger Ebert has been the film critic of the *Chicago Sun-Times* since 1967, and won the Pulitzer Prize in 1975. He has an archive of more than ten thousand reviews and other movie pieces at www.rogerebert.com.

Chris Fujiwara is the author of *The World and Its Double: The Life and Work of Otto Preminger* (Faber & Faber, 2007) and *Jacques Tourneur: The Cinema of Nightfall* (Johns Hopkins University Press, 1998) and the general editor of *Defining Moments in Movies* (Cassell Illustrated, 2007). He writes on film for the *Boston*

Phoenix, Cineaste, Film Comment, and other publications and edits *Undercurrent,* the film-criticism magazine of the international film critics' association FIPRESCI.

J. Hoberman has been a film critic at the *Village Voice* for thirty years.

Richard T. Jameson's recent writing has appeared in *Queen Anne & Magnolia News* (Seattle) and *Steadycam* (Munich) and on MSN.com and Amazon.com. Previously he edited the magazines *Movietone News* (1971–1981) and *Film Comment* (1990–2000), as well as the National Society of Film Critics anthology *They Went Thataway: Redefining Film Genres* (Mercury House, 1994).

Peter Keough has been the film editor of the *Boston Phoenix* since 1989.

Stuart Klawans has written about film for the *Nation* and other publications since 1988. He is the author of *Film Follies: The Cinema Out of Order* (Cassell, 1999) and *Left in the Dark: Reviews and Essays, 1988–2001* (Nation Books, 2002).

Dennis Lim is the editorial director at the Museum of the Moving Image in New York and editor of the Museum's Web site Moving Image Source. He is also a contributing editor at *Cinema Scope* and a regular contributor to the *New York Times* and the *Los Angeles Times*. Previously the film editor at the *Village Voice*, he edited the *Village Voice Film Guide* (John Wiley & Sons, 2006). He teaches in the graduate journalism department at New York University and is currently writing a book on David Lynch.

Rob Nelson writes about movies at MinnPost.com; his work also appears in *Film Comment, Cinema Scope,* the *Boston Phoenix,* and on the Walker Art Center's film/video blog (www.blogs.walkerart.org/filmvideo). The recipient of three awards each from the Association of Alternative Newsweeklies and the Society of Professional Journalists, he teaches film studies at the Minneapolis College of Art and Design, has served on festival juries in Los Angeles and Vancouver, and is a regular attendee of the Cannes, Toronto, Full Frame, and Sundance festivals. His article about *The Insect Woman* was recently published in the Smithsonian Institution's Shohei Imamura booklet, *A Man Vanishes.*

Gerald Peary, a longtime film critic for the *Boston Phoenix,* heads the film program at Suffolk University, Boston. His books include *John Ford: Interviews*

(University Press of Mississippi, 2001) and the coedited anthologies *The Classic American Novel and the Movies* (Ungar, 1977) and *Women and the Cinema* (Dutton, 1977). A University of Wisconsin PhD, Peary was a Fulbright scholar in Yugoslavia and acting curator of the Harvard Film Archive, and is curator-programmer of the Boston University Cinematheque. He is writer-director of the feature documentary *For the Love of Movies: The Story of American Film Criticism*, which screened as a work-in-progress at the 2007 Telluride Film Festival.

John Powers is film critic at *Vogue*, critic at large for NPR's *Fresh Air with Terry Gross*, and a columnist for *L.A. Weekly*. He is the author of *Sore Winners (and the Rest of Us) in George Bush's America* (Doubleday, 2004). His work has appeared in *New York*, *Rolling Stone*, *Harper's*, the *Nation*, the *Washington Post*, the *New York Times*, and the *Los Angeles Times*. He codirected the BBC documentary *I Am a Sex Addict* with Vikram Jayanti.

Peter Rainer is film critic for the *Christian Science Monitor*. He also reviews DVDs for Bloomberg News and is heard on *Film Week* for the NPR affiliate KPCC-FM and XM satellite radio. Previously he was film critic for *New York*, the *Los Angeles Times*, the *Los Angeles Herald Examiner*, and *New Times Los Angeles*, where he was a finalist in 1998 for the Pulitzer Prize in criticism. From 1989 to 2004 he was chairman of the National Society of Film Critics. He edited the critical anthology *Love and Hisses* (Mercury House, 1992) and wrote and coproduced the A&E biographies of Sidney Poitier and the Hustons.

Carrie Rickey has been the *Philadelphia Inquirer's* film critic for more than two decades. She has reviewed films as diverse as *Water* and *The Waterboy*, profiled celebrities from Lillian Gish to Will Smith, and reported on technological breakthroughs from the video revolution to the rise of movies on demand. Her reviews are syndicated nationwide, and her essays appear in numerous anthologies, including *The Rolling Stone Illustrated History of Rock & Roll* (Random House, 1992), *The American Century: Art and Culture, 1950–2000* (W. W. Norton, 1999), and *American Movie Critics* (Library of America, 2006).

Jonathan Rosenbaum was film critic for the *Chicago Reader* from 1987 to 2007 and is the author, coauthor, or editor of sixteen books, including *Moving Places* (Harper & Row, 1980), *Midnight Movies* (with J. Hoberman, Harper & Row, 1983), *Greed* (BFI Publications, 1991), *This Is Orson Welles* (editor, HarperCollins,

1992), *Placing Movies* (University of California Press, 1995), *Movies as Politics* (University of California Press, 1997), *Dead Man* (BFI Publications, 2000), *Movie Wars* (A Cappella, 2000), *Abbas Kiarostami* (with Mehrnaz Saeed-Vafa, University of Illinois Press, 2003), *Essential Cinema* (Johns Hopkins University Press, 2003), *Movie Mutations* (coedited with Adrian Martin, BFI Publications, 2003), and *Discovering Orson Welles* (University of California Press, 2007). His Web site is www.jonathanrosenbaum.com.

Richard Schickel reviews movies for *Time* and Time.com. He is the author of more than thirty books, the latest of which is *Film on Paper* (Ivan R. Dee, 2008), and is the director-writer-producer of a similar number of documentaries, the latest of which are *Bienvenue Cannes, Spielberg on Spielberg,* and *The Men Who Made the Movies: William A. Wellman,* all broadcast in 2007. He is currently working on a five-hour history of Warner Bros., to be released in 2008.

Matt Zoller Seitz, a finalist for the Pulitzer Prize in criticism, was film critic of *New York Press* from 1995 to 2006. He is now a film critic for the *New York Times,* the publisher of the film and TV criticism Web site The House Next Door (www.mattzollerseitz.blogspot.com), and an independent filmmaker, whose first feature, *Home,* is available on DVD through Vanguard Cinema.

Michael Sragow is the movie critic for the *Baltimore Sun.* He edited the Library of America's two-volume collection of James Agee's writing as well as *Produced and Abandoned: The National Society of Film Critics Write on the Best Films You've Never Seen* (Mercury House, 1990). His work has appeared in *Rolling Stone,* the *Atlantic,* and the *New Yorker.* He has just completed the first biography of the film director Victor Fleming for Pantheon.

David Sterritt is chairman of the National Society of Film Critics, film professor at Columbia University and the Maryland Institute College of Art, and past chairman of the New York Film Critics Circle. He was film critic of the *Christian Science Monitor* for decades and writes often for *Cineaste, Film International,* PopMatters.com, and *MovieMaker.* He holds a PhD from NYU and has served on the New York Film Festival selection committee. His writing has appeared in *Cahiers du cinéma,* the *New York Times, Film Comment,* and many other publications; his books include *Guiltless Pleasures: A David Sterritt Film Reader* (University Press of Mississippi, 2005).

Amy Taubin is a contributing editor for *Film Comment* and *Sight and Sound* magazines and a frequent contributor to *Art Forum* magazine. Her book *Taxi Driver* was published in 2000 in the British Film Institute's Film Classics series. Her critical essays are included in many collections. She was a film critic for the *Village Voice* from 1987 to 2001, where she also wrote a column titled "Art and Industry." She teaches at the School of Visual Arts in New York City.

Charles Taylor is a columnist for the *Newark Star-Ledger* and Bloomberg News. A contributor to the *New York Times, Newsday,* the *Los Angeles Times,* and *Dissent,* he has written on movies, books, music, and politics for Salon.com., the *New Yorker,* the *Nation,* the *Boston Phoenix, Slate,* the *New York Observer, Sight and Sound,* and other publications. He lives in Brooklyn.

Kevin Thomas was film reviewer for the *Los Angeles Times* from 1962 to 2005 and continues to write reviews and features for the paper since retirement. He has received the National Lesbian and Gay Journalists Lifetime Achievement Award for support of gay cinema and the Distinguished Alumnus Award from Gettysburg College in 2000; other honors include awards from the Los Angeles Film Critics Association (which he helped found in 1976) and the National Society of Film Critics when he retired. He is past president of the Los Angeles Film Critics Association and has served on many film-festival juries.

Desson Thomson has been a film critic for the *Washington Post* since 1987, where he also writes about cultural events. Raised in England, he moved to the United States in 1975 and attended American University. He joined the *Post* in 1983 and wrote for the Style section before becoming a critic. After reuniting with his birth father in Scotland in 2002, he changed his last name from Howe to Thomson and has been writing under that name ever since. When he's not reviewing movies he is a scriptwriter, an avid soccer player, and lead singer for the band Cairo Fred.

Peter Travers has been the film critic and senior features editor for film at *Rolling Stone* magazine since 1989. He appears regularly as a film commentator on ABC, and his film analysis has been featured on shows from *Charlie Rose* to *Good Morning America.* He can be found online each week by logging onto www.rollingstone.com. Travers is the author of *The 1000 Best Movies on DVD,* published by Hyperion (2005), and the editor of *The Rolling Stone Film Reader,* published by Pocket Books (1996). He is also a former chair of the New York Film Critics Circle.

Kenneth Turan is film critic for the *Los Angeles Times* and National Public Radio's *Morning Edition* and director of the *Times* Book Prizes. A graduate of Swarthmore College, he has been the *Times* book-review editor and a staff writer for the *Washington Post*. He is the coauthor of *Call Me Anna: The Autobiography of Patty Duke* (Bantam, 1987), teaches at USC, and is on the board of directors of the National Yiddish Book Center. His latest books, *Never Coming to a Theater Near You* (2004) and *Now in Theaters Everywhere* (2006), are published by Public Affairs Press.

James Verniere is the film critic for the *Boston Herald*. He was born in Newark, New Jersey, has a master's degree in English literature from Rutgers University, and once taught at the Clinton Correctional Institute for Women. His work has previously appeared in the National Society of Film Critics anthologies *The A List* (Da Capo, 2002) and *The X List* (Da Capo, 2005).

Stephanie Zacharek is a senior writer for the online magazine *Salon*. Her work has also appeared in the *New York Times*, *Entertainment Weekly*, *Rolling Stone*, *New York*, and *Sight and Sound*.

Permissions

Index